GODLESS

—— v. ——

LIBERTY

The Radical Left's Quest to Destroy America's
Judeo-Christian Foundation

DD Simpson

NEWMAN SPRINGS PUBLISHING
320 Broad Street
Red Bank, NJ 07701

First originally published by Newman Springs Publishing 2021

ISBN 978-1-63881-088-9 (Paperback)
ISBN 978-1-63881-089-6 (Hardcover)
ISBN 978-1-63881-090-2 (Digital)

Printed in the United States of America

I dedicate this book to the love of my life, Mi Bonita.
Thank you for making me laugh every day.

Contents

Preface..7
Introduction..9
Chapter 1: The Separation of Church and State........................15
Chapter 2: The Moral Decay of Society.....................................42
Chapter 3: Less Than Liberty...79
Chapter 4: Abortion, Euthanasia, Sexual Orientation 103
Chapter 5: Donkeys and Elephants..132
Chapter 6: Racism 165
Chapter 7: The Death of Journalism..187
Chapter 8: Judeo-Christian Values and the Bible....................230
Chapter 9: Only the Father Knows 260
Chapter 10: Author's Summation...270
Epilogue...305
Articles 311

Preface

I feel it's essential before moving forward to acknowledge that I'm a sinner and doubt very much Jehovah would tap this southpaw out of the bullpen to throw the first stone. I wish to shed light on this underwhelming disclosure if for no other reason than to let it be known that I'm not above anyone when it comes to being free of sin. I'm just a regular guy, who like many in this great country of ours, has grown tired of seeing the blatant disrespect toward two of the greatest gifts ever bestowed upon humanity: the Bible and the United States Constitution. The time is past due for the craziness known as the radical left agenda to take their godless damn hands off our sacred documents and for the people of this great nation to rise and be heard.

In the following pages, I will address several sensitive, third-rail issues: abortion, homosexuality, racism, euthanasia, religion, and politics. I will give legal, political, and biblical views to each of these topics. However, I would not be able to write this book without invoking my conservative opinion, along with some of my brutally honest Brooklyn attitude. In those instances, I will make clear that these are my viewpoints and not facts. To the one or two libs that accidentally purchased this book, feel free to disagree with my written commentary; but unlike what hip professors with male buns have taught you, facts are not open to debate, hence why they're called facts.

In *Godless v. Liberty*, I reserve my harshest criticism for those dishonest public figures taking part in the attack against America and our Judeo-Christian way of life. I refer to these elitists as idiots. For the record, this is my personal opinion and, to the best of my knowledge, has not yet been proven a fact. With that said, if I should write something that upsets one of these divas, which I'm reasonably confident I will, I hope they can find a way to cope without running to their $350-an-hour shrink to unload why they felt offended for the six hundredth time this week. But if the outrage is too much for Hillary, Cher, Maddona, Fonda, Alec, LeBron, Bette, Depp, Michelle, or any of the other idiots mentioned in this book and they choose to pay me a visit in the middle of the night carrying a pitchfork and torch, try to remember to bring a few wine coolers and any 45 by Neil Diamond. I'll keep a light on.

Since everything is about identity these days, I've created my own group. I am a BOWFOG: a bald, old, White, fat, opinionated guy. Sadly, at the moment, we BOWFOGS are an endangered species in America; so if you should see one, please be kind to us.

To clarify, any mention of "left," "libs," and "Dems" in this book refers to today's secular radical left and not great historical liberal minds such as Locke, Voltaire, and Jefferson.

Unless noted, all verses used are from the King James Bible. On occasion, I will use God's name Jehovah, which appears in this format several times throughout the King James Version, including in Exodus 6:3: *"And I appeared unto Abraham, unto Isaac, and unto Jacob, by the name of God Almighty but by my name JEHOVAH..."*

My sincere gratitude to my three wise men: Raymond Long, Jeff Gossack, and Wil Serano, for allowing me to tap into their years of experience and knowledge.

Lastly, since most of the material cited throughout is familiar to theologians, historians, and political scientists, I have taken the liberty to omit the usual scholarly apparatus of footnotes. However, where deemed necessary, I've provided pertinent references and origins.

Introduction

*The fundamental basis of this nation's law was given to Moses
on the Mount... If we don't have a proper fundamental moral
background, we will finally end up with a totalitarian government
which does not believe in rights for anybody except the state.*

—President Harry S. Truman

In the summer of 1787, fifty-five delegates representing thirteen states gathered in Philadelphia to amend the lesser-known Articles of Confederation. The neophyte government was tottering on the brink of collapse. States were openly threatening war against one another while inflation was running rampant. The threat of anarchy worsened when a Revolutionary War veteran led a group of armed men in Massachusetts to revolt against the state's draconian tax policies and debt collection. Shay's Rebellion, named after its leader, had exposed a significant flaw in the central government's yielding most of the powers to the states.

From all appearances, George Washington was content living out his days as a Virginia farmer with his wife, Martha. Having triumphed over the most powerful empire of its day, the retired general grew weary of the prospects that it would all be for naught if his fellow Americans defeated themselves in the end. So, once again, Washington answered the call to duty. Upon his arrival at the Constitutional Convention, the American Cincinnatus was elected unanimously as president to preside over the proceedings. Everyone there knew if there were any hope of saving the Union, it would be with the universally respected Washington at the helm.

After four months of compromises, rewrites, and a creative balancing act of separation of powers, the convention created something far exceeding their original intent. The four-page document consisting of seven articles and fewer than five thousand words was signed by thirty-nine delegates on September 7, 1787. At the time, none of the men present inside the oxygen-starved Independence Hall could've ever imagined that arguably the most important document ever created by man would last for over 230 years and counting.

Two years later, the first ten amendments were added to the Constitution. Known as the Bill of Rights, these amendments recognized that we are all born with God-given inalienable rights. Never before had any governing power acknowledged God as the bestower and not a king, queen, or dictator. By shifting the power to the people, a revolutionary seismic event occurred. Under the new Articles listed in the Constitution, the fundamental idea of government of the people, by the people, and for the people was born. These laws were meant to protect ordinary citizens from government overreach while also keeping checks and balances for those entrusted with power.

As James Madison poignantly put it, *"If men were angels, no government would be necessary."*

Like the Bible, some believe the words in the United States Constitution are left up to interpretation. For the record, I am not one of them. Our framers painstakingly formulated each word carefully with the intent that the document should be followed as written. The concept is known as originalism, and something the left despises.

However, the framers anticipated the need for an evolving document to keep up with a growing nation, so they added Article Seven of the Constitution, which outlines the procedures for proposing and ratifying an amendment. The task of making changes to the Constitution was intentionally made arduous. Three-fourths of the state legislators, those elected representatives of the people, are needed to amend the document. That is why on many critical issues, the secular left in Congress, knowing they don't have the votes for their radical ideas, take the easier route via the judicial system to help create policy. The Dems find activist judges willing to give their personal leftist interpretation of what they *feel* the meaning of a text should be. This is why these radicals will do anything, and I mean anything, to have activist judges on the Supreme Court. Unfortunately, this shortcut initiated by Congress and carried out by the judicial branch has given nine unelected, unaccountable, lifetime appointees more power than our framers ever intended. In doing so, they've bypassed the will of the people.

Let's take a look at an example of judicial activism.

Amendment 1 of the United States Constitution states,

"Congress shall make no law respecting an establishment of religion, or prohibiting the free exercise thereof…"

One would think this straightforward, unambiguous wording would leave little wiggle room. However, on the Cornell Law School's website, they explain the religion clause in the First Amendment as follows:

"It forbids Congress from both promoting one religion over others and also restricting an individual's religious practices."

These words provided by the *geniuses* at Cornell, along with the infamous Thomas Jefferson phrase, *"Separation of Church and State,"* are absent from our Constitution. In other words, they only exist thanks to the liberties taken by higher education and some in the courts who believe they know better than our Founding Fathers.

How about that? I think I might've just stumbled upon the definition for elitist snobs.

In fairness, I can't blame Cornell for repeating words offered in a Supreme Court decision. However, since my master's and PhD degrees do not come from an Ivy League school (I'm still waiting to hear back from Cornell's admissions regarding my application that I sent back in 1983) and my resume includes law school but lacks an actual law degree, the following may sound absurd but both institutions are wrong. Yes, shockingly, BOWFOG is correct regarding this highly problematic issue known as judicial activism. The Supreme Court and Cornell Law School have taken liberties our Founding

Fathers had never intended. Don't believe me. Read the religious clause as written and then read their interpretation one more time.

First Amendment as written: "Congress will make no 'law' establishing a religion…"

Supreme Court/Cornell Law: "Congress is forbidden from promoting one religion over others."

In conveniently changing a few words, the secular left, ACLU, and those atheists offended by God's mere mention can rely on their *interpretation* and not the specific text itself. For example, adding the word *promoting* into the clause grossly broadens the scope and forever changes the argument's foundation. So with the new meaning inserted into our First Amendment, the Supreme Court can rule against prayer at a public school event because it's, you guessed it, *promoting*. Of course, if the argument were about *establishing a law*, well, they wouldn't have a leg to stand on because Congress did no such thing. The real irony here is the second part of the religious clause, better known as the Free Exercise Clause, states, "*Or prohibiting the free exercise thereof.*" Somehow, this part is all too often conveniently passed over by those on the left sitting on the Supreme Court. It's as if our framers never wrote the words. But they did. So instead of safeguarding our liberty to practice religion freely, the Court ruled that it was more important to protect atheists' "feelings."

Sorry, Jake, but praying with your teammates on the field before a public high school football game may traumatize the godless idiot sitting in section 33, row F, seat 6 (Santa Fe Independent School District v. Doe, 2000).

It's amazing what a few lawyers, a pocket thesaurus, organizations sharing a common hatred toward God and a malevolent misinterpretation of our Constitution can do to undermine our inalienable rights.

GODLESS, 1

LIBERTY, 0

Before moving forward, I should provide *Merriam Webster's* definition of the word *secularism*:

"*An indifference to or rejection or exclusion of religion and religious considerations.*"

Now here's my definition:

Those who believe Baby Jesus is trespassing when He appears in a public Nativity scene, despise when the Ten Commandments are on display in public schools, or anyone who dares to mention God's name in the presence of an atheist.

There's a reason the Bible and Constitution are under attack from the godless left. Modern-day liberal politicians despise anything that takes power and attention away from them. In their secular society, the government should be at the center, unlike in the Judeo-Christian world, where we reserve this honor for Jehovah. Sadly, many look toward these godless politicians to cure all their ills. Since God, morality, and spiritual goodness is the antithesis of a secular society, interpretation, instead of fact, is relied upon to slowly but systematically tear away at our Constitution. The end result is a modern-day society that makes Sodom and Gomorrah look like Mayberry.

In the following chapters, I will illustrate how the Supreme Court, liberal policies, and a subverted Constitution have done more to deteriorate our country than any foreign enemy of ours could ever dream. I want to think all is not lost, but if history has taught us anything, we will need to suffer greatly before we learn. If this were not the case, wars would be far fewer and peace more frequent.

A final point. While writing this book, there were occasions when I struggled to find the right words to describe how I felt about those whose views differ from mine. There are my fair share of "idiot" bombs and "hypocrite" tossed about, but still, something was missing. I desperately searched for a word, a phrase, or anything that could encapsulate how I felt, but it alluded me. Then one day, I heard a distinctive voice on the radio that I immediately recognized to be that of conservative talk show host Rush Limbaugh. The station was playing a montage in tribute to the recently deceased radio legend when I experienced a eureka moment. In the sound clip, Rush was explaining the "core difference" between conservatives and liberal leaders. It was in that instance I realized I was looking at things from the wrong perspective. I was too busy trying to understand the left that I failed to consider how they viewed conservatives. But not

Rush. He nailed it and, in doing so, articulated the striking contrast in a way that only the Rusher Maha Rushie could:

> *In many peoples minds, conservatives especially, we are all in the arena of ideas, and we're competing for dominance. We want to genuinely persuade our opponents that we're right and they're wrong. We want to do it by being accurate and honest about what we believe. We don't want to attract believers to our cause by lying to them, by telling them things which aren't true. We want to have credibility when the whole thing is over with. So, we assume the other side is the same way. We assume everybody is out playing by the rules, and we're all engaged over the battle for the minds of the American people. So, to us, it's a question of right versus wrong. I don't think the liberals are much concerned about that. Liberals don't look at conservatives as wrong.* Liberal leaders look at conservatives as evil. It's not right versus wrong, it's good versus evil, and they, the liberal leadership, they are good. We conservatives, just by virtue of being conservatives, they say we're evil. *So, in the battle of good versus evil, good may do anything to triumph over evil. They break the law because there is nothing but stopping evil.* (Rush Limbaugh, 1951–2021)

Chapter 1

The Separation of Church and State

If we forget that we're one nation under God, then we will be one nation gone under… Freedom prospers when religion is vibrant, and the rule of law under God is acknowledged.

—President Ronald Reagan

The blustery cold winter of 1789 caused travel throughout the northeast to halt, delaying the First Federal Congress by over a month. The most pressing issue of the day for these delegates was the tallying of the electoral votes cast for the United State's presidency. Finally, after both houses of Congress established a quorum, the sealed ballots were opened and tallied to reveal George Washington's unanimous selection as America's first president.

On Thursday, April 30, 1789, the fifty-seven-year-old retired general navigated his way up a set of stairs inside Federal Hall. By the time the Virginian farmer made his way to the second floor, a large crowd had assembled outside in anticipation of witnessing history. As the onlookers blanketed the lower Manhattan street below, a cautious Washington stepped out onto the balcony to a hero's welcome. Purposely attired in all-American-made clothing, rather than donning anything made from across the Atlantic, the impressive six-foot-two president-elect took his rightful place under the portico.

Washington placed his left hand on a Masonic Bible, retrieved at the very last moment by secretary of the Senate Samuel Otis, and then sternly erected his right hand up toward the heavens. The chancellor of New York, Robert Livingston, administered the oath. When done, the newly sworn-in president leaned over and, in reverence, kissed the Bible as the chancellor announced to the crowd below, "Long live George Washington, president of the United States."

The following is an excerpt of President Washington's inaugural address:

> *Fellow Citizens of the Senate and the House of Representatives...*
>
> *It would be peculiarly improper to omit, in this first official Act, my fervent supplications to that Almighty Being who rules over the Universe, who presides in the Councils of Nations, and whose providential aids can supply every human defect, that his benediction may consecrate to the liberties and happiness of the People of the United States, a Government instituted by themselves for these essential purposes: and may enable every instrument employed in its administration to execute with success, the functions allotted to his charge. In tendering this homage to the Great Author of every public and private good, I assure myself that it expresses your sentiments not less than my own; nor those of my fellow-citizens at large less than either. No people can be bound to acknowledge and adore the Invisible Hand, which conducts the Affairs of men more than the People of the United States.*

A day that started with church bells ringing throughout the city nonstop for thirty minutes finished with a fireworks display to honor America's first president. A new era in world history had begun.

It should not be overlooked that Washington's first act as president was kissing the Bible, and his second was expressing, through softly spoken words, the love, respect, and homage due the Almighty from a grateful nation, a Judeo-Christian nation.

Eight years after his swearing-in, the father of our nation published his farewell address in Philadelphia's *American Daily Advertiser.* He cautioned the fragile young republic against permanent foreign alliances and to resist political factions here at home. Washington feared the latter would give rise to a "spirit of revenge" via "cunning, ambitious, and unprincipled men." It was as if our first president could see today's corrupt politicians and know that these cancerous bureaucrats would put their interests before the nation.

Washington's letter was filled with ominous warnings, fatherly advice, and a hope of unity. In it, he expressed what he believed the key was to our nation's success:

> *Of all the dispositions and habits which lead to political prosperity, religion and morality are indispensable supports. In vain would that man claim the tribute of patriotism, who should labor to subvert these great pillars of human happiness, these firmest props of the duties of men and citizens.*

I sometimes wonder what George Washington would think of the United States today. Would he be proud to have fathered the most powerful nation in the world, or would he be terrified to see that his warnings have gone unheeded? And what about the document Washington was the first to sign in 1787? Would he be pleased to know that the United States Constitution has lasted as long as it has, or would he be saddened to see his fellow citizens using every effort to undermine and pervert the words written in its text?

Under Attack

The attack on the United States Constitution began in the middle of the last century, starting with prayer in schools, a daily practice for the first 150 years of our republic is now outlawed. In the 1962 Supreme Court case of Engel v. Vitale, nine men in black robes that the people never elected to hold any office decided the atheist's feelings took precedence over God. Using Thomas Jefferson's *"wall of separation,"* the justices perverted the words to say what they wanted them to mean and not as they were written. The separation of church and state was not meant to keep God out of schools but rather to keep the state out of churches. Allow me to repeat these words: keep the state out of churches. The letter between Jefferson and the Danbury Baptist that referenced the "wall of separation" made this point very clear. Our newly elected third president was reassuring the concerned congregation that the federal government could not interfere with their church under the religion clause of the First Amendment:

"Congress shall make no law respecting an establishment of religion or prohibiting the free exercise thereof."

As one can clearly see in this Amendment, there's no mention of the term "separation of church and state."

In the Danbury letter dated November 7, 1801, the Connecticut church expressed concerns to Jefferson over the words "free exercise of religion." To them, the First Amendment clause suggested that the religious right was "government granted" rather than from God, fearing that someday those in power may try to regulate religious expression. They believed that freedom of religion was a God-given inalienable right that the government should be powerless to restrict unless those activities caused someone to work ill to his neighbor. Or as Thomas Jefferson described religious freedoms:

"It does me no injury for my neighbor to say there are twenty gods or no God. It neither picks my pocket nor breaks my leg."

Jefferson fully agreed with the concerns addressed by the congregation. In a letter dated January 1, 1802, he replied to the Danbury Baptists, assuring them that their free exercise of religion was indeed an inalienable right that the government would not interfere with. In the text, Jefferson uses the phrase "a wall of separation between church and state" and how this "wall" would prevent the government from interfering or hindering religious activities. Today we use the words "separation of church and state" to stop religious expression, completely the antithesis of the Founders' intentions.

In 1879, the Supreme Court heard oral arguments in a case dealing with polygamy. In Reynolds v. The United States, Reynolds argued that since his "faith" required him to marry multiple women (*God help him*), the law was violating his First Amendment rights of free exercise of religion. The Court unanimously voted against his claim, upholding polygamy to be against the law.

However, the real significance in the case was not if a man could marry more than one wife, but the argument made by Reynolds directly citing the "separation of church and state." He invoked the phrase found in Jefferson's letter hoping to use it to his advantage. The Supreme Court was not content with Reynolds just using the eight-word separation clause but instead had the entire section of the letter reprinted to show how its intent was to protect the church from government and not the other way around.

Late in the nineteenth century, a case came before the Supreme Court that had great importance in whether Christian values would stay at the core of our great American experiment.

In Church of the Holy Trinity v. United States (1892), Supreme Court justice David Brewer declared that the United States was a "*Christian Nation.*" I won't bog you down with the case law, but the significance of Justice Brewer's words when writing his opinion reaffirmed God's importance to our republic, along with the arm of the state staying out of church business.

Note: The Court's ruling was unanimous, 9–0. In the sixteen-page written decision, the Court provided over eighty historical precedents that America was indeed a Christian nation. The Court further noted that of the forty-four states currently in the Union, all had some direct God-centered declaration in their constitution

In another unanimous 9–0 decision defending Christian faith (Vidal v. Girard, 1844), Supreme Court justice Joseph Story championed the scriptures by rhetorically stating, "Why not the Bible, and especially the New Testament… Where can the purest principles of morality be learned so clearly or so perfectly as from the New Testament." (*Amen to that!*)

Can you imagine a justice on the Supreme Court today openly endorse the Bible from the bench? The sentiment alone proves how far removed we are from our framers' intent of establishing a Judeo-Christian nation.

Fact check: I believe this would be a good time to stop and debunk a false narrative that atheists have been floating around for years that we are not and never have been a Christian nation. Of course, this is nonsense and falls under the "if you tell a lie big enough and keep repeating it, people will eventually come to believe it" category. However, in fairness, the godless pack of leftists may have a strong argument, which lies in the Treaty of Tripoli.

Here's the line in the treaty atheists regurgitate to make the argument that we are a godless country:

"As the Government of the United States is not, in any sense, founded on the Christian religion."

They hammer this point home by explaining that the treaty was formulated by none other than the *diest* himself (according to the atheist), George Washington.

Case closed, right? So, in the ruling of GODLESS v. LIBERTY, the winner is...well, not so fast. If we continue reading the omitted words found after the semicolon, the text takes on an entirely new meaning. Here's the line in its entirety:

> As the Government of the United States is not, in any sense, founded on the Christian religion; as it has in itself no character of enmity against the laws, religion, or tranquility, of Mussulmen; and, as the said States never entered into any war, or act of hostility against any Mahometan nation, it is declared by the parties, that no pretext, arising from religious opinions, shall ever produce an interruption of the harmony existing between the two countries.

In the 1796 treaty, the United States wanted to clarify that we were a different Christian nation than those over in Europe that openly held hostilities toward the Muslim world. Yes, we were a

Christian nation, but not the kind that Tripoli was accustomed to dealing with at the time.

GODLESS, 1

LIBERTY, 1

One last point regarding context. As one can see, a creative edit can change the meaning of an entire text. The same can be said for those who use terms like *deist* and *militia* to prove a point without giving the reader the proper context of their meaning. The example here of "diest" and "militia" has a significantly different interpretation today than when the United States first began. So when someone refers to George Washington as a *diest* or miscategorizes the use of the word *militia* to attack our Second Amendment, ask them from what reference they're basing their assertion. I call this game the Three Card Monty of Truth.

"Call Me"

I want to share an anecdote that occurred during the early stages of writing this book. I was having a phone conversation with a doctor friend of mine who attended a Jesuit College. The good doctor is a learned individual with one of the more open minds that I have the pleasure of knowing. I began to explain how I believe our Constitution has been slowly and deliberately under attack since the middle of the last century. Perhaps to be polite or maybe to sincerely show some interest in my thesis, he asked for an example. The first one I gave him was the 1962 Supreme Court ruling that banned prayer in public schools (Engel v. Vitale). After making my argument as to why I thought this was a devastating defeat to Christianity and in violation of the First Amendment, my friend disagreed with me by siding with the Court. I was stunned. What part did I not make clear? There had to be a misunderstanding, but to my dismay, there wasn't.

The good doctor was kind enough to expand on his reasoning. He explained that when he visited his in-laws how he felt very uncomfortable when they said grace in his presence before dinner. His thinking was since he felt obligated to take part in their prayer, then he could see how some students might feel the same.

I told him he made an "interesting" point. (Note: If someone ever tells you something is interesting, they're really thinking, *WTF*.) I then apprised him that nowhere in the Constitution was it written that American citizens were restricted from practicing their religion freely. Conversely, the First Amendment specifically directed its concerns at Congress and the federal government by purposely limiting their roles in the Free Exercise Clause.

He then said it wouldn't be fair to some students who might feel compelled to participate due to peer pressure.

"Interesting," I said again, but this time with a slight bite of my lower lip.

Doc went on to say, "But you know, if there was one good thing about prayer in schools, it was the values it instilled in the students."

Unable to hold back any longer, I bypassed the indifferent one-word response of "interesting" and went right to the "WTF" in full. "That's the entire point, you idiot. The idea is to teach our young respect, appreciation, and civility. Commencing the school day by giving thanks to our Creator, yeah, I would think that's a pretty good way to start." I finished by asking a rhetorical question drenched in sarcasm: "So maybe this prayer *thing* isn't such a bad idea after all?"

In an unrelated matter, if, by chance, Doc is reading this, I haven't received a Christmas card from you in quite some time. I hope everything is okay. I'm still at the same address, and unlike you, I haven't changed my cell number, and in case you were wondering, yes, I've been working on my tact. I hope to hear from you soon.

In all seriousness, I believe most people are reasonable and have more in common than not. It's the extremes on each side that can make things unbalanced.

So I think what my (once) good doctor friend was trying to convey before his cell phone mysteriously lost its signal was that if either side should become too dominant, then we run the risk of being at the mercy of the powers that be. I would never want anyone forcing me to pray, but at the same time, I should be able to practice my beliefs in public without prejudice. Unfortunately, due to the relentless war by the unyielding radicals on Christianity, my views are considered too extreme. However, their quest to rid God from society, make abortions on demand, do away with borders, and blow up our Constitution is considered mainstream in their warped minds. We call this little soap opera disaster "The End of Our Republic."

Side note: I think it's fair to say that extremes in anything rarely turn out well. Just ask Jim Fixx, who's credited with inventing the jogging craze of the seventies. He bragged about how he could eat whatever he wanted because the calories would simply burn off. Mr. Fixx died of a heart attack at fifty-two while enjoying a scenic jog in Vermont. It's rumored his last words were "Super-size me."

The Democrats would love to do away with the pesky Electoral College and go to a popular vote. After all, in recent decades, the Democrat presidential candidates have won the majority vote but lost on the electoral count. On the surface, their gripe is understandable. The people and not the states should elect the president, right?

At the Constitutional Convention, this issue came up. The smaller populated states were concerned that federal elections would be decided by a handful of the larger states, so a *compromise* was struck. As is the case in most concessions, the Electoral College is not perfect and should be open to improvements. However, having New York, Califonia, and Texas decide who the next president will be every four years excludes a large portion of our country. Perhaps Maine's "ranked-choice voting" is a viable option as well as the splitting of electoral votes as they do in Nebraska and the aforementioned state.

As for those of you slamming the table demanding it has to be a popular vote, keep something in mind. In the 1860 presidential election, Abraham Lincoln won only 40 percent of the popular vote but 59 percent of the Electoral College. I think there's little doubt, if not for President Lincoln and his undying commitment to keep the Union together, slavery and the Confederate States of America would've had a different future.

God Must Go

Tragically for the past half century, the Supreme Court has ruled that the "wall of separation" equated to God's eviction from the public square even though this phrase doesn't appear in the

Declaration of Independence or the US Constitution. If this wall was Jefferson's intent, why then did he attend a church service conducted in the House of Representatives two days after penning the Danbury letter? Why did he reference God four times in the Declaration of Independence? And, if the wall was truly meant to be an impenetrable divide, why would Jefferson write, "That they are endowed by their Creator with certain unalienable Rights." Wouldn't those signing the Declaration of Independence object to any reference to God/Creator if the intent was for there to be an impenetrable wall? Let's stop the nonsense. There was no objection in 1787 because it was never our Judeo-Christian Founders' wishes.

At the Thomas Jefferson Memorial in Washington, D. C. stands a nineteen-foot statue in honor of our third president. The open-air, shallow-dome circular structure sits on twenty-six columns made out of white Imperial Danby marble from Vermont. Inside the portico, there are several inscriptions carved into the white Georgia marble walls. There's an excerpt from the Declaration of Independence, several famous quotes by Jefferson, and what I have concluded to be an ominous warning by our third president. The quote inscribed on the northeast interior wall reads:

> *God who gave us liberty. Can the liberties of a nation be secure when we have removed a conviction that these liberties are the gift of God? Indeed I tremble for my country when I reflect that God is just, that his justice cannot sleep forever...*

Over the years, the Supreme Court has ruled against God numerous times. With each decision, God, along with our Constitution, would lose again and again. I think it's important to point out that none of the following cases would have seen the light of day if it wasn't for the travesty that took place in 1947. So if you've never witnessed a slippery slope before, here we go:

1947: Everson v. Board of Education (5–4)

In this controversial Supreme Court ruling, Justice Hugo Black read in part the majority opinion:

"The First Amendment has erected a wall of separation between church and state. That wall must be kept high and impregnable."

Of course, ever since, secular liberals have taken Black's words to mean, "God must go." No longer would the second part, the Free Exercise Clause, be honored. With the Court's radical decision, the beginning of the end of one of our nation's most precious rights had been stripped away from the American people without any elected representative present to protect what had been the law of the land for the previous 150 years.

The secular left's crying call of *separation* was so often used that most Americans believe it's in our Constitution. The thought makes me think of the famous quote by Dr. William James: "There is nothing so absurd but that if you repeat it often enough people will believe it."

Note: In my view, the Everson ruling has to be considered one of the worst decisions ever reached by the highest court. I put it up there with Dred Scott v. Sandford (1857), The Civil Rights Cases of 1883, Plessy v. Ferguson (1896), Korematsu v. United States (1944), and Roe v. Wade (1973). With such a dubious record throughout their history, there's no wonder why our framers made the judicial branch the least powerful of the three. That's right. They're not coequal branches, but if you say it enough…well, you get my point.

To illustrate how preposterous the notion of an absolute separation of church and state is, all one has to do is look at the government's oversight when it comes to opening a house of worship. If there were an impenetrable wall, why would churches have to register for building permits, adhere to health regulations, or follow any tax codes? Or, be forced to close their doors during a pandemic by godless governors? What happened to that great big, impenetrable wall the secular left loves to tell us was the intentions of our framers?

Here's one better.

Since Europeans have landed on North America's shores, pastors have conducted sermons on virtually every conceivable topic possible. For the first 150 years of our republic, pastors could *freely* discuss all political matters with their congregation. The idea was that these church leaders would be held accountable by their flock and a higher authority if they abused their trust. Just as a reminder, the secular left tells us we must maintain a *wall* and that *wall* must be impregnable. If that's the case, why then is a church threatened with the loss of their charitable exempt status if they don't abide by a law the government set forth against the very institution they're supposed to leave alone? The mafia refers to this as a "kind request," whereas the law more accurately calls it *extortion*.

Since I disagree with the secular left regarding the meaning of *separation*, I'd rather not make an argument that may sound like I'm defending the practice. I'm merely pointing out the hypocrisy. However, I am left wondering why the government would go to such great lengths in shutting down the voices of church leaders? Since I only spent enough time in law school to purchase—mind you, purchase, not read—*Black Law's Dictionary*, I'm not exactly an expert on the law. So let's see if we can figure this one out together.

The First Amendment not only protects churches from the government, but if my memory serves me correctly, wasn't there something about freedom of speech in there as well? So here's the real question: why does the government threaten to punish churches financially for something permitted for the first two-thirds of our nation's existence? Maybe, and I'm just shooting in the dark here, the communist proabortion godless leaders on the left know there's a pretty good chance that people who go to church are less likely to be in-line with their liberal agenda. And for those parishioners on the fence, the powers that be are certainly not going to want anyone sharing information from the pulpit that may disagree with their atheist ideology.

So, in summary, the government is violating three-fifths of the First Amendment against places of worship: those being religion, speech, and assembly. In case anyone was curious why "assembly" is included in this trifecta disaster, it's because if the church doesn't do what the government wants, they're going to cripple them financially. The government's threat to take away their tax exemption forces religious groups to adhere or risk no more wafers on Sunday. And, like any good syndicate, the government has plenty of muscle to carry out this menacing extortion scheme in the form of the IRS.

Note: In May of 2017, President Trump signed an executive order curtailing the SS, excuse me, I mean IRS, limiting their scope. The order reads in part:

"To the greatest extent practicable and to the extent permitted by law to respect and protect the freedom of persons and organizations to engage in religious and political speech."

In my view, this is a prime example of how *tolerance* in lieu of religious liberty can be dangerous. Although many may commend former President Trump in his efforts to right a wrong created by the godless Obama administration, the fact remains, another president may come along and choose to do otherwise—precisely what our framers were trying to avoid when they penned the First Amendment.

To better explain the contrast between religious liberty and religious toleration, allow me to share an excerpt from Kevin Seamus Hasson's *The Right to Be Wrong: Ending the Culture War Over Religion in America:*

> *Religious toleration is not a gift of God, but the gift of the government, and what the government gives, the government can take. Religious liberty is carved into the bedrock of natural law. Religious toleration is always written in sand.*

The whole thing has been turned upside down, starting with the "Amazing Kreskin's" insight into Jefferson's Danbury letter.

Allow me to take the Everson Supreme Court ruling one step further. The Court made its decision without the use of any precedent, because there wasn't any. In my hope to gain some perspective on this perplexing monumental decision, I went back to 1947 to see if there was something I was missing.

"God save the United States and this Honorable Court" were the first words the justices heard as they took their seats to open the session that year. In an unobstructed view along the chamber walls, the nine male jurists dressed in black robes faced a piece of ivory vein Spanish marble that sculptor Adolph Weinman used in creating his frieze masterpiece depicting Moses holding the Hebrew-inscribed Ten Commandments.

*Did someone forget to mention to Mr. Weinman about the separation of church and state? I'm sure he would've been just as happy to chisel out some cartoon characters. Maybe instead of Moses holding two tablets, he could've had a secular Bugs Bunny chomping on a carrot.

The chief justice, Fred M. Vinson, an army veteran, had to be aware that in 1947 all the chaplains in the military, both houses of Congress and in his own Court, were all funded by the American taxpayers (strike one regarding separation). A learned man of the law and history, I will further assume he was familiar with our Founding Fathers' reliance on Christianity and the Bible when establishing our nation (strike two). Lastly, in 1947, all previously established precedent for the justices to base their ruling on whether or not America was a Christian nation was one-sided. Of course, that would be on the side of Christianity.

Reminder: In the 1892 Church of the Holy Trinity v. United States, the Court referenced nearly eighty precedents declaring the United States a Christian nation and unanimously ruled that Christian principles remain the basis of our country's laws and institutions. I believe Justice Brewer's written opinion for the unanimous 9–0 Court summed up what everyone in this country already knew in 1892: *"We are a Christian nation."*

In short, before 1947, Baby Jesus was welcomed in the public arena and safe from the godless left. However, what should've been strike three against the attack on God in the Everson v. Board of Education case, turned out to be a devastating blow against religious liberty. With the "wall" established as a precedent, the Court's next target was prayer in schools.

GODLESS, 2

LIBERTY, 1

1948: McCollum v. Board of Education (8–1)

The Court wasted little time reaffirming its newfound precedent in Everson—otherwise known as the "wall of separation doctrine"—in declaring that teachers weren't permitted in public schools to provide religious instruction even though the participants were seeking such tutelage. For the first time in our nation's history, the released-time program would have to occur off all publicly owned property.

GODLESS, 3

LIBERTY, 1

Let the craziness commence…

1962: Engel v. Vitale (6–3)

With momentum on their side, the secular movement gained another victory when the Supreme Court ruled prayer in public schools was prohibited.

In this landmark decision, the Court redefined the word *church* to mean any religious *activity* performed in public. Thanks to the secular movement in the judiciary branch—otherwise known as judicial activism—they could now redefine the meaning of the word *church*.

What such insight, I'd love to invite the justices over my house to tell me what the hell my wife brought home last week from her pottery class. I think it's a cup, but it could be a bowl pretending to be a plate. With such a vivid imagination by the black-robed idiots, I wouldn't be shocked if they told me it was a bloody flying saucer.

Just to hammer this point home, they (nine idiots in black robes) redefined a word that anyone with any degree of knowledge knows means an "institution" and changed it to "any public activity." I would have to think Mary Lou Retton is envious of the acrobatics performed by these old white-haired men.

Stop and think about the following.

Our most precious right has been taken away under the premise of a nonofficial document (the Danbury letter) authored by a person who never worked on the Constitution or the Bill of Rights

(Jefferson). However, for the ninety members who did work on the First Amendment, not one is on record referencing Jefferson's phrase. But we are led to believe by black-robed mind readers that this was our framers' *intent*. Sorry Mary Lou, the gold goes to team Antichrist for nailing their dismount while plunging their dagger into our Bill of Rights. And yes, that's two Marry Lou Retton references in as many chapters—you're welcome!

To summarize, in 1962, using zero precedents, the US Supreme Court ruled the removal of prayer in public schools. A year later, in 1963, the Court reaffirmed their decision by ruling in both the Abington v. Schempp and Murray v. Curlett cases that Bible reading was not permitted in public schools. A few years later, in the DeKalb v. DeSpain case, the Court declared a nursery rhyme unconstitutional because it "*implied*" God. That's right. It didn't mention God, but because someone may *think* it was referring to God, the verse had to go. Did I hear someone say THINKPOL (the name given to George Orwell's Thought Police)? *Seriously, have we lost our minds!*

Note: Article 1, section 5, paragraph 3 mandates a written record of all proceedings conducted by Congress. The words "separation of church and state" are nowhere to be found at any time during the US constitutional proceedings.

GODLESS, 4
LIBERTY, 1

1971: Lemon v. Kurtzman (8–1)

"Any public display of religion must be secular."

What the hell does that mean? If one wants to have a Christmas tree in a public school, they better not refer to it as a Christmas tree? Heaven forbid thinking about inviting Baby Jesus if his presence "promotes" Christianity. So the Christmas tree will be renamed the holiday tree, and Baby Jesus is invited as long as the Son of God remains secular in nature. You just can't make this stuff up!

GODLESS, 5
LIBERTY, 1

1985: The government creates the "endorsement test" to avoid the appearance of bias toward any single religion.

Let me see if I can understand this one. Our liberal judges are doing a back handspring with a lemon twist dismount to appease the atheist, but God forbid I should say "God forbid" in front of people who don't believe in God.

Holy cow! I think I need a drink.

Godless, 6

Liberty, 1

1989: County of Allegheny v. ACLU (5–4)

The Court decided the displaying of a Christmas nativity scene and a banner that read, "Gloria in Excelsis Deo" (Latin for "Glory to God in the Highest") at the county building was unconstitutional.

Tanqueray and tonic, please. Hold the fruit.

Godless, 7

Liberty, 1

1992: "Endorsement Test"

If an atheist feels the Ten Commandments is pushing them outside their own beliefs, then God must go.

Make it a double. Thank you!

Godless, 8

Liberty, 1

1992: Lee v. Weisman (5–4)

The Court deemed that prayer at a public school graduation in Providence, Rhode Island, unconstitutional.

"Jake, here's your diploma. Now, if you even think about thanking God, you'll have detention for the rest of your life."

I think I'm going to need something a little stronger!
GODLESS, 9
LIBERTY, 1

2000: Santa Fe Independent School District v. Doe (6–3)

The Court ruled that student-initiated prayers at a public school football game were unconstitutional and did not fall under the Free Speech and Free Exercise Clauses of the First Amendment.
Pour the Tanqueray bottle into an IV bag, and then find a vein.
GODLESS, 10
LIBERTY, 1

Fact check: Although it may seem that every explosive case ends up in the Supreme Court, the reality is that less than .000001 percent of all appeals make it there each year. I think the odds of seeing Maddona, Joy Behar, or Nancy Pelosi wearing a MAGA hat are slightly better than getting a case before the highest court.

5–4

So how is it, in a country established under Judeo-Christian values, that God is now being treated like the skunk at a picnic by the High Court? Can they not see that the further away we get from the Almighty, the worse our society has become. I would argue that court rulings alone cannot be held responsible for our nation's decay, but they certainly haven't helped. The most powerful country the world has ever known has lost its moral compass, and because of this, I'm afraid we will go the way of every empire that preceded us.

The pressing question is, how did the Supreme Court evolve into an equal branch of government that could wield such enormous, untethered power? For starters, it was never the Founding Fathers' intention to have the judiciary branch as an "equal." In Alexander Hamilton's "Federalist No. 78," the Revolutionary War hero proclaimed that since the judiciary had neither the military power (the president) or the purse (congress), then by default, it would be the weakest of the three branches. But as we are all too aware, this is far from the reality that exists today.

Helping to propel the judiciary into the juggernaut that currently exists is the abdication of responsibility by Congress. All too often, senators and representatives find it easier to pontificate on hotbed issues than address them. It's no wonder Congress had an approval rating of only 17 percent in the summer of 2019. By sidestepping their responsibilities as the voice of the people they represent, many issues have been left to the Supreme Court to decide: Deferred Action for Childhood Arrivals (DACA), abortion, prayer in schools, and immigration reform, to name a few.

Abraham Lincoln voiced his concern with the possibility of such a precedent:

> *The candid citizen must confess that if the policy of the government, upon vital questions, affecting the whole people, is to be irrevocably fixed by decisions of the Supreme Court—the people will have ceased to be their own rulers, having, to that extent, practically resigned their government into the hands of that eminent tribunal.*

It was men, similar to our Supreme Court in appearance and authority, who presided at the Oracle of Delphi. In the parable, once a year, Apollo would visit the temple virgin known as the Pythia. There, the son of Zeus would give the Pythia the ability to see the future. The annual announcement would have a significant impact on commerce, crops, and prospective wars. The high priests wearing black robes were the ones entrusted to reveal what they heard. However, depending on how their allegiances and biases aligned would sometimes influence their hearing. Of course, this was not supposed to be the case. They were only to repeat what was said and reveal it to the people.

There were disagreements on occasions among the nine men in black as to what the Pythia had conveyed. In cases when they couldn't reach a consensus, they took it upon themselves to put it to a vote. During one of these stalemates, all the priests heard the Pythia but disagreed on what she had spoken. The question at hand was whether or not to go to war, an answer the king of Thrace eagerly awaited. Four men without partiality heard her say it would not be advantageous to do so while five of the men discerned that the gods would be with them in battle. It just so happened these five men and their influential friends would gain financially from such a conflict.

The 5–4 decision proved to be disastrous for the king and the over fifty thousand soldiers he lost on the first day of battle. He'd later learn that the decision had nothing to do with what the Pythia said and everything to do with the egocentric bias of a handful of men with unchecked power.

I'm always amazed when I hear of a 5–4 Supreme Court decision. These men and women who sit on the Court are some of the country's finest legal minds. They've been in the legal world most of their adult lives and have an understanding of the law I think few can ever truly appreciate. My question then is, how can nine knowledgeable people see, read, and hear the exact same thing and come up with different conclusions?

I will risk the faux pas of answering my own question.

While I was in the New York City Police Academy as a cadet, the instructors would go over the Constitution and, more specifically, the Bill of Rights. I learned the difference between a legal search and seizure from an illegal one (the Fourth Amendment) and when it was time to read someone their Miranda Rights (the Fifth Amendment). As a police officer, I would further familiarize myself with the state penal law codes and the vehicular traffic law. The extent of legal material taught in the academy over the six-plus months is an introduction to the system and in no way makes anyone who graduates the next Oliver Wendell Holmes Jr. However, most police officers like myself continue their education after the academy's training days have ended. In my police career, I made hundreds of arrests and issued thousands of summonses. In all those instances, I never once had a gray area. If I put nine cops in my shoes, I'm confident that all nine would have come to the same conclusion as I had. Sure, I may have had to look up a code or violation number, but the fact the person committed a crime was never in doubt. Probable cause is the burden of proof for a police officer to take away someone's liberty of freedom. However, if my cuffs came out, there was zero doubt in my mind that the person committed a crime.

So, in my experience, the law was reasonably straightforward. This leads me to conclude that the legislation is clear; it's the people (lawyers) and their prejudices that make them cloudy. If not, how else can one explain so many crucial 5–4 decisions?

The Court is supposed to rule on matters without bias, but we see rulings split down ideological lines repeatedly. Thus, one can predict with some degree of certainty how members of the Supreme Court will vote. That is, except for the crucial *swing vote*. In recent years, this vote had belonged to justices Sandra Day O'Conner; Anthony Kennedy; and, before Amy Coney Barrett joined the Court, Chief Justice John Roberts. Some of the most critical decisions were not voted on by Congress and signed into law by the president, but instead by a single unelected individual sitting on the Supreme Court.

Here are some examples of crucial *swing vote* rulings by Sandra Day O'Conner:

- Planned Parenthood v. Casey (1992)
  In another 5–4 decision, O'Conner's decisive vote affirmed a women's right to an abortion. The case reaffirmed the 1973 decision of Roe v. Wade.
  GODLESS, 11
  LIBERTY, 1
- Lee v. Weisman (1992)
  By her one vote, Justice O'Conner affirmed that prayer is not protected at graduations and other public school events.
  GODLESS, 12
  LIBERTY, 1
- Stenberg v. Carhart (2000)
  O'Conner's swing vote overturned Nebraska's ban on partial-birth abortions. The ruling meant that a federal

judge in a 5–4 decision had the power to overturn the will of the people in a state matter that was voted on by officials elected by the people of that state.

GODLESS, 13

LIBERTY, 1

- Grutter v. Bollinger (2003)

All men are equal under the law…sometimes. At least that's what the 5–4 decision declared when affirmative action was upheld with Justice O'Conner's swing vote.

GODLESS, 14

LIBERTY, 1

- McCreary County v. ACLU of Kentucky (2005)

In this case, Justice O'Conner's deciding vote deemed the Ten Commandments displayed in several Kentucky courthouses unconstitutional. This would be the same Ten Commandments displayed behind the justices at the Supreme Court and that our Founding Fathers referred to as the spiritual foundation to our laws. Thanks to one person's vote, God loses again.

GODLESS, 15

LIBERTY, 1

Swing Vote Deux:

Justice Anthony Kennedy said of the term *swing vote*, "The cases swing. I don't." Kennedy may not have been a big fan of the label, but his single vote decided several crucial cases more times than not. Here are a few examples:

- Planned Parenthood v. Casey (1992)

Kennedy, along with the other swing vote of O'Conner, upheld Roe v. Wade.

- Lawrence v. Texas (2003)

The striking down of a state sodomy law paved the way for same-sex unions throughout the nation.

- US v. Windsor (2010)

  The Supreme Court of the United States (SCOTUS) overturned a federal law depriving benefits to same-sex couples.
- Obergefell v. Hodges (2015)

  After thousands of years of religious doctrine defining "marriage" as a union between a man and a woman, Kennedy's swing vote made same-sex marriage the law of the land.

  GODLESS, 16

  LIBERTY, 1

Next!

It didn't take long after Justice Anthony Kennedy's retirement in 2018 to see that Chief Justice John Roberts would, in all likelihood, be the next swing vote on the Court. However, the title wouldn't last long. Two years later, after the sudden passing of the progressive Ruth Bader Ginsberg, conservative Amy Coney Barret was sworn onto the Supreme Court. The shift swung the Court to a 6–3 conservative majority, neutralizing Roberts's pivotal swing vote.

Most reasonable legal scholars would agree that the Supreme Court has evolved into our society's moral arbitrator. A scary proposition since SCOTUS has had its fair share of blunders over the years. In the long run, this pendulum of democracy can be destructive toward our republic. Unfortunately, there are those on the left who'd rather see this armageddon when it comes to our three branches of government. And since the courts are the weakest of the three, they've become ground zero for progressives.

When it comes to abortion, prayer in public schools, displaying the Ten Commandments, affirmative action, and a host of other issues, the elite in Congress have hijacked them not for the people they represent but for their own political advancement. Instead of debating these crucial issues on the House floor to allow the people to have a say through their elected representatives, some in power would instead hand it off to the de facto legislature, aka SCOTUS.

Side note: A few years back, I was helping my wife study for her citizenship test. I decided it might be helpful for the two of us to visit Washington, D. C., so that she could see our government in action. Our first stop on our tour was Article 1 of the Constitution: the Capitol Building's legislative branch. After explaining both chambers of Congress and how the Senate and House of Representatives functioned, I took her to see Article 2: the executive branch's home known as the White House. After a brief history lesson on the presidents and their powers, we finished by visiting Article 3 of the Constitution: the judiciary branch's Supreme Court. While we were there, I overheard someone say, "This is where they pass the laws." When I looked over to see who was butchering their civics lesson, I observed a father tutoring his young son. My wife could see I was distracted, so she asked what was disturbing me. After explaining my frustration over the disbursement of misinformation, she encouraged me to go over and politely correct the gentlemen. As I explained to her, one learns to mind their business while growing up in a big city like New York so I declined. However, my fearless Colombian wife walked up to the young boy and father and began explaining how it was the big dome building across the way responsible for the lawmaking and that it was the president who signed them into law (*now she was the bloody expert*). The young boy looked up at my wife and asked, "So what do they do here?" as he pointed to the Supreme Court building. Not missing a beat, my clueless but bonita partner said, "That's a wonderful question, and I know just who would love to answer that for you." For the next few minutes, I explained to the father and son how the Supreme Court acted like Templar Knights when it came to protecting our Constitution. When cases are brought before them to interpret, they are to act without bias and follow the law. I finished by telling them a bit of trivia few know of when it comes to the Supreme Court rendering their decisions. On the very top of every ruling offered by the justices, it begins with the words: *"The opinion of this court."*

It's this author's opinion that the Court has evolved into the very thing our Founders feared the most: an unchecked power ruled by the unelected few, otherwise known as oligarchies.

The Court wasn't always the threatening body it appears to be today. In 1832, Chief Justice John Marshall and the Supreme Court handed down a decision that conflicted with President Andrew Jackson's policy. The president didn't fray but instead made an illuminating observation:

"John Marshall has made his decision; now let him enforce it."

A Thankful Nation

On October 3, 1789, George Washington presented his first proclamation as president to set aside a Thanksgiving holiday at Congress's request. The celebration was for the establishment of a new government and the completion of the Bill of Rights. In George Washington's National Thanksgiving Proclamation, he states:

> *Whereas it is the duty of all nations to acknowledge the providence of Almighty God, to obey His will, to be grateful for His benefits, and humbly to implore His protection and favor—and whereas both Houses of Congress have by their joint Committee requested me "to recommend to the people of the United States a day of public thanksgiving and prayer to be observed by acknowledging with grateful hearts the many signal favors of Almighty God especially by affording them an opportunity peaceably to establish a form of government for their safety and happiness..."*

Further down in the proclamation, Washington drives home the point of God and the purpose of government:

> *To render our national government a blessing to all the people, by constantly being a Government of wise, just, and constitutional laws, discreetly and faithfully executed beyond—to protect and guide all Sovereigns and Nations (especially such as have*

a shown kindness unto us) and to bless them with good government, peace, and concord—To promote the knowledge and practice of true religion and virtue, and the encrease {sic} of science among them and us—and generally to grant unto all Mankind such a degree of temporal prosperity as He alone knows to be best.

George Washington signed the proclamation:

"Given under my hand at the City of New-York the third day of October in the year of our Lord 1789."

Thomas Jefferson suspended the holiday, only to be resumed by President Lincoln in 1863. Our sixteenth president proclaimed a national day of "*Thanksgiving and Praise to our beneficent Father who dwelleth in the Heavens.*"

As one can see, men like Washington and Lincoln, considered by most to be the two greatest leaders our country has ever produced, believed our nation's survival ran through the Almighty, not around Him.

In my view, "the separation of church and state" has been yet another hoax carried out by the left. Anyone who values the history of our country knows we are indeed a Judeo-Christian nation. That is why one month after opening in 1800, the Capitol building—that would be the one with the big white dome located in D. C.—was designated a church. I will say, if our framers intended to have a separation of church and state the way our modern-day secular courts have ruled, they sure did a terrible job implementing their policy. Or, and I'm just shooting in the dark here, that was never what our Founding Fathers had in mind. But as long as the left keeps repeating their lies, they hope to convince the rest of us simpletons that God doesn't belong. I beg to differ.

In case anyone still believes our framers wanted a secular government, here's a brief history lesson:

In Washington's inaugural address, he called upon the people to acknowledge God in prayer. He was not alone in issuing proclamations for prayer. State governors throughout the early days of our republic did the same. In fact, John Hancock, in none other than Massachuttes, issued the proclamation twenty-two times as governor for the citizens to take time and pray for the salvation of our country. These notices were printed and paid for at the behest of the government using tax dollars to publish a state proclamation for prayer.

I'd be curious what the reaction would be of Elizabeth Warren or Bernie Sanders if today such an idea were floated about. Money to subsidize abortion clinics: "Yea." For prayer: "Nay."

Chapter 2

The Moral Decay of Society

Our constitution was made only for a moral and religious people.
It is wholly inadequate to the government of any other.

—President John Adams

Something has changed in our society, and it hasn't been for the better. We can pretend that's not the case, but I think it's fair to say that life at the turn of this century has seen a steep decline in morals, ethics, and religion than at the beginning of the previous one. It's important not to mistake our technological advances for human ones. Sure, the modern world is a wonder of sorts. We can drive and fly virtually anywhere, and with the use of smartphones, we have the universe at our fingertips. So you would think churches would be packed with parishioners thanking the Good Lord for all His blessings, but this couldn't be further from the truth. How is it then that we have more of everything but we're less happy as a whole? I have a theory, and it begins and ends with God.

Our Founders were well versed in the Bible and its invaluable principles. One such advocate for the teachings of the scriptures in public schools was Benjamin Rush. A prominent physician, social reformer, and signer of the Declaration of Independence, Rush said, "If we were to remove the Bible from public schools, we would be wasting so much time punishing crimes and taking so little pains to prevent them."

Maybe that's why, for the first 150 years of our nation's existence, the Bible was part of every public school curriculum. Then came back-to-back liberal Supreme Court decisions in the early sixties that dismissed prayer, the Bible, and God from classrooms.

Side note no. 1: Although the United States makes up only 4.4 percent of the population on Earth, it incarcerates 22 percent of the world's prisoners, 655 per 100,000. Making it the highest incarceration rate in the world as of 2020.

Side note no. 2: When President Dwight D. Eisenhower was asked if he had any regrets while in office, the thirty-fourth president replied, "I have two, and they're both sitting on the Supreme Court." Ike was referring to Chief Justice Warren and Associate Justice Brennan. The Warren Court, as it has become known as, grossly expanded judicial power while doing everything to attempt to limit God's.

Goodbye, God; Hello, School Shootings

The following is the prayer behind the 1962 Engel v. Vitale SCOTUS case that deemed praying in public schools unconstitutional:

> *Almighty God, we acknowledge our dependence upon Thee, and we beg Thy blessings upon us, our parents, our teachers, and our Country.*

Under the guise of the establishment clause created by the 1947 Everson v. Board of Education case, the Court delivered a devastating blow toward Christianity still felt to this day. Again, this was the US Supreme Court making a ruling on something that Congress (the legislative branch) never attempted. Let's suppose Congress did pass a law mandating prayer in schools. Then the Court would've had every right to deem it unconstitutional. But as we know, that was not the case.

Side note: Prior to the 1962 ruling, there were isolated, sporadic shootings in schools. These were extremely rare and none on the mass level we are tragically all too familiar with today. While prayer existed in schools, the term "mass school shooting" did not.

From 1903 to 1963, there were a total of sixty-eight people killed in school shootings. That's slightly over one killing a year before God and the Bible were ruled unconstitutional.

In 1966, the University of Texas experienced the first mass shooting in US school history. A twenty-five-year-old student fatally shot fifteen and wounded another thirty-one during a ninety-six-minute shooting rampage from the school's tower.

From 1967 to 1991, there were an additional 126 souls killed by gunfire.

Below is a list of shooting deaths starting from 1992 provided by K12 Academics:

1992–1993: 55 souls
1993–1994: 51 souls
1994–1995: 20 souls
1995–1996: 35 souls
1996–1997: 25 souls
1997–1998: 40 souls
1998–1999: 25 souls
1999–2000: 25 souls
2000–2001: 19 souls
2001–2002: 4 souls
2002–2003: 14 souls
2003–2004: 29 souls
2004–2005: 20 souls
2005–2006: 5 souls
2006–2007: 38 souls
*Virginia Tech (32 of the 38)—Blacksburg, Va.
2007–2008: 3 souls
2008–2009: 10 souls
2009–2010: 5 souls
2010–2011: 7 souls
2011–2012: 44 souls
*Sandy Hook Elementary (28 of the 44)—Newton, Ct.
2012–2013: 17 souls
2013–2014: 15 souls

2014–2015: 19 souls
2015–2016: 10 souls
2016–2017: 16 souls
2017–2018: 43 souls
*Marjory Stoneman Douglas H. S. (17 of the 43)—Parkland, Fl.
2018–2019: 17 souls

Note: The above numbers do not include students who survived gunshot wounds and homicides from other than a firearm (knives, blunt instruments, etc.).

Since the 1962 Engel v. Vitale ruling, there have been 760 shooting deaths in schools. That's an average of over 14 killings per year compared to 1 during the first half of the twentieth century. It's my opinion that there's been no greater contributor to this nightmare in our society than decisions generated by the Supreme Court. The removal of the fundamental foundation of Judeo-Christian values from our schools has had tragic consequences. If one disagrees between the correlation of taking God out of schools and the horrific uptick in violence that has followed, I ask what else it could be? Is it sugary drinks, violent video games, drugs, or a host of other societal factors? Maybe, but none of those exist on the scale it does today if children are raised on biblical principles as their foundation in life instead of the next Xbox game and a Red Bull.

Gun Control

How about mental institution control? Well, obviously, that's not as sexy, but the truth is, if we want to stop future tragedies like Sandy Hook and Marjory Stoneman Douglass, the best place to start is getting control over the people who shouldn't be walking the streets. So how many people is that?

Mental facilities began emptying in the 1960s and have seen a steady decrease in patients ever since. Today in a country with over 330 million people, only 25,000 are under care in these institutions. However, if we went back fifty years ago, the US population was under 200 million, but the admittance rate hovered around 500,000.

Simple math indicates that many people among us are in desperate need of mental health. But instead of addressing the issue, we have the Dems screaming to do away with the Second Amendment. My question is, do you really think that all the people who are shot in Chicago, Baltimore, New York, and the rest of these inner cities are law-abiding, permit-carrying citizens? Of course not. So instead of politicians doing something to address the issue at hand, mental health, they scream for more gun control. How about more God! If people were honoring Him instead of being lured into Satan's world, there's no question these events would happen less frequently.

But don't stricter gun laws help make cities safer?

The statistics show just the opposite. The top ten states with the most restrictive gun laws in the country have cities with the most violent crimes. Take Illinois, for example. The state is home to some of the nation's strictest gun laws but had an average homicide rate in Chicago of over 560 from 2016 to 2020. With the highest per capita murder rate in the nation, Baltimore was named the most dangerous city in America by *USA Today* even though Maryland's gun laws are among the nation's toughest. So we're told by the Dems if we'd only give up our Second Amendment, none of these tragedies would ever happen again. I'm just shooting in the dark here, no pun intended, but how does that make any sense. Think about it. In the most draconian states, people who cannot acquire a gun permit are being killed by thugs carrying unlawful firearms. But we're supposed to believe if we, the law-abiding public, gave up another one of our liberties, we will all be safe. The scary part is that many people believe this lie.

Public Schools

In Atlanta, eight educators with financial incentives to achieve better test scores for their students went to prison for "fixing" the numbers. A little further north, Baltimore is spending over $16,000 per student. So what do you get for the third-highest per capita spending in the country? Well, for starters, out of thirteen high schools, not one student was proficient in math. Before you go and blame this all on the Democrats, back in 1967, the city had a Republican mayor. I don't know how and I can't prove it, but I think all Baltimore's current issues stem from that lone Republican who held office way back when. I know that sounds a bit bizarre, but hear me out on this one. Since Baltimoreons keep on electing the same Democrat officials decade after decade, the only rational explanation I can think of is that they've been trying to fix the mess this one lone Republican made fifty-something years ago. By the way, it's Baltimoreons, not Balti-morons, or so I've been told.

In Queens, Principal Khurshid Abdul-Mutakabbir of Maspeth High School, unlike the Baltimore high schools, doesn't have a problem with state scores. According to the Board of Education, the school boasts an excellent 99 percent proficiency in both math and reading. The institution is in such demand that parents are selected by lottery for the chance to get into the much sought-after public school that holds the city's lowest student to teacher ratio at 19–1. So what's the problem? Well, it seems Principal Khurshid Abdul-Mutakabbir may not be a big fan of us Catholics. You see, Principal Khurshid Abdul-Mutakabbir's "lottery selection" somehow rejected all five hundred Catholics who applied. Just so there's no misunderstanding, not one Catholic out of the five hundred who applied to Principal Khurshid Abdul-Mutakabbir's public high school was accepted. And what was Principal Khurshid Abdul-Mutakabbir's explanation: "It was a clerical error." Sure it was, Principal Khurshid Abdul-Mutakabbir, sure it was.

I always appreciate simplistic explanations. It sort of reminds me when Representative Ilhan Omar was kind enough to explain to this simpleton New York City ex-cop what happened on 9/11: "Some people did something." But then again, would anyone expect anything less from a woman who married her brother?

I can go on with example after example of inept, corrupt morons running inner-city public schools and local government, but I think I've painted enough of a picture. It's a mess, and the mess is broken. Even the good schools have issues. But as one can see, this was not what our framers had in mind.

The four documents deemed to be the foundation of our laws are the following:

- Declaration of Independence (1776)
- Articles of Confederation (1777)
- Northwest Ordinance (1787)
- Constitution of the United States (1787)

The Northwest Ordinance established the new territories as one district under Congress's jurisdiction. The laws set in the document outlawed slavery, the proper treatment toward the indigenous Indians, and the path to statehood, which eventually led to Ohio becoming the seventeenth state admitted into the Union in 1803.

To ensure academia standards were maintained in the territories, the framers added Article III to the Northwest Ordinance, which read:

"Religion, morality, and knowledge, being necessary to good government and the happiness of mankind, schools and the means of education shall forever be encouraged."

In case anyone missed it, the government—in one of the most important documents created by our framers—encouraged religion to be taught in public schools. But as our school system rots from moral decay and knowledge is offered as an elective instead of the standard, the secularists would still have us believe that God in schools is the problem.

As we live in a world that is increasingly turning upside down, I can't help but be reminded of the prophet Isaiah's words when he said, *"Woe unto them that call evil good, and good evil; that put darkness for light, and light for darkness; that put bitter for sweet, and sweet for bitter!"* (Isa. 5:20).

Should anyone be surprised by how our school systems have deteriorated since God was shown the door? The more the secular left gains control of our future's most precious institution, the less productive schools have become.

Understanding the impact education has on society, Abraham Lincoln's timeless observation on the issue should give pause when it comes to our future:

"The philosophy of the schoolroom in one generation will be the philosophy of government in the next."

God help us!

Civility

Political theorist and patriot Samuel Adams believed that by observing the people of a nation and their manners as a whole, he could tell what direction a country's fate was heading.

Adams noted, *"Neither the wisest constitution, nor the wisest laws, will secure the liberty and happiness of a people whose manners are universally corrupt."*

Side note: Adams uttered those words 250 years ago. So if Samuel Adams were around today, would he think we're on the way up as a nation or on the way down? Sadly, I think we can all agree on the answer to that question. For this author, it's what has motivated me to write this book, along with the hope of restoring our Judeo-Christian values as a nation. It's my belief that manners are an intricate part of the fabric that we, as human beings, need to help cultivate a society. The right set can bring happiness, prosperity, and respect whereas without can deteriorate our liberties. Remember, the rotten apple in a basket does not grow healthier from the vibrant apples it encompasses, but rather, the decaying fruit slowly poisons the rest of the bushel. Unfortunately, the more people use their middle finger to communicate with one another, the further into the abyss we go. Perhaps the lady on her cell phone discussing her third abortion while waiting in line at Walmart or the person driving through a red light because they're late for work individually doesn't seem to be a significant threat to our civilization. However, accumulatively, these types of selfish, self-centered acts aren't sustainable in a thriving nation. That's why Satan's desensitizing of society's moral compass has pushed the godless left agenda into believing that right is wrong and wrong is right. Think about the obvious for a moment.

How can a rational person defend the killing of the unborn? They can't because it's pure evil. But through the creative, hard-to-argue euphemisms of "pro-choice" and "women's rights," society can now justify the evil wrongdoing.

Born during the Revolutionary War, Daniel Webster (1782–1852) is considered one of America's greatest orators. He holds the distinction between having served in both the upper and lower houses of Congress.

During a Fourth of July speech, the statesman affirmed the importance of morals in society and their leaders:

> *To preserve the government we must also preserve a correct energetic tone of morals. After all that can be said, the truth is that liberty consists more in the habits of the people than in anything else. When the public mind becomes vitiated and depraved, every attempt to preserve it is vain. Laws are then a nullity, and Constitutions waste paper... Ambitious men must be restrained by the public morality: when they rise up to do evil, they must find themselves standing alone. Morality rests on religion. If you destroy the foundation, the superstructure must fall.*

The only commander-in-chief to have previously served in the House of Representatives was our twentieth president, James A. Garfield. Perhaps Garfield's previous experience in Congress provided him with a unique perspective of the people's civic responsibilities when it came to electing their leaders. Garfield said of the issue:

> *Now more than ever before, the people are responsible for the character of their Congress. If that body be ignorant, reckless, and corrupt, it is because the people tolerate ignorance, recklessness, and corruption. If it be intelligent, brave, and pure, it is because the people demand these high qualities.*

With Congress's approval rating consistently hovering in the high teens, low twenties, I think it's fair to assume what Garfield's sentiment would be toward today's society and their chosen representatives.

Rules of Civility and Decent Behaviour

Though he never received a formal education, George Washington taught himself by reading and experimentation. Washington felt so strongly about the importance of good manners that he would practice transcribing the 1595 composition of the French Jesuits's set of directives. As a young boy, the future president penned a book that consisted of 110 rules to live by in life. The title of young Mr. Washington's masterpiece is *Rules of Civility and Decent Behavior in Company and Conversation*.

In Washington's book, he uses biblical principles as the foundation for good civility. Here are a few examples:

- Rule 22:
  Show not yourself glad at the misfortune of another though he were your enemy.
  In Proverbs 24:17, the Bible states:
  "Do not rejoice when your enemy falls, and do not let your heart be glad when he stumbles."
- Rule 34:
  It is good manners to prefer them to whom we speak before ourselves...
  In Philippians 2:3, the Bible states:
  "Regard one another as more important than yourselves. Do not look out merely for your own personal interests, but also for the interests of others."
- Rule 56 (my personal favorite):
  Associate yourself with men of good quality, if you esteem your own reputation, for 'is better to be alone than in bad company.

In Proverbs 13:20 and 1 Corinthians 15:33, the Bible states:

"He who walks with wise men will be wise, but the companion of fools will be destroyed."

"Do not be deceived, evil company corrupts good habits."

- Rule 73 (My wife thinks I need to read this one more often):

Think before you speak. Pronounce not imperfectly nor bring out your words too hastily but orderly and distinctly.

In James 1:19, the Bible states:

"Let every man be swift to hear and slow to speak."

At an early age, my father gifted Washington's book to me. Outside of the Bible, it's been the most influential book in my life. To this day, I find myself saying "please" when asking, "thank you" when receiving, and "excuse me" when uncertain. I've handed down these principles to my daughter; and please, God, she will hand them down to her children.

If we continue to remove God and His principles from everyday life, we are doomed. Such a combination of less God and more government will have people lined up for visiting day at prisons rather than at church.

Side note: I volunteer for the United Way in a program known as Reading Pals. I want to stress to anyone feeling depressed, angry, upset, or overwhelmed to go and volunteer. No medication in the world can help more than helping others. Trust me, I would know. Name an antidepressant, and I'll bet you at some point I was on it. There was Paxil, Zoloft, Xanax for the anxiety, Cialis for the side effects from the Paxil, and I'd finish with Ambien because I couldn't sleep trying to remember if I took my meds. I was a mess. Just imagine how much fun I was to be around. To put it bluntly, I was so self-absorbed that I made Narcissus look like Mother Teresa.

One day, a friend gave me some tough love advice by telling me to stop feeling sorry for myself and start thinking of others. I reacted precisely how a selfish, self-centered jerk would. I told him to go to hell and stormed off. Later, when I came down from my self-pity tantrum, I went back and asked my lifelong friend, who happened to be my priest, for help. Father Gerald's advice is the same that I pass along today. The secret is this: I'm still a self-centered, narcissistic jerk, but by not thinking of myself every waking moment and being forced to think of others, I take a break from being that jerk. And you want to know something, it feels pretty good.

When people ask why I enjoy volunteering, I tell them it's better than taking meds. And although good deeds only go so far with the Man upstairs, I made a promise to Him that I would help myself by helping others. Trust me, it's a win, win, win.

Through the United Way, I was kindly offered to participate in a unique event known as HandsOn Broward: Real Men Read (See *Sun Sentinel* article on page 311). The gathering invited local men from the community to read a book to the Thurgood Marshall Elementary School students. Principal Michael Billins was the brainchild behind the idea. He stressed that many of the children were without fathers in the inner-city South Florida school and that, in all likelihood, it would be their first time hearing a male voice read to them. Principal Billins reflected on his African American childhood and his own experience of growing up in a home without a father. He felt the combination of a male role model and reading was extremely important to his students' future success.

Before the rest of the male participants and I went to our assigned classrooms, Principal Billins asked if anyone had any questions. Standing off to the side was a distinguished-looking individual who asked in a stern voice, "How many of your students in the school are below their respective grade's reading level?" When the principal inquired why he was asking, the fellow volunteer explained that he was the head of corrections and wanted to know how many extra beds they'd be needing.

The exchange seemed to suck out whatever good energy was in the room. Perhaps sensing his approach might've been a tad aggressive, the correction superintendent apologized for how he phrased the question and then stressed to the rest of us volunteers present the direct correlation between illiteracy and incarceration. As the Warden candidly put it, "We either take care of the issue today [literacy], or I'll be dealing with it in about five or ten years from now."

Socialism

"The American people would never knowingly vote for socialism, but under the guise of liberalism, they would adopt every fragment of the socialist platform."

The famous quote dates back nearly a century and is credited to ACLU founder Norman Thomas. He foresaw a day when America would unknowingly become a socialist country. Like a thief in the night, private property will be replaced by a commune while the government takes full control of production and distribution. But this could never happen in America, or could it?

In August of 2020, Joe Biden gave his acceptance speech at the Democrat National Convention. Absent that night were any of the future President's classic gaffs such as "You ain't Black if you vote for Trump" and "Put y'all back in chains." What made the latter comment extra special was his adlib Southern drawl when he delivered the "you all" part. For a second, I thought it might've been Hillary Clinton bragging about how much she loved her hot sauce to a NYC hip-hop radio show (The Breakfast Club interview, April 18, 2016) or Al Gore at any Black function. But no. This was Uncle Touchy-Feely Joe doing his *thang y'all*. Then there was the former vice president mistaking his wife for his sister or his sister for his wife, I'm still not sure, and sadly, neither is he. And let's not forget this oldie but goodie Joe said at a town hall hosted by the Asian and Latino Coalition: "Poor kids are just as bright and just as talented as white kids…" Nothing racist, elitist, or bias in that comment, right? But this is Uncle Joe. Remember he says things he doesn't mean.

Getting back to that flawless DNC speech, Biden spoke of awe-inspiring *love being more powerful than hate and how light is more powerful than dark.* He failed to mention how having your dad as a vice president is more powerful than a good resume. *You're welcome, Hunter!* However, the words that rang alarm bells were the ones no one in the media, left or right, picked up on. They were when Joe said, *"Fairness over privilege."*

Uncle Joe's dog whistle was music to the ears of the left socialist part of the Democrat Party, but for me, they're an ominous warning of what's to come.

The first obvious question is, who exactly is going to define the terms *fairness* and *privilege*? Once someone in power takes it upon themselves to arbitrarily separate the wheat from the chaff, what exactly are Uncle Joe and the government going to do to right this supposed wrong? Here's a suggestion, I don't think it was fair for Biden's son to make millions in China and Ukraine while his father was the lead representative to both countries. So maybe we should confiscate Hiden' Biden's property and funds he accumulated from this privilege and, in the name of *fairness*, give them to, let's say, me. That would be silly, right? Well, this is precisely where the righteous left is going with this *fairness/privilege* campaign minus the "me" part. After all, BowFOGs are seen as the bad guys in this modern-day Robin Hood scenario. So I think it's safe to say I'd be on the "donating" end of this utopian paradise.

So who will be the gatekeepers watching over the redistribution of the *fairness scale*?

They are the '*do as thee, not as me*' clan who love to tell everyone how they should live and die, otherwise known as the elite. These high-and-mighty people love to make rules for us to obey but never intend to follow themselves. Don't believe me? Let's take a peek at a few examples:

- For those of you who may not be familiar with the mayor of Chicago, her name is Lori Lightfoot. During the pandemic of 2020, the first Black mayor of the city gave a stern warning to her constituents: "We will cite you, arrest you, and jail you if you violate the city's shutdown." Included in the draconian regulations was the closing of hair salons. However, for the mayor whose salary is five times as much as many Chicago police officers, this rule didn't apply to her. When confronted by a reporter for violating her own ordinance regarding the closure of hair salons, the self-righteous mayor replied, "I'm the public face of this city. I'm on national media. I'm out in the public eye." "I'm a hypocrite." Oops, sorry, the last one was an observation, not a quote.

However, since we're on the topic of Lightfoot and hypocrisy, here's a doozy. In the summer of 2020, during the rioting in Chicago, the mayor banned protestors (not rioters, but actual constitutionally protected protestors) from demonstrating on the block she resides. Lightfoot justified her unconstitutional measures by stating, "I have a right to make sure my home is secure." I would think her constituents have the same rights. However, for those in poorer communities, Lori Lightfoot would disagree.

On a separate note, Lightfoot won "The Mayor with the Best Hairstyle in America Contest." With the black shoe-polish running down his face, Giuliani finished second, while the deceased Ed Koch came in at a distant third.

- Nancy Pelosi, Crazy Nancy, Nervous Nancy, or, how about this one, Maskless Nancy. After months of chastising anyone who would listen that we must wear masks or die, Congress's wealthiest person was caught on video in a hair salon walking around without a mask. Maskless Nancy said, "I take full responsibility," and then proceeded to blame the owner of the salon for "setting her up." You just can't make this stuff up. By the way, can anyone explain to me what the phrase "I take full responsibility" means? For what it's worth, here's my two cents. Once someone says those words and in the next breath starts to blame other people, they lose all credibility. I know how shocking this must be for many people to hear that a politician could be a lying hypocrite. However, this author takes full responsibility for this observation. Who knows, maybe the Catholic proabortion Maskless Nancy will pray for me the way she had for Trump. On second thought, please don't!

As people around the country lost their jobs, and sadly, in many instances, their loved ones, the congresswoman from Califonia went on a late-night talk show to proudly show off her $15 pints of ice cream stored in her $24,000 fridge. I have no animosity toward the "public servant's" financial success, but I would like to know how the disconnected "let them eat ice cream" congresswoman and her husband, Paul, made all that money.

From all accounts, Paul Pelosi is a very successful businessman. Mr. Pelosi owns a large stake in StarKist Tuna, which in turn owns a packing plant in American Samoa. Back in 2007, when the nation's minimum wage was increased by nearly 40 percent, Nancy had American Samoa exempted from the bill. Why is that, one might ask? Well, maybe, and I'm just shooting in the dark here, it had something to do with Paul Pelosi's lucrative investment in the company.

So let me see if I have this one right. The Dems have been clamoring for a $15-an-hour minimum wage increase, except in places that may financially affect them or their spouses. The hypocrisy should come as no surprise. Crazy Nancy was the same politician denouncing a wall between the US and Mexico while at the same time living in a mansion in San Francisco surrounded with ten-foot walls and a security system that cost in the upper-six figures.

- Congresswoman Dianne Feinstein and Nancy Pelosi have a lot in common. They're both from Califonia, are incredibly wealthy, and love telling everyone to wear a mask. However, while walking through an airport in Califonia, *shockingly*, Feinstein was photographed not wearing one. Fortunately, her private pilot was wearing his N95 while carrying the congresswoman's pooch.

A kind reminder to the pilot: you're a pilot, not a dog sitter. Maybe next time, the eighty-nine-year-old Feinstein can do a Paris Hilton impersonation and carry her own dog. After all, I would think you'd be more concerned with that ten-ton tuna can you're about to take off in than playing Jeeves.

The mask and dog are just more examples of hypocritical nonsense from the left. However, when Feinstein went after Amy Coney Barrett during her Seventh Circuit Court of Appeals confirmation hearing in 2017, a constitutional line had been deliberately crossed.

As the senator, whose career has spanned over six decades, looked down from her throne, sorry, I mean dais, Feinstein decided to voice her personal concerns over the "dogma" that she described as "living loudly within" the practicing Catholic Barrett. I could promise you, if the nominee were an atheist, Feinstein would've been more respectful of that person's godless beliefs than the attack she displayed toward the good Christian woman who sat before her that day. I'll have to assume the lawmaker skipped over that freedom of religion thingy in the Constitution when she attended law school. Oh, that's right, the lawmaker never went to law school.

- Allow me to introduce you to Pennsylvania's health secretary, Dr. Rachel Levine. Not exactly a household celebrity, but for a few weeks in May in 2020, her name was uttered throughout the Keystone State in the same *reverence* Bucky Dent's is up in Boston. In case your not a baseball fan, the New York Yankee shortstop hit a three-run homer in 1978 to once again crush Sox fans' hopes of killing the great Bambino Curse. After that, it's forbidden to say "Bucky Dent" in the state of Massachusetts without adding his middle name, which rhymes with the word *sucking*.

As for Dr. Rachel "blank-ing" Levine, the health secretary came under some credibility issues when she defended her agency's handling of the virus. At the time, a staggering 70 percent of the state's deaths (6,600 souls) came from inside nursing homes and personal-care facilities. Levine's office announced that the agency was simply following a March directive from the Centers for Disease Control (CDC) that stated in part: "Nursing homes should admit any individuals that they would normally admit to their facility, including individuals from hospitals where a case of Covid-19 was/is present." The "credibility issue" came when it was discovered that the health secretary had her ninety-five-year-old mother moved out of a personal care home weeks earlier. The optics of "it's safe for you people but not for my mother" set off protests throughout Harrisburg. Levine provided an explanation that only seemed to inflame an already volatile situation when she pointed out that her elderly mother requested to be moved and that she was merely complying with her wishes. If true, I will say this about Levine's mother; she has much better instincts for safety than her daughter. Or, and I'm just shooting in the dark here, Levine used her governmental position to protect her and her family's interests while ignoring the safety of the thousands left behind in nursing homes.

Regardless of which scenario is closer to the truth, the fact remains that thousands of seniors have died because of incompetence at the highest level of government, and somehow, these idiots still have taxpaying jobs. For Dr. Levine, that "job" would be an annual salary of $155,000 plus benefits.

- Former vice president Al Gore has to be my favorite loser of all time. After conceding to Bush on election night of 2000, the whitest White guy in political history had the coconuts to call "W" back to tell him he'd changed his mind. Of course, the bigger mistake was making the first phone call to concede, but the second had to be by far the more humiliating. After a thirty-six-day legal battle, the Democrat nominee conceded for a second and final time.

Gore went through a tough time after his defeat. He put on a ton of weight, separated from his wife, and sported the worst beard ever grown on a human or a goat. But Al wouldn't go down as my favorite loser of all time if he'd stopped there. The former VP persevered and eventually found his calling. No, not the Internet, he'd already invented that, and besides, Al needed something bigger. Drum roll, please... Gore came up with "global warming." The guy who gets audiences to laugh with, "Hi, my name is Al Gore. I used to be the next president of the United States," was back! Unfortunately, his "global warming" was a tough sell, with winters in Wisconsin cold enough to freeze pigeons in mid-flight, so the brainiacs on the left came up with "climate change" instead.

With Al's newfound good fortune, he was once again in the pilot's seat. I mean that literally. With his new lease on life and an Oscar for best documentary sitting on his mantle, Gore began jetting around the world to warn everyone that CO_2 gases, that would be the carbon dioxide gases emitted through the combustion of fossil fuels, are killing our planet.

I don't know about you, but I'm thankful that Mr. Gore is burning fuel to fly all around the planet like a modern-day Paul Revere, warning us that we're going to all die if we use one more plastic straw.

For the record, I'm all for conservation and believe our planet is in constant flux. So I don't need another elitist telling me to adjust my thermostat while they fly around in private jets to houses the size of the Taj Mahal. *Al, thanks for the effort, but you're still a loser at the end of the day. Granted a very wealthy loser, but a loser nonetheless.*

- Next in line for "private-jet hypocrite of the year" goes to John Kerry. Kerry wasn't born a snob. He earned his elite status the old fashion way by marrying into it.

   Tapped as President Biden's climate czar, one would think this crusader for cleaner air would do almost anything to save the planet. Well, you're right. Kerry was so dedicated to lowering carbon emissions that in 2019 he flew halfway around the world in a private jet to Iceland to receive the Arctic Circle Prize for his leadership in the field of climate change. I know what most of you are thinking; who knew the penguins had award shows? As for me, I was thinking how obnoxious it was for some elite-ass cracker to fly around in an earth-destroying Gulfstream jet just to have his ego stroked.

So was Kerry embarrassed when called out on his blatant hypocrisy? After all, private jets have been estimated to emit forty times more carbon per passenger than commercial flights. Answer: hell no! Instead, the embellished war hero explained to us little people the reason behind his actions: "If you offset your carbon, it's the only choice for somebody like me who is traveling the world to win this battle."

Okay, let's try taping the brakes on this nonsense. Firstly, how does one "offset" their carbon? Exactly how does that conversation go:

"Hey, John, what are your plans for this weekend?"

"Well, I just flew back from Iceland on my private jet, so I thought I'd cut back on my carbon output by staying home in my twenty-thousand-square foot air-conditioned summer cottage this weekend."

I guess when one reaches elite status, they automatically start to believe everyone else is stupid. But really, John? You're going to justify flying around in a private jet to accept an award to put over your mantle and then tell us it's okay because you're "offsetting" your carbon. John, have you forgotten how many homes you and your lovely ketchup-rich wife own? If you really want to save the world, all you have to do is donate your homes to the poor and move into an efficiency-apartment. If it would help make the transition smoother, you can take a bottle of Grey Poupon and one Rolls-Royce.

- In a taped address that aired on the second night of the DNC Convention in 2020, Bill Clinton sharply criticized President Donald Trump for his handling of the coronavirus. If the former president stopped there, there's a reasonably good chance Bubba wouldn't have made it into *Godless v. Liberty*. But instead, the sex addict went on to say that the "Oval Office should be a command center" and how "there's only chaos" in the White House. I have to agree with Bill on this one. The Oval Office should be used as a command center and not as a short-stay tryst like some local roadside Motor Lodge Inn. Now I could be wrong, but wasn't Bubba the president who was caught with some intern wearing a blue dress playing the popular college dorm game "hide the cigar"? And forgive my foggy memory but wasn't he responsible for that loathsome act of adultery taking place in the Oval Office?

I don't think the psychoanalysis field has advanced far enough to have come up with a name for Bubba's disorder. I was thinking "narcissistic sociopathic pedophile sex addict" but settled on "Hillary's husband syndrome" instead.

To put things in perspective, Bill's complete lack of self-awareness would be comparable to Jefferey Dahmer criticizing how someone ate their turkey leg at Thanksgiving dinner.

Hey, Jeffrey, I'll eat the leg my way, and you can eat it… never mind.

Speaking of guys named Jeffrey, my condolences go out to Slick Willy on the loss of his close island-hopping pedophile buddy Jeffrey Epstein. Rumor has it that Bubba is missing his friend so much that he's considering buying Michael Jackson's Neverland estate to help *lift* his mood.

- Since we're on the topic of morally corrupt pieces of sunshine, allow me to introduce three men who have never told the truth in their entire lives: Teddy Kennedy, Harry Reid, and Adam Schiff.

  Ted "Chappaquiddick" Kennedy was yet another Irish Catholic politician with poor driving skills and questionable ethics. Ted's character, or should I say lack thereof, was on full display when he gave the "Robert Bork's

America" speech. What can best be described as a political drive-by assassination, Kennedy took to the Senate floor to announce to the nation that Bork was essentially the worst human being on the planet and should not be allowed anywhere near the Supreme Court.

Kennedy: *"In Robert Bork's America women would be forced into back-alley abortions, Blacks would sit at segregated lunch counters, rogue police could break down citizens' doors in midnight raids, schoolchildren could not be taught about evolution,"* and so on until the senator from Massachusetts scared the bejesus out of most of America. For the first time, the Senate's advise-and-consent turned into seek-and-destroy. The fiasco even birthed a new verb, *borked.* Of course, Kennedy knew he was lying, but if ruining one man's life is what it took to preserve abortion, then integrity be damned!

For former Speaker of the House Harry Reid, lying was a bloodsport. Protected by Article 1, Section 6 of the United States Constitution, Reid and the rest of his cohorts are exempt from civil and criminal liability for things they say in speeches or debates from Congress's floor. The loophole that lawfully allows one to defame and slander political opponents would be equivalent to giving a serial arsonist a Speedway gas station to manage. With matches in hand, Reid began firebombing at will from the Senate floor.

In one of his more notorious attacks, Reid claimed that 2012 presidential candidate Mitt Romney hadn't paid any taxes for ten years. In a political chess move, Reid put the onus on Romney by saying, "Let him prove that he hasn't paid taxes," and then shamelessly questioned the candidate's "trust." You just can't make this stuff up.

By the time Romney released his taxes to counter Reid's false claims, the damage had already been done to his campaign. In response to the McCarthyism tactics, Reid justified his actions by rhetorically asking, "Romney didn't win, did he?"

After Reid retired, there was an opening in the Democrat Party for a spokesperson to continue the left's long tradition of unethical politics. Allow me to introduce the congressman from Califonia's 28th District, Adam Schiff.

Shifty Schiff is one of those types of people everyone knows. He's the awkward guy at the summer barbeque wearing a v-neck cashmere sweater, trying to fit in by talking about the incredible cycle of photosynthesis. But I have to give Schiff credit for finding his niche in life. Where else but in Congress could a guy go with no talent, morals, or ethics and still be considered a great leader by half his colleagues?

As chairman of the Intelligence Committee, Schiff had access to a lot of sensitive information. When it served him, some of that material or closed-door testimony would mysteriously, and may I add illegally, find its way to the press. During Mueller's two-year witch hunt, Schiff repeatedly lied to the American people saying there was "absolute evidence" that Trump colluded with the Russians during the 2016 presidential campaign. However, after spending $48 million, Mueller and his cronies could not find what Schiff described was in "plain sight."

Fast-forward to October 2020. For years it was suspected that Joe Biden abused his position as vice president to enrich his family, but there was never a smoking gun. Enter Hunter Biden, a modern-day version of Michael Corleone's older brother Fredo. The not-too-bright Hunter, similar to Fredo, is probably a nice enough guy who's more in his element when he's partying with a bunch of hookers and an 8 Ball. However, ask either Fredo or Hunter to close the drapes or pick up a laptop from a computer repair store and chances are something not so good will happen. (I go into more detail about the infamous computer in a later chapter and how it ushered in journalism's death). But for Shifty Schiff, he was able to explain everything away with two words we may have all heard of before: *Russian disinformation!* That's right. Without any investigation, Sherlock Schiff was able to save the government an additional $48 million by declaring the Russian bastards were at it again. The fact that neither of the Bidens denied the computer or emails belonged to Hunter makes Shifty Schiff's Perry Mason moment a bit weak. But maybe after being wrong about the last Russian disinformation campaign, Schiff knew something the rest of us didn't. Or, and I'm just shooting in the dark on this one, Schiff is a lying sack of shit who will say or do anything to further his and his party's quest for more power.

It's these types of political hacks like the congressman from Califonia that George Washington tried to warn us about in his Farewell Address, saying that partisanship would lead to the "ruins of public liberty."

• New Jersey governor Phil Murphy was dining out during the pandemic while all the other restaurants in his state were under a strict shutdown order. Mind you, that would be the same order he issued.

Side note: I can't help but think of the comic genius Mel Brooks and his character Louis the XVl in *History of the World Part 1*. There's the king in the middle of enjoying skeet shooting when his trusted advisor, Count de Monet (Count the Money), approaches him to let him know the people are revolting because they feel that the king has no regard for the peasants. King Louis (Mel Brooks), shocked in hearing such news, profoundly protests, "They are my people. I am their sovereign. I love them." With that, the king gives the command "Pull" for his next target to be unleashed. Instead of the traditional clay disk used in skeet shooting flying across the horizon, it's one of his peasants being hurled through the sky. King Louis takes aim with his musket and shoots at the screaming lad but misses. He gives a quick critique of his lack of marksmanship by quip-ping, "Drifting to the left."

I hope Governor Murphy enjoyed his fine dining while the rest of his peasants humbly ate at home. Rumor had it when the governor was informed of the outcry by his constituents, he proclaimed, "But I love my people—*pull!*"

In fairness, Murphy doesn't seem to be the sharpest tool in the shed, the brightest star in the sky, maybe one or two fries short of a Happy Meal, a few cards away from a full deck, and, I'm reasonably confident, somewhere in Jersey there's a village missing its idiot. But I still don't think the governor deserves all the blame. Remember, peo-ple had to wake up, get dressed, drive to the local school, enter the school, and pull a lever that read "Murphy" for this guy to be where he is. So I'm seriously starting to worry that maybe the toxic fumes in Bayonne are less contained than we think or maybe people should stop marrying their cousins in the Garden State. All that aside, can someone please explain the following thought process to me.

Early on in the pandemic crisis, Murphy was on with Tucker Carlson of Fox. The governor was self-praising his autocratic policies that he thought would help stem the spread of the virus, all in the name of helping the public, of course. Carlson pushed back on the governor by asking, "By what authority did you nullify the Bill of Rights in issuing this order? How do you have the power to do that?"

The governor, who swore an oath to uphold the Constitution of the United States of America, cavalierly responded, "That's above my pay grade. I wasn't thinking about the Bill of Rights…"

Cancel the missing person's report; we found the idiot. His village is located in Trenton. By the way, con-gratulations are in order for New Jersey. They're not only number one in the country for the highest property taxes, but they also have the top dumbest governor in the union.

In case those kissing-cousins can't count, that's two number 1s. Yee-ha!

• Before the Wuhan virus hit, Mayor Bill "Past the Bong" de Blasio was taking two SUVs to the gym every day. By the way, Hizhonor lives in Manhattan, and his gym is fourteen miles away in Brooklyn. So let me see if I have this right. The guy who wants to stop building skyscrapers in New York City because they're harmful to the environment thinks taking two SUVs in rush hour traffic to the gym is perfectly acceptable. Got it!

As schools remained closed in the fall of 2020, the mayor went to the airways to spew his ideology on redistribution of wealth and how the government had all the answers to correct this inequality. Evidently, getting the children back in the classrooms and opening businesses throughout the five boroughs took a back seat on his priority list. The following is the mayor's answer to the city's quest for utopia. I'm sure Engels and Marx would be very proud of their comrade de Blasio.

De Blasio: *"You really want to change things in this city? Then everyone better change a lot of the way they live more foundationally. If you just talk about it and feel self-satisfied, God bless you. That is not actually going to change things. What changes things is redistribution of wealth. Tax the wealthy at a much higher level. And I just feel like this is a lot of cocktail party comfort going on rather than people honestly dealing with this issue. Help me tax the wealthy, help me redistribute the wealth, help me build affordable housing in White communities if you want desegregation."*

Having grown up in NYC, I never knew that there were "White communities." Maybe the mayor should change the famous Brooklyn sign to read: *"Welcome to Brooklyn, America's Fourth Largest White Community."*

Once again, the left wants to control where people live, how they live, and who they live with. Here's an idea, maybe we can do this without the government playing the role of a Century 21 real estate agent.

Let's see what good old Benjamin Franklin thought about the government giving out freebies.

Franklin: *"I am for doing good to the poor, but... I think the best way of doing good to the poor is, not making them easy in poverty, but leading or driving them out of it. I observed... that the more public provisions were made for the poor, the less they provided for themselves, and of course, became poorer. And on the contrary, the less was done for them, the more they did for themselves, and became richer."*

In reference to the Ten Commandments, Franklin goes on to say:

"Six days shalt labor...industry and hard work will increase, and with it, plenty among lower people; their circumstances will mend, and more will be done for their happiness by enabling them to provide for themselves, than could be done by dividing all your estates among them."

I think it's fair to say that Franklin and de Blasio have opposing views when it comes to what the government's role should be. De Blasio wants to tilt the scales in favor of one's skin color (the very definition of racism) compared to providing an opportunity for those willing to work hard. Common sense should dictate that the more big government gets involved in an open and free society, the less liberty we will have due to such an intrusion.

Side note: I found it interesting in comrade de Blasio's speech that he failed to offer to redistribute his $258,750 annual salary or pay back the one billion taxpayer dollars that went mysteriously missing while his wife, Chirlane McCray, was put in charge of the city's disastrous mental health project. I can't decide what's more ironic, that the money allocated for mental health can't be accounted for due to amnesia or the love of capitalism by a communist? I'll have to think about that one.

Revolution

For those who believe Vladimir Lenin's Bolshevik revolution commenced in 1917, they'd be wrong. The seeds were sown decades earlier in 1887 when Lenin's older brother Aleksandr, and four of his revolutionary comrades, were executed for conspiring to assassinate Czar Alexander III. The event made the USSR's future dictator fully committed to overthrowing the imperial leadership and replacing it with what he believed was a more just form of government, socialism. With the combination of indoctrinating himself with Karl Marx's manifesto and a fervent, if not obsessed, commitment to revolution, all Lenin needed now was the opportune time to implement his coup.

Side note: Today's left is promising that their "type" of socialism is different from that of the Marxist-Leninist socialism, which has killed hundreds of millions of people worldwide. I recall George Santayana saying something about, "Those who cannot remember the past are condemned to..." I wish I could remember how the rest of that goes, but I guess it's not that important.

In the winter of 1905, Lenin thought his time had arrived. With the combination of Russia's humiliating defeat to Japan and an unskilled leader in Czar Nicholas II, the fuel for a revolution through political dissent was in place. On the twenty-second of January, a group of workers descended on the czar's Winter Palace in St. Petersburg to voice their displeasure. What happened next would be forever known in Russia as the Bloody Sunday Massacre. The Imperial forces indiscriminately opened fire on the crowd, and when they stopped, over one hundred of their fellow countrymen laid dead and another three hundred plus wounded. Any trust the Russian people had in their government before the massacre was forever irrevocably fractured.

As ripe as the moment was for a revolution, Lenin's splintered Bolshevik party could not agree on how best to move forward. Lenin supporters, the Majoritarians, advocated for military force while his Bolshevik opposition, the Minoritarians, sought a more democratic path toward socialism. So with the czar regaining control and the Bolsheviks splintered, Lenin was forced into exile.

Lenin, born Vladimir Ilyich Ulyanov, knew he had to be patient and wait for the political climate to worsen. Seventeen years later, during World War I, he found an unlikely ally in Germany who assisted him in his return. By making assurances to the Russian people to overthrow the provisional government and replace it with a communist state led by the working class, Lenin achieved his life's ambition. All it took was timing, the tickling of the ear of those desperately in need, and a complete disregard for humanity.

Forgive the interruption, but I just recalled the rest of that quote from George Santayana: *"Those who cannot remember the past are condemned to…repeat it."*

Of course, we know from the history of the twentieth century, when it comes to the utopia of communism, the promises of prosperity, bread, and equality were replaced with death, hunger, and godlessness. I'm left asking myself, why then are today's liberal politicians pushing the same agenda? And why is it that those who are most vulnerable and in need of the government's help are always the ones that pay the harshest price?

Like Lenin, today's left has been patiently waiting for the right opportunity to pounce their agenda on the American people. Helping are those in Congress who for decades have willingly abdicated their responsibility to the courts. The revolution we see today did not start with the AOCs of the party. She is just a half-wit cog in the wheel—the ultimate goal by the radical left is global communism in the name of "fairness." In this world of fairness, there won't be any more borders or walls, just an equal, diverse community that we'll live and love together as one. Did I hear someone say, "Summer of love?" Hell no! This infatuation is for every season. Oh, but a few small details. The elite will *begrudgingly* stay in power, not because they want to, but because they feel *obligated* to make sure things go accordingly. They'll keep the walls erected around their property while tearing down all other barriers. And guns will be a thing of the barbaric past, except for those same few elites who'll have plenty of guns for their security team in case some of us ingrates get curious about what's on the other side of that wall they live behind. It will be in the name of *fairness* as to why BOWFOGS will be ordered to attend mandatory diversity training, and if that doesn't indoctrinate someone like myself into believing that white people are pure evil, then it's off to Katie Couric's deprogramming camp. All in the name of that "F" word—*fairness*.

Fortunately, our framers had a different philosophy of governance. They believed people should be free to make decisions for themselves. That limiting people's prosperity would only curtail the growth of our nation. For our Founding Fathers, "Life, Liberty, and the Pursuit of Happiness" meant less government, not more. So the framers drafted a document known as the Constitution, and in it, they mapped out each branch of the government. When done, the legislative branch representing the people would have the most authority, followed by the executive and judicial. Our framers were well aware of the courts' potential abuse of powers, having witnessed the British judiciary system, so they intentionally left the judicial branch as the weakest.

As Congress abdicates its role more and more to the courts, three critical things occur. First, the judiciary branch, by default, becomes increasingly more powerful. Second, by skipping the legislative process, the citizens lose their representation in government. And lastly, an essential component of a healthy republic is bypassed, that being compromise.

For the progressives in Congress, this new way of doing business has many benefits. For starters, by the Supreme Court ruling to disallow prayer in schools, the left was able to pass through an agenda that nearly 85 percent of the electorate at the time opposed. The same can be said when it comes to abortion and affirmative action. So with no political exposure and bypassing the people's representatives, Congress found the perfect conduit to carry out their agenda—a judicial activist Supreme Court. Of course, the losers in this trade-off are the American people who see their voice in Congress hushed by a Supreme Court growing ever more powerful.

The left will have you believe that the antiquated piece of paper signed by a bunch of old white slave owners in 1787 needs to be replaced. And here, my friends, is where the rubber truly meets the road. Our Constitution is under attack by a bunch of red pinko Marxists who promise to cure every need, tickle every ear, and will magically make everyone's life better. The only thing the leaders will ask (demand) in return for delivering this utopian paradise is to denounce individualism and change our nation's motto from "*In God We Trust*" to "In State We Trust."

Understand, these revolutionary ideas cannot occur if our country is flourishing. So, like any good confidence game, the con waits in the weeds until the mark begs for them to take power. By the time the scam is exposed, people are dead, lives are destroyed, and hell on earth has a new address.

Above all else, after reading this book, I hope you take away the fact that God loves you, and the left is looking to rip up the greatest document man has ever produced and replace it with the never-ending disaster known as socialism!

The Dems' Agenda

Back in July of 2020, in a church eulogizing representative John Lewis, former President Barak Obama said, "If all this takes eliminating the filibuster, another Jim Crow relic, in order to secure the God-given rights of every American, then that's what we should do."

The former president was referring to what he believed were obstacles that stood in the way of civil rights legislation. Of course, he purposely conflated several issues that had no bearing but served the purpose of justifying one of the most critical components to our Senate; the filibuster. And why would he want to disparage such a thing? So he could plant the seeds to what's coming next by the Democrat Party: a full-court press power grab absent of compromise. Not surprisingly, the former president failed to mention that the Jim Crow laws were a by-product of a racist Democrat-controlled Supreme Court that, in 1883, ruled the Civil Rights Act of 1875 unconstitutional. That would be the same Civil Rights Act that was preventing the practice of racist segregation throughout the Democrat South. History tells us that the vacuum created by SCOTUS's decision produced the Jim Crow laws and not the filibuster. But if the former president says it enough times, then maybe we can keep our doctor. Oh, sorry, my bad. I'm conflating Obama's lies.

Probably the most disgusting part of Obama's statement was that it was said in a church during a funeral service. In the President's defense, maybe he was used to a lack of decorum in a house of worship after spending twenty-plus years listening to Reverend "The Racist" Wright and his anti-White sermons. However, that aside, let's look at how dangerous Obama's words are.

The filibuster is in place in the Senate for a reason, and as I've explained, it has nothing to do with Jim Crow. Our Founding Fathers knew if both chambers of Congress needed a simple majority to push through their agenda, then eventually, majority rule would become the standard instead of *compromise*. Take away the filibuster, and the greatest deliberative body the world has ever known ceases to exist, and mob rule becomes the law of the land.

Does the former president not know this? Of course, he does. He taught constitutional law at the University of Chicago for over a decade. So why then the push to undo an intricate part of our democracy? Well, it goes back to the left's quest to tear down our system and create what they feel a perfect union should be, which is one without opposition or *compromise*. And here's the rub: once they're back in power—a simple majority in the House of Representatives, a supermajority in the Senate, and the executive branch—their revolution will commence. And all this done in the name of justice, or should I say, their sense of justice.

It's worth noting that in 2005 there was a first-term senator from Illinois who gave a compelling argument as to the importance of the filibuster and his opposition to ending it:

"If the majority chooses to end the filibuster if they choose to change the rules and put an end to Democratic debate, then the fighting and the bitterness and the gridlock will only get worse."

So who said these compelling words in defense of that old "Jim Crow relic." Well, amazingly, that would be the same guy who is now on a seek and destroy mission against the filibuster: Barack Hussein Obama II. You just can't make this stuff up!

Righteous indignation may work for a movie plot on how the underdog doesn't compromise and holds firm to their core beliefs. However, what makes our system of government everlasting is division and *compromise.* If history has taught us anything, it's that autocratic power only lasts so long until someone stronger comes along. This cycle brings us back to the caveman days, where the one with the bigger club ruled everything his way until someone came along with an even bigger club, and so on, and so on. It's this "mob rule" that is being offered by the left under the guise of righteousness, fairness, and equality.

Once the Democratic Party regains full power, say au revoir to many things that have worked well for our republic. How about that pesky thing called the electoral college? Well, since it cost Hillary Clinton the 2016 election, you can bet that the protection of the small states will be discarded to make way for what the left deems as fair.

Here's what else is on the Dems' wish list:

- packing the Supreme Court
- adding Puerto Rico and D. C. as states
- one-party rule
- no borders
- no more guns
- a new constitution
- free health care, lodging, and education for illegals
- abortion on demand
- federally controlled elections
- diversifying the suburbs

And who's going to pay for all this? Who cares! The left knows this is not sustainable. So their goal is not to make things better for the masses but to make them more dependent on the state. It's kind of like an enterprising drug dealer who gives his product for free until his clients are entirely reliant on his services. In this scenario, the drug dealer is the government, and the client the addicted citizen. I'm just surprised that some people in this country believe the yarn the left is spinning. Even though this liberal ideology has been proven to be a disaster throughout the twentieth century, some think drinking this socialist Kool-Aid will be different this time. Maybe we can ask those in Jonestown how their afternoon refreshment tasted. Oh, sorry, I forgot it's too late. And if the American people don't wake up, it will be too late for us as well.

Timberrrr

The attacks on Confederate statues started slowly until during the pandemic summer months in 2020 when anarchists decided George Washington, Abraham Lincoln, Teddy Roosevelt, and that no-good Italian explorer's statue all had to come down. Why? Remember the excuse used to take prayer out of school: the atheist felt *offended*. Well, bingo! If it was good enough to stop little Jake and Mary from getting spiritually closer to their Creator, well, hell, then it should be good enough to destroy our history.

For the record, that no-good Italian that I'm referring to in jest is, of course, Christopher Colombus. I doubt my offhanded comment will offend Tony, Vinny, Paulie, and Mary; but please allow me to make amends if it does.

When I was in school, we were taught Colombus did something that no one else in his time had done. He successfully sailed to a new land and, in doing so, opened up the modern world. My teachers left out all that stuff about his brutal treatment of the indigenous people. My guess is he wouldn't win any awards at the local Rotary Club, but it doesn't discount his historic discovery. He was the one who had the *cojones* to ask King Ferdinand and Queen Isabella for money to sail in a direction no one had ever returned from successfully. Was he a nice guy? Probably not, but that's not why we honor him with a statue. He did something extraordinary that changed the world. It would be like finding out Neil Armstrong cheated on a college test and decided that he was no longer worthy of having his picture displayed at the Kennedy Space Center. Or what if we uncovered that Martin Luther King Jr. was an adulterer or a plagiarist, or both? Would that change his accomplishments as the most influential civil rights leader this country has ever known? I think not. So perhaps it would be a good idea for everyone to step off their moral high horse and gain some perspective. After all, nobody is without sin. And please, spare me any Hitler comparisons. There's a difference between sin and some deranged evil POS.

As for the Confederate statues, having served in the United States military and willing to die for the freedoms I hold so dear, the thought of honoring anyone who committed treason against our great nation sickens me. That said, the statues are part of our history and should be used to educate future generations. But to borrow the words of the human thesaurus Dennis Miller, "That's just my opinion, I could be wrong."

Note: The first objective during the October Revolution in Russia (1917–1923) was to tear down all the statues that the new order deemed unworthy. Sound familiar?

The Prince

In the sixteenth century, an Italian diplomat named Niccolo Machiavelli wrote what some consider the first modern study on political philosophy. Published after his death in 1532, Machiavelli proposed in his book *The Prince* that immoral means can be justified for princes when it came to glory and survival, that perception itself can be more potent than reality. His win at all cost and unconventional view on ethics brought to pass the pejorative term *Machiavellian*.

A half a millennial before the mafia character played by Chaz Palminteri in *A Bronx Tale* claimed that it was better to be feared than loved, Machiavelli was already putting his thesis on paper. By expressing the importance of absolute obedience from the prince's subjects, power would remain secure and unchallenged. Machiavelli advises the prince to become a "great liar and deceiver." Regardless of whether the ruler keeps his word is insignificant, it's the illusion he does is what's crucial. According to Machiavelli, men had to be either pampered or crushed since adversaries would likely seek revenge for minor injuries but not for fatal ones. As for the masses, the goal was to keep them comfortable enough to lessen the chances of an insurrection due to the prince's totalitarian rule. This concept of governing through the "ends justifying the means" was to produce stability, not justice.

Another way Machiavelli believed the sovereign would maintain control was by keeping his subjects "satisfied and stupid." The Romans perfected this philosophy among their citizens with the "bread and circuses" conducted at the Forum.

Today the government relies on the same "food and entertainment" to keep control of the masses. Nothing in modern times has contributed more to accomplishing the "satisfied and stupid" doctrine than the invention of television and fast-food joints. Through the media, we're told everything from what to wear, how to think, and what we should like or dislike. Politicians routinely use the bully pulpit of television to spread misinformation. At the same time, supposed "unbias" news outlets skew content to their audiences that best represent the network's political views. Our freedom of the press has turned into an entertainment mogul worried more about ratings and profits than justice and facts. We have a society of morbidly obese individuals who have a television remote in one hand and a Big Mac in the other. And now, thanks to Uber Eats, the smartphone, and Alexa unlocking the front door, this individual has a better chance of having a heart attack watching the Jerry Springer show than getting laid.

The point I'm making here is that none of this crazy nonsense gets off the drawing board without the tools of deception and manipulation. Whether it's governing as the Prince or spurring on a revolution, the concept is the same. In some ways, it's similar to picking the jury in the OJ Simpson trial. The ideal formula is stupidity mixed with an illusion of self-importance. After all, if the people are intelligent enough to want to be well informed, there's no way they will buy the crap that's being sold to them. So, in a nutshell, here's the left's game plan: create a false narrative, drum up lots of anger, and, when all else fails, blame it on the racist White cops and climate change.

Now that the loyal subjects are fat and stupid, and religion has been tossed to the curb along with that Judeo-Christian document known as the United States Constitution, there are still a few more hurdles to overcome before the left can declare total victory and begin ruling like the Prince. Of course, we know there can never be an actual victory for people who live in a world of perpetual turmoil. After all, how can one be content sipping a $7 café mocha latte while glancing over an article in the *New Yorker* describing the perils of suburban field mice being forced to relocate due to overdevelopment and not feel there's so much work that still needs to be done?

Here's the kicker: once the left accomplishes their goal of total and untethered power, only the Lenins and Stalins will be the survivors. Everyone else will have served their purpose and will become expendable. That's when the millennial man-bun Jake and nose-ring Mary cry, "That's not fair." But for some reason, like Charlie falling for Lucy's football trick over and over again, people think this time will be different. Why do you think King George said if General Washington were to resign his commission after winning the Revolutionary War that he'd be "the greatest man in the world." It goes against human nature to give power up willingly after acquiring the taste for it. In fact, the only thing corruptible people in power yearn for is more power…and maybe a Fresca.

After all the hard work is done, undoubtedly, they'll be someone ruthless enough to come along and consolidate the power. In Stalin's case, he went about killing off his competition, a strategy he came across from reading a book he kept on his nightstand, *The Prince*. By the time godless Jake and Mary wake up to the con, they're so scared they'd be happy to serve the motherland, fatherland, or whatever politically incorrect collective noun the Antichrist chooses.

Maybe I've lost my mind, but here's an idea. How about we keep the filibuster, limit the Supreme Court to nine justices, let the legislature legislate, and while we're at it, respect the document that has served this nation for over 230 years. I know, that's just crazy talk. But let's see what Honest Abe had to say about the Constitution in an 1857 address in Kalamazoo, Michigan:

> *Don't interfere with anything in the Constitution. That must be maintained, for it's the only safeguard of our liberties. And not to Democrats alone do I make this appeal, but to all who love these great and true principles.* (Abraham Lincoln)

Chapter 3

Less Than Liberty

The ultimate tragedy is not the oppression and cruelty by the bad people but the silence over that by the good people.

—Dr. Martin Luther King Jr.

In our country's quest to form a more perfect union, there have been numerous times when our nation has failed miserably. The scar that's cast the darkest shadow is, without question, slavery. I often wonder how the owners of this barbaric institution were able to sleep at night, knowing the abomination they were committing against humanity. There's no depth low enough that humankind won't race to in the name of evil. When one stops to think of the brutality man has committed toward their fellow man, there's no wonder why so many Christians eagerly await Jesus's Second Coming. My only question is, how many more acts of atrocity will need to occur before the Kingdom comes? No one can say when the day will be, but it's no mystery when it does come who won't be invited into God's Kingdom:

> *Or do you not know that wrongdoers will not inherit the kingdom of God? Do not be deceived: Neither the sexually immoral nor idolaters nor adulterers nor men who have sex with men nor thieves nor the greedy nor drunkards nor slanderers*

*nor swindlers will inherit the Kingdom of God. (1
Cor. 6:9–10 NIV)*

So much for that family reunion.

Moving on. Until that day is upon us, we're left to rely on imperfect governments to make decisions that directly affect our lives. Even though our Constitution has been a beacon of hope for so many, the fact remains it hasn't always been just.

I've chosen eight Supreme Court cases to illustrate just how imperfect our government's judicial branch has been throughout the republic's history. Each describes an injustice that may be difficult to believe occurred in these United States of America. But occur they did. And since history has a way of repeating, I doubt we've seen the last of inequities within our mortal system.

1. Dred Scott v. Sanford (1857)

> There was no reason to believe when Dred Scott was born into slavery at the turn of the nineteenth century that his life would be any different than the rest of the four million men, women, and children subjected to bondage at that time. Over the years, Scott was sold several times, forcing him to travel throughout the South and Western territories. While with one of his owners, an army surgeon named Dr. John Emerson, he met and married fellow slave Harriet Robinson.
>
> In 1846 the couple sued for their freedom in the St. Louis Circuit Court. The suit was predicated on the "once free, always free" state doctrine. Since the Scotts spent time in the slavery-free Wisconsin Territory before returning to Missouri, the two believed that under the statute, they should be freed. After years of appeals, the case finally made its way to the United States Supreme Court.
>
> In 1856, the Court, in a 7–2 decision, ruled against Dred Scott. The travesty wasn't only a defeat for Scott but all Blacks throughout the country.

Chief Justice Roger Taney, a protector of the South from what he perceived as unwarranted northern aggression, never wavered in his support for the institution of slavery. In his hammering majority opinion against Scott, Tanney said:

The blacks had no rights which the white man was bound to respect; and that the negro might justly and lawfully be reduced to slavery for his benefit. He was bought and sold and treated as an ordinary article of merchandise and traffic, whenever profit could be made by it.

Taking the matter a step further, the unconscionable chief justice planted the seeds that would later lead to the Civil War when he declared Congress's 1820 Missouri Compromise unconstitutional, spreading slavery to all territories.

Without any help from the courts, Dred Scott, his wife, and two daughters eventually bought their freedom. Although the time was short, he lived a little over a year as his own master before succumbing to tuberculosis on September 17, 1858.

Presidential trivia: On March 4, 1861, Republican Abraham Lincoln was sworn in as the sixteenth president of the United States. Administering the oath of office on that brutally cold afternoon was none other than Democrat chief justice Roger Taney. With the wind howling at twenty miles per hour and temperatures well below freezing, I'm guessing that the chief justice's reception toward the new president was not nearly as warm.

In history, the "what if" game can be nauseatingly futile. However, to underscore the importance of an individual or group's impact on society, I pose: what if the Supreme Court did not rule the Missouri Compromise unconstitutional? What if Dred Scott was deemed a citizen and not an article of property? What if, instead of slavery spreading into the territories, the North and South found a less bloody way to eradicate their differences? What if men weren't idiots?

2. The Civil Rights Cases of 1883

Before there was Brown v. Board of Education, there was the Civil Rights Act of 1875. President Ulysses S. Grant signed the act into law as part of the post-Civil War Reconstruction era. The federal government implemented the law to protect all Union citizens, especially the rising persecution of African Americans in the South. The Civil Rights Act was covered by the Fourteenth Amendment's Equal Protection Claus, which *guaranteed* African Americans equality when it came to *public accommodations*. From now on, there could be no more discrimination against the Black community when it came to busing and serving on juries, hotels, and restaurants. With slavery abolished, the slow road toward integration and true equality among all races was now the law of the land. Then the Supreme Court came along.

The Court consolidated five similar civil rights cases to form a single decision. In their 8–1 ruling, the justices put the march toward civil rights on hold for nearly a century and unleashed discrimination felt to this day. In their not-so-infinite wisdom, the Court decided the Thirteenth Amendment eliminated "the badge of slavery" but had no constitutional justification in prohibiting racial discrimination. So, in layman's terms, the Supreme Court winked to all their good-old-boys in the South, letting them know to do as they please. Hence, the Democrat Jim Crow era began.

Behind every horrendous ruling, one will find an equally awful justice writing his opinion to justify the indefensible. In this case, Justice P. Bradley had the dishonor of putting his name to the majority opinion. He argued that the Thirteenth Amendment dealt solely with abolishing slavery and that the legislature went too far by enacting the Civil Rights Act. As for the Fourteenth Amendment, the only segment of society in violation was the federal government by interfering with private businesses' rights to choose who they wished to accommodate. Somehow or someway, Bradley either failed to see the liberties trampled upon against the African American people or, similar to Chief Justice Taney in the Dred Scott case, simply didn't care.

My Hero!

The lone dissent in the 8–1 decision was Justice John Marshall Harlan. I sometimes wonder what it must've been like to be the only rational person to adjudicate the case with integrity. Andrew Jackson once said, "One man with courage makes a majority." Maybe Harlan's dissenting vote wasn't enough to sway his fellow justices, but his unwavering principles have lived on as an example that just because a group is in the majority doesn't necessarily mean they're morally right.

As for Justice Harlan's scathing dissenting opinion, he illustrated that the Thirteenth Amendment did a lot more than "prohibit slavery as an institution." He referenced Section II of the Amendment that seemed to be blindly ignored by his colleagues that "Congress shall have power to enforce this article by appropriate legislation."

So let's see if we're all on the same page.

Congress, those would be the people elected into office and held accountable by their constituents, passed the Thirteenth and Fourteenth Amendments, successfully legislated the Civil Rights Act of 1875 and did all this by following the laws set forth in the United States Constitution. But eight idiots in black robes with their own agenda who weren't accountable to anyone decided to undo everything previously signed into law. Unbelievable!

Prediction: Awful rulings like this will happen again. Why? Because there's no shortage of idiots in government. So as our country heads toward the socialist abyss, I remind everyone of Dante's words:

"The hottest places in hell are reserved for those who, in a time of great moral crisis, maintain their neutrality."

Side note: While traveling in the academic community as a guest speaker, I no sooner begin to criticize the Supreme Court when some young, wide-eyed scholar pridefully brings to my attention Brown v. Board of Education as if the case was foreign to me. I allow the future Clarence Darrow or RBG to make their argument of how the Supreme Court ended the deplorable practice of segregation in schools. I would nod my head in a look of defeat and then agree with everything the student previously said. After a slight pause to allow for a false sense of confidence to come over the barrister-to-be, I would inquire if they were familiar with the 1875 law passed by Congress, banning segregation throughout our nation. "That can't be," is the usual response. After all, according to the skeptical student, if the law was passed back in the nineteenth century, why was it necessary for the Supreme Court to act in the middle of the following century? "Well," I'd begin to explain, "that's because, in 1883, SCOTUS ruled Congress's 1875 desegregation law unconstitutional. The only thing SCOTUS was doing in the Brown case was undoing the previous Court's travesty."

3. Kelo v. City of New London (2005)

The North Star of American liberty is property. So important was this philosophy to our founders that Jefferson went as far as to say, "Property is our fence to liberty." Many of the liberties set forth in the Bill of Rights encompasses the subject of personal property. The often forgotten Third Amendment discontinued the practice of soldiers billeting in civilian homes. The Fourth protects said residence from illegal searches and seizures. Added within the Fifth Amendment, one will find the "Taking Clause," also referred to as "eminent domain." It reads, "Nor shall private property be taken for public use without just compensation."

New London, Connecticut, is the quintessential picturesque Norman Rockwell small town where families commonly pass down their home from one generation to another. However, in the spring of 1998, the local city planners came up with a plan that would end any such heirloom from continuing and bring into question the legal definition of eminent domain.

The project was known as the "Municipal Development Plan." The city's goal was to acquire private property through the eminent domain law. The government has this legal right to expropriate property for public use as long as a payment of compensation is made to the owner(s). After all, when hospitals, highways, or schools are built to benefit the community, undoubtedly, the argument for public use is established.

However, that was not going to be the case in this small New England town. The purpose behind the government taking private property was to turn around and sell it to a private developer. Even to most non-legal eagles, the slick move was clearly in violation of the eminent domain clause, which outlines explicitly that the property can only be taken for public use. Well, when there's a lot of lawyers sitting around getting paid by the hour, it should come as no surprise that one of these snakes found a loophole. And what was the "secret sauce"?

First, let's follow the bouncing ball.

Jim and Margie bought their dream house. They've lived there all their adult life, raised two children, and now, after 360 monthly payments to Hanover Trust, they're ready to enjoy their mortgage-free home and live happily ever after. But wait one second. After a knock on the door, they hear what Ronald Reagan had described as the nine most terrifying words in the English language: *"I'm from the government, and I'm here to help."* The government's "*help*" is to take Jim and Margie's house for a compensation yet to be determined. The couple is aware of the eminent domain clause and, being good Christians, don't want to impede what they assume will significantly benefit their community. So the retired Korean War veteran, Jim, looks over at the pencil-pushing bureaucrat and asks, "So what does the municipality plan on building, a hospital or a school?" "No," says the idiot. "We're going to sell it, along with the fifteen other homes we're confiscating, to the private pharmaceutical company Pfizer. They've discovered that a little blue pill could help with a man's erection, so they're going to need more land to satisfy manufacturing expansion." (No pun intended, and yes, this was the reason behind the land grab.) By the time Jim retrieved his shotgun from the closet, the idiot was in his Prius hanging a k-turn on Franklin Street. When the grandfather of five finally calmed down, he remembered what it said in the Constitution regarding the government could only take property for public use. He reassured his wife that they had nothing to worry about and that justice would be served.

Okay, snakes, I mean lawyers, let's get back to that loophole.

The secret sauce was in the tax revenue increase that Pfizer would generate for the city. Since more money equates to more fire, police, and other local municipal services, the eminent domain spirit of taking property for public use could now be justified by the local government. If successful, every piece of private property in the country would be at the government's mercy, something I believe our framers went to great lengths to avoid. But still, the argument by the government, although creative, was still weak. The law's spirit was about dealing with public progress and not generating a more significant tax revenue so public officials could get a hefty pay increase, right?

The case worked its way through the system until reaching the Supreme Court. In a narrow 5–4 decision, the majority of liberal justices on the bench sided with the town of New London and their use of eminent domain to generate economic development. In Justice John Paul Stevens's majority opinion, he wrote, "The City has carefully formulated an economic development plan that it believes will provide appreciable benefit to the community, including—but by no means limited to new jobs and increased tax revenue. Because that plan unquestionably serves a public purpose, the takings challenged here satisfy the public use requirement of the Fifth Amendment."

Before I share Justice Sandra Day O'Connor's minority opinion, I want first to explain why this case is a travesty.

My immediate concern is for the families forced to relinquish their property by the government for private use in the name of economic development—creating a scary precedent moving forward. My next concern may sound ridiculous, but who would've ever thought a privacy case in 1965 would lead to legalizing abortions in 1973.

There are whispers that the Democrat left wants to *diversify* the suburbs in the name of *fairness*. As for me, I think it's a dangerous proposition when the government acts as a utopian real estate agent. I'm afraid the god-like power created by dictating who is worthy of a three-thousand-square-foot split ranch will be too tempting for the left to resist. So here's my next *prediction*. There will come a day when eminent domain will be used in the name of diversity and equality, completely erasing any remnants of our Founders' protection toward the sanctity of private property and the liberty it affords us. I can hear politicians decrying that their effort is for the greater good of society. I don't know who will be told to leave, stay, or be awarded a house by the state; but I can tell you which neighborhoods won't be affected. Here's a hint: if you have to ask, you probably couldn't afford to live there.

Here's Justice Sandra Day O'Connor's minority opinion in the Kelo v. City of New London:

Under the banner of economic development, all private property is now vulnerable to being taken and transferred to another private owner, so long as it might be upgraded...nothing is to prevent the State from replacing any Motel 6 with a Ritz Carlton, any home with a shopping mall, or any farm with a factory.

In my view, the common sense dissent is nearly perfect. My only wish would've been if Justice O'Connor gave her five idiot colleagues a dose of Moses (Charleston Heston) while reading her opinion: "Take your stinking paws off my 'property,' you damn dirty apes."

4. Plessey v. Ferguson (1896)

Allow me to sum up this Supreme Court travesty in one sentence: *separate but equal my ass!*

The South's Jim Crow legislation was serving the purpose of those who felt that the Blacks were inferior. Leave it to the Democrats to come up with another great euphemism in *separate but equal* to mask their fundamental objective of keeping the Blacks suppressed. On the surface, it sounds reasonable, just like *Black Lives Matter*. However, similar to BLM's racist terrorist organization, once one starts peeling away the layers, it's easy to discover that the deeds and not creative slogans are what defines a movement.

During the Civil War, Louisiana was liberated by the North under General Benjamin Franklin Butler's command. While federal troops occupied the state, African Americans went to integrated schools, could fall in love and marry whom they wished, and sit in any railroad cart of their choosing. It was this New Orleans that Homer Plessy grew up in as a child. Maybe that's the reason why years later when his city fell under Jim Crow's segregation policies, the man with one-eighth African blood volunteered to be arrested for sitting in a "White Only" section.

On June 7, 1892, the Citizens Committee with a sympathetic railroad and a private detective possessing arrest powers launched their plan. After purchasing a first-class ticket, the insurance salesman Plessy took his seat in the restricted area and was subsequently arrested by the detective for violating the state's separate-car law. The case was now in the system, where it would eventually end up at the Supreme Court.

In the 7–1 decision, the only bright side was the man who will be forever known as the "Great Dissenter," Justice John Marshall Harlan, once again showed what courage was all about. Standing alone, *my hero* gave another fiery dissent directed at his colleagues. It's this author's opinion that Harlan's written dissent is the greatest ever written. Below is an excerpt compliments of the Great Dissenter:

> *But in view of the constitution, in the eye of the law, there is in this country no superior, dominant, ruling class of citizens. There is no caste here. Our constitution is color-blind, and neither knows nor tolerates classes among citizens. In respect of civil rights, all citizens are equal before the law. The humblest is the peer of the most powerful. The law regards man as man, and takes no account of his surroundings or of his color when his civil rights as guaranteed by the supreme law of the land are involved... In my opinion, the judgment this day rendered will, in time, prove to be quite as pernicious as the decision made by this tribunal in the Dred Scott case. (Justice John Marshall Harlan)*

It would take over a half-century before "separate but equal" was finally rooted out from our society.

5. Buck v. Bell (1927)

Carrie Buck (1906–1983) was a Charlottesville native who, in 1924, was involuntarily committed to a state psychiatric hospital due to her diagnosis of epilepsy and feeblemindedness. She became the first of nearly eight thousand other Virginians who were sterilized over a six-decade period. The law that allowed the state of Virginia to perform such procedures was passed in the interest of the "health of the patient and the welfare of society."

In a page out of the Nazi's playbook on eugenics, the United States Supreme Court deemed that the sterilization of individuals suffering from imbecility, epilepsy, and feeblemindedness was permissible, upholding the Virginian law. Writing for the 8–1 majority opinion, Justice Oliver Wendall Holmes Jr. concluded that the compulsory sterilization of the intellectually disabled did not violate the *due process clause* of the Fourteenth Amendment. Holmes callously added, "Three generations of imbeciles are enough," referring to Carrie Buck's daughter, mother, and herself. The Supreme Court Justice wasn't done pontificating on his strong opinion:

> *It is better for all the world if instead of waiting to execute degenerate offspring for crime, or to let them starve for their imbecility, society can prevent those who are manifestly unfit from continuing their kind... We must sterilize those who sap the strength of the State [to] prevent our being swamped with incompetence.*

The legal precedent established by SCOTUS in Buck v. Bell allowed for over sixty thousand sterilizations nationwide. All this in the hope of curtailing "genetically inferior children" onto future generations.

By 1974, the law's core was repealed by most states when the science showed evidence that Buck and many others did not suffer from "hereditary defects."

For reasons beyond my comprehension, SCOTUS has never taken the appropriate steps to overturn Buck v. Bell. In fact, in 2001, the US Court of Appeals in Missouri cited the Supreme Court case during a proceeding that involved the sterilization of a mentally disabled woman. In short, Buck v. Bell is unbelievably still the law of the land.

Note: The lone dissent in Buck v. Bell came via the only Catholic associate justice on the bench, Pierce Butler (1866–1939). He believed people should be judged by qualities on the inside rather than the external ones those in the eugenics community obsess over. As for Justice Holmes, many scholars in the legal field believe that he is one of the greatest justices to have ever don the black robe. His written opinions have gone down as some of the most eloquent writings to have ever come from the bench. When there was a debate as to whether or not there should be limitations on the First Amendment's freedom of speech, Holmes ingeniously clarified the conundrum by penning his legendary phrase: "*Falsely shouting fire in a theater and causing a panic.*" In my view, Oliver Wendell Holmes Jr. is an excellent example of great men in history who've accomplished extraordinary things but far from perfect.

6.   Korematsu v. United States (1944)

Japanese American Fred Korematsu was born in 1919 during a racially charged time in San Fransico. The local press fueled tensions by referring to Asian Americans as "yellow peril" and "unclean." The bigotry was so strong that Fred would have to go to Chinatown if he wanted to go out for dinner or get a haircut.

On the morning of December 7, 1941, Fred's life would be directly impacted by events happening 2,400 miles away in Hawaii. The Japanese had just attacked Pearl Harbor, causing President Roosevelt to declare all Japanese immigrants over the age of fourteen to be enemy aliens. A few months later, on February 19, 1942, FDR escalated restrictions by drafting Executive Order 9066, authorizing the War Department to prepare the removal for anyone with Japanese ancestry living on the West Coast. All suspected enemies of the state were to be relocated to inland internment camps.

For the twenty-one-year-old Fred, he had no desire to report to one of the mandatory "assembly centers." Instead, he desperately wanted to stay with his girlfriend, Ida, in the restricted zone of San Francisco. It was Fred's girlfriend who came up with the idea for him to go for a $300 plastic surgery procedure. After the surgery, Fred changed his name on his draft card to Clyde Sarah. Neither attempt worked very well. Two weeks later, Fred was stopped by a police officer while walking down the street in the restricted area of San Leandro. It didn't take long for the officer to ascertain the young man's true identity and proceeded to place the young Japanese American under arrest.

While being held at the Presidio military base in San Francisco, Fred was paid a visit from Ernest Besig, a representative of the Northern Califonia ACLU. The civil liberties advocate was looking for the right set of circumstances to challenge the Exclusion Order in court. After listening to Mr. Besig, Fred agreed to his representation. Immediately, the ACLU attorneys filed to dismiss the charges, claiming they were unconstitutional but were denied. Before long, the case began receiving national attention.

When Fred's case went to trial, the prosecution called only one witness, the FBI agent who interrogated Fred after his arrest. The agent testified that Fred admitted he was of Japanese descent and within the restricted zone when arrested. To no surprise, Fred was found guilty of the Exclusion Act and sentenced to a meaningless five-year probation. Meaningless, because right after the verdict, Fred was relocated to an internment camp in Utah.

While in the camp, the ACLU filed an appeal on Fred's behalf. His attorney, Wayne Collins, explained in the legal brief that "the imprisonment without cause, without justification and without trial in defiance of the very letter and spirit of the Constitution."

On December 18, 1944, in a 6–3 decision, a majority of the Supreme Court blatantly ignored Fred Korematsu's constitutional rights of equal protection, freedom of movement, and due process by upholding his lower court conviction.

The three dissenting associate justices had sharp criticism for the government. Justice Owen Roberts wrote that "assembly centers" were nothing more than a euphemism for prison. In Justice Robert Jackson's dissent, he wrote, "Guilt is personal and not inheritable." Justice Frank Murphy cut to the heart of the issue by stating, "[The] Exclusion Order goes over the brink of constitutional power and falls into the ugly abyss of racism."

In 1983, Federal Judge Marilyn Patel vacated the lower court's conviction of Fred Korematsu. In her decision, Patel wrote that the government relied on "unsubstantiated facts, distortion, and the representation of a military officer [Gen. DeWitt] whose views were seriously infected by racism."

Fred moved on with his life, marrying a girl he met while in Detroit. The couple had two children, and some years later, moved back to the Bay Area. Fred never told his children about his big case or the two years he spent in an internment camp. They would later learn about it in school.

In 1998, President Clinton awarded Fred Korematsu the nation's highest civilian honor, the Medal of Freedom.

Note: Trump v. Hawaii was a Supreme Court case that involved a ban on residents from seven countries entering the United States. The controversy behind the case was that some believed the countries on the list were singled out because they were predominately Muslim nations. The Court upheld the ban on a narrow 5–4 vote, rejecting the anti-Muslim claim. Chief Justice John Roberts used the opportunity to address the travesty that took place seven-decades earlier:

"Korematsu was gravely wrong the day it was decided, has been overruled in the court of history, and to be clear—has no place in law under the Constitution."

In my view, the Korematsu case should be a reminder to all those who hold our liberties dear that they should never be taken for granted nor should our constitutional rights ever be suspended in times of war or a pandemic.

7. Roe v. Wade (1973)

I go into the Court's controversial decision in greater detail in chapter 4. In short, I feel the unborn are the most vulnerable and the least protected in our upside-down society. Once again, the Supreme Court ignored the will of the people and the representatives they voted into office by taking the decision of abortion away from the states. The issue was taken further into the moral abyss when the jurists bestowed upon themselves the role of gods by deciding what constituted a life. For the justices, their "secular roulette wheel of viability" landed on twenty-four weeks.

8. Stone v. Graham (1980)

Each case that I've chosen on this list illustrates how the Supreme Court doesn't always get it right. Over their existence, they've ruled people as property, segregated citizens, condoned eugenics, upheld the taking of constitutionally protected property, and rubber-stamped the internment of an entire group of people based solely on their race. These travesties against humanity were all committed despite our Constitution, not because of it.

In the SCOTUS case of Stone v. Graham, I'm left scratching my head, wondering what the hell five out of four justices were thinking when they decided that displaying the Ten Commandments in public schools was unconstitutional. Mind you that the Ten Commandments are on display throughout the Supreme Court building in over fifty-nine depictions. Of course, the Court explains this away by saying, "those" Ten Commandments are secular similar to that of the Code of Hammurabi and Justinian's Code. Dr. McCoy, take it away: "Are you out of your Vulcan minds?" That's like saying, although we all know the sky is blue, we're going to refer to it as "a color in the spectrum" as not to offend anyone. I call BS on this one. The sky is blue, and the Ten Commandments is not a secular document. It is the foundation for our laws in the Western civilization that was passed down to Moses by our Creator.

It gets better, or should I say worse. Here's a summary of the majority's opinion in Stone v. Graham:

Posting of religious texts on the wall serves no such educational function. If the Ten Commandments are to have any effect at all, it will be to induce the schoolchildren to read, meditate upon, perhaps to venerate and obey, the Commandments...

Holy shit! This book aside, that has to be the single dumbest piece of crap ever written—and I mean ever. We're not talking about some first-year law student who just pulled in on the back of a pickup truck from New Jersey. Those words were written by a Supreme Court Justice (William J. Brennan Jr.) sitting on the highest court in the land with fancy degrees hanging in his study, undoubtedly next to photos of pompous other idiots like himself that our society has come to worship. And the best this godless idiot can come up with is to enlighten gun-toting, Bible-clinging simpletons like me that the Ten Commandments have no educational value. Heaven forbid little Jake and Mary should see the Ten Commandments in school and learn something. They may be less inclined to, I don't know, lie, steal, and do a "Menendez Brothers" on their parents. Now I know, that's just crazy talk by this BOWFOG, but maybe there's something to these laws Jehovah passed down to Moses on Mount Sinai. And maybe, just maybe, they can instill goodness in all of us, starting with our children. Remember, nobody is forcing Jake and Mary to read the Ten Commandments. It won't be on any test, and they can walk by and choose to ignore the posting or not. The fact that there's a remote chance they may stop and read it has the cowardly Court shaking in their boots and making rulings that God must go.

In all sincerity, are we so far removed from our Judeo-Christian roots that learned men can look at the Ten Commandments and believe this is a "threatening document" for our students to read?

The left is on a crazy train going full speed ahead off a cliff, and they're all cheering as if this was a good thing. Here's my *prediction* on just how crazy this crap is going to get. There will come a day when a mother gives birth to a living, breathing baby, and as long as the umbilical cord is still attached, mommy dearest, in the name of privacy, will be allowed to terminate the life of the newborn. Crazy? Well, let's see what the Virginia governor had to say about a similar scenario minus the umbilical cord.

This was Ralph Northam during a radio interview in 2019:

"The infant would be delivered, the infant would be kept comfortable…and then a discussion would ensue between the physicians and the mother."

In case you missed it, that *"discussion"* was whether or not to kill the baby.

Question: Am I the only one who finds it disturbing that we're living in a world that deems the Ten Commandments taboo but *discussing* murdering a newborn is perfectly normal?

God, help us!

Minersville School District v. Gobitis and West Virginia State Board v. Barnette

I want to end this chapter by discussing two Supreme Court decisions that I felt didn't reach the "travesty" bar set in the previously mentioned eight cases but were still controversial nonetheless. The two legal proceedings had to do with a religious group, a hand salute, and an unwillingness to participate.

There are some people who find the Jehovah's Witnesses to be a mystery. Maybe it's from a lack of knowledge, or perhaps, it's more about what they've been told. Contrary to popular belief, their goal is not to irritate people by knocking on unwanted doors. Their purpose is to follow the example Jesus gave the church when sharing the "good news" in spreading the Gospel "from house to house" (Acts 5:42, 20:20). If one were to inform a Jehovah's Witness their visits aren't welcomed, they would cease any future visits.

It's true they don't believe Jesus died on a cross but rather an upright stake, nor do they celebrate Christmas, vote, or accept blood transfusions. There's another thing the Witnesses won't participate in, and that is the reciting of our country's Pledge of Allegiance. One may think this author, as a red-blooded American, might take exception to what appears to be a slight toward our great country. But similar to those who kneel during our National Anthem, I'm grateful we live in a place that allows such displays of defiance without persecution. However, in my view, there is a glaring difference between the two acts. One is done to disrespect our nation, while the other believes it's staying true in honoring the Word of God.

Over the years, while studying different religions and their congregations, I've observed that the Jehovah's Witnesses as a whole are law-abiding citizens who are respectful toward governmental authority. Similar to other Christian religious teachings, there are parts I agree with and some I don't. Where the divergence appears is with specific translations and their interpretations.

In their attempt to maintain a balance between God, the government, and their faith, the elders within the Jehovah's Witnesses often remind their congregation of two scriptures:

In Matthew 22:21, Jesus said, "Render to Caesar the things that are Caesar's; and to God the things thing's that are God's." And in Romans 13:1, it says, "Let every person be in subjection to the governing bodies."

These scriptures educate all Christians on how as loyal servants of God, they should interact with those in authority. For the Jehovah's Witnesses, the words allow them to follow the laws set out by the government without dishonoring God. However, in Exodus 20:4–5, the scripture created a direct conflict between their *beliefs* and the United States government.

First, let's take a look at the scripture:

> Thou shalt not make unto thee any graven image, or any likeness of any thing that is in heaven above, or that is in the earth beneath, or that is in the water under the earth. Thou shall not bow down thyself to them, nor serve them: for I the Lord thy God am a jealous God…

So how did we get from Exodus 20:4–5 to the Jehovah's Witnesses not wanting to pledge their allegiance to the flag?

It all started back in the 1930s when some lunatic by the name of Adolf Hitler went on a *cleansing* campaign. We are all familiar with his brutal persecution and human atrocities toward the Jewish people. What some may not be aware of is the scope of his evil had also included homosexuals, gypsies, and, yes, Jehovah's Witnesses.

But why the Witnesses?

The Nazis were about nationalism and claimed the Witnesses' behavior represented a threat to the "national community."

So what was this *behavior* that posed such a threat?

The Jehovah Witnesses refused to extend the German greeting, commonly known as the Hitler salute. They believed the salute was a form of idolatry and in direct conflict with Exodus 20:4–5. For their defiance, German Witnesses were arrested. Unlike the Jewish people, the Witnesses could escape persecution by simply signing a document renouncing their religious beliefs and giving their allegiance to the Third Reich. Staying true to their faith, most, if not all, of the Witnesses chose not to sign the document and, in doing so, sealed their fate. From 1933 to 1945, nearly 1,500 Jehovah's Witnesses were killed while thousands of others spent years in concentration camps.

In the United States, Joseph Rutherford, the president of the Jehovah's Witnesses governing body, saw what was transpiring in Germany and believed there was a commonality between the Hitler salute and our Pledge of Allegiance—something this author disagrees with entirely.

In the 1940 Supreme Court case, Minersville School District v. Gobitis, the Court ruled in favor of the school board that could now "compel" students to recite the Pledge of Allegiance despite a student's religious objection—something this author strongly disagrees with as well.

So how is it that I can disagree with Rutherford's stance on the Pledge of Allegiance but agree with Jehovah's Witnesses' right not to participate? One word: *comply.*

By the school board commanding their will, the impactful words found in the pledge would be reduced to nothing more than a recital by a parakeet. After all, what's the purpose of living in a free country if your allegiance has to come via coercion?

In the Court's 8–1 decision, the First Amendment's exercise clause was all but ignored. The lone dissenter, Chief Justice Harlan Fiske Stone, made his voice heard in a rare move by reading his entire opinion from the bench. Here's an excerpt:

> History teaches us that there have been but few infringements of personal liberty by the state which have not been justified as they are here, in the name of righteousness and the public good.

Three years later, when the Supreme Court took on the West Virginia State Board v. Barnette case, the Court reversed itself by ruling in favor of protecting religious liberties. No longer could school boards "compel" students to recite the Pledge of Allegiance.

Side note: In my view, there's a difference between those who kneel during the National Anthem and those who choose not to recite our Pledge of Allegiance for religious reasons. Some may feel otherwise, and maybe someday we can openly debate the issue, something we can't do in many countries around the globe.

During a keynote speech to the Federalist Society shortly after the 2020 election, Supreme Court Justice Samuel Alito sounded the alarm:

> *Tolerance for opposing views is now in short supply. In certain quarters religious liberty has fast become a disfavored right. For many today, religious liberty is not a cherished freedom. It's often just an excuse for bigotry, and it can't be tolerated even when there's no evidence that anybody has been harmed… The question we face is whether our society will be inclusive enough to tolerate people with unpopular religious beliefs…*

Can I get an Amen!

Before I move on from this topic, I want to remind everyone what the Witnesses went through while Hitler was in power. All they had to do was sign a piece of paper, but instead, they held to their convictions. So what do you suppose today's knee-bending athletes would do if faced with similar adversity, sign the document or remain kneeling?

To help answer that very question, I wrote an op-ed that was published in South Florida's *Sun Sentinel* newspaper on September 10, 2020. To put the piece in perspective, it was the summer of 2020 and athletes from all the major sporting teams decided, in "solidarity," to conduct a one-game boycott.

Keep on Walking

Last week, professional players from all major sporting teams across America walked-off basketball courts, ballfields, hockey rinks, and soccer fields to show their support for the Black Lives Matter movement.

I have a message for all those gifted athletes:

Why stop at only one game? After all, if you genuinely believe that you are on the right side of history, then please, sacrifice your multi-year, multi-million dollar contracts to teach us, the working-class simpletons of the world, how you think things should be. While you're at it, to truly make your boycott standout, how about getting rid of those overproducing carbon dioxide McMansions you like so much, along with those Earth-destroying private jets, yachts, and fancy cars you proudly show-off. And, if you really want to help me see things from your elitist perspective, how about relieving yourself of all that opulent bling around your neck and hanging from your ears. Sorry, but I'm having difficulty seeing you from all that glare coming off your blood diamonds.

In case my sarcasm hasn't resonated or was lost in translation, allow me to be more forthcoming. I'm tired of spoiled, overpaid, pampered divas thinking they have the moral high ground to tell the rest of us law-abiding citizens of this great country that cops are the bad guys and white people are inherently evil. I'm tired that some individuals feel it necessary to disrespect our flag by kneeling. I'm tired of the division I see amongst my fellow citizens. I'm tired that civility and civics have taken a back seat to riots and ultimatums.

I'm tired of insincere acts of solidarity. Muhammad Ali stepped away in his prime to protest *the Vietnam War. Now that was a sacrifice. These people boycott one game and think they're Mahatma Gandhi. Let them go three weeks the way he did without eating, and I may still disagree, but at least then I can respect their convictions.*

Our country has a healthy judicial system. It may not always get it right, but I challenge anyone to find something better on this planet. So, how about we not rush to judgment, let the system run its course, and while we're at it, let's temper down the rhetoric before our Republic is no more.

So getting back to my original question regarding what would these athletes do if faced with the same adversity as the Jehovah's Witnesses, I'll take a shot in the dark and say the only decision these spineless kneelers would've had was to figure out which line they needed to sign on? Right after that, I'm pretty confident players like Kaepernick and the rest of his sycophants would've been the first ones clicking the heels of their Knobelbecher Nazi boots as they snapped to attention, extending their right arm forward while shouting, "Heil Hitler."

Note: If Tom Brokaw decides to write a book on today's millennial athletes, I have a title for him: "The Worst Pieces of Selfish, Self-Centered, Narcisstic, Mocha-Latte Drinking, Apple Phone Basement-Dwelling, AOC-Bernie Loving Pieces of Crap Generation of All Time." Or we can go with the working title of "The Worst Generation."

Chapter 4

Abortion, Euthanasia, Sexual Orientation

I feel the greatest destroyer of peace today is abortion.

—Mother Teresa, 1979 Nobel Lecture

There's a unique legal and moral component that conflicts with my ethical beliefs as a Christian in the above three topics. Abortion and same-sex marriage is the law of the land while euthanasia is heading in that direction. However, does this make any of the three morally right? In addressing the legal and biblical aspects for each, I hope to show that it's not gays or women that need protecting but Christianity.

Roe v. Wade

There's no issue more polarizing in modern American history than the one of abortion. In this chapter, I will attempt to illustrate why I believe the act has nothing to do with privacy or a women's right to choose and everything with the taking of an unprotected, innocent human life. For those who condemn abortion, this chapter may help strengthen your convictions. But as for the many who support the murdering of society's most vulnerable, I doubt I will change many minds over the next several pages. To be perfectly candid, that isn't my intention. My goal is to shed light on a very divisive, dark topic. In doing so, maybe as a society, we can see the morally ill-advised road we've started down and quit pretending wrong is right and right is wrong.

In my view, the act of abortion is part of a sequence of poor choices leading up to that final awful act. I compare it to a teenage gangbanger shooting his or her victim. Everyone looks at the last event as the tragedy, which in part it is; however, I see it as a string of tragedies, starting with the gangbanger's spiritually devoid home that in all likelihood was absent of a mother, father, or both. The other events to occur—the dropping out of school, doing drugs, obtaining a gun, committing crimes—all stemmed from that initial lack of a family nucleus.

There certainly may be different sets of circumstances leading a woman to terminate a pregnancy. But I wholeheartedly believe if God were embraced instead of cast aside by the secular left, there'd be fewer abortions in our country. So instead of using a women's "right to choose" to eliminate the so-called problem, maybe as an advanced civilization, we can eliminate the issues that lead up to so many unwanted pregnancies.

In 1973 the same unelected officials who were declaring the right to privacy involving medical procedures in Griswold v. Connecticut (1965) took a leap more historic than Neil Armstrong's. It was eight years later when the Court used the confidentiality precedent set in Griswold in deciding Roe v. Wade. No longer was abortion about killing a defenseless unborn child, but rather a privacy issue protected by the Fourteenth Amendment. The left immediately clamored to the phrase "right to choose" as their rallying cry. If "right to choose" sounds familiar, it's because it should. The South used the same argument when defending the deplorable practice of slavery by shifting the debate to the states' right to choose. They didn't want it to be about the Black people's bondage because they knew they couldn't make an argument for something so universally evil. So the wealthy plantation owners in the South that were grossly profiting over the immoral practice of slavery decided instead to make it about state rights.

Lesson advice: If you have a morally weak argument, change the argument.

Who was Jane Roe?

Norma McCorvey was raised in a broken home by an alcoholic mother and absent father. In 1969, at age twenty-one, Norma met a guy while playing pool in a lesbian bar called The White Carriage *(imagine telling that story to the family over Thanksgiving dinner)*. The two spent that summer traveling around Dallas, playing in pool tournaments and making some money along the way. At some point in between playing, drinking, and dropping acid, the billiard partners began an intimate relationship.

By the end of the summer, Norma decided to go back home to Louisiana to stay with her mother and find work. After the man she'd been dating for a few months dropped her off, the two went their separate ways, never to see each other again. A short time later, Norma discovered she was pregnant. The young woman had previously given up two children to adoption immediately after giving birth. Faced with going through another pregnancy that she didn't want, Norma considered having an illegal abortion. She traveled back to Dallas to see if she could find someone to perform the procedure. Instead of finding a doctor, Norma crossed paths with two lawyers looking to overturn the Texas law against abortions.

In 1970, the two feminist attorneys, Linda Coffee and Sarah Weddington, met with Norma in a Dallas restaurant to discuss their legal options. One of the lawyers asked if she felt abortions should be legal and safe for all women. Without hesitation, Norma said, "Sure, of course." With that, Coffee and Weddington filed a lawsuit against the state of Texas with Norma as the lead plaintiff. Understanding that the legal process would take longer than her pregnancy, Norma reluctantly brought her baby to term and then immediately gave the child up for adoption.

As for the legal battle, it was just getting started.

A federal three-judge panel ruled that Texas's law against abortion unconstitutional. Dallas County District Attorney Henry Wade ignored the ruling, which prompted an immediate appeal. The Supreme Court agreed to put the case on their docket. So, on

December 13, 1971, and again on October 11, 1972, both arguments were heard. On January 22, 1973, in a 7–2 landmark decision, the Supreme Court affirmed that the Constitution's Fourteenth Amendment's due process clause gave women the legal right to have an abortion. Outlined in the ruling was the status of a fetus not being a person in the constitutional sense. Writing for the majority opinion, Justice Harry A. Wade explained that the right to liberty under the Constitution attaches only after birth. Another obstacle the justices had to overcome was deciding on the timeline permissible to terminate a fetus. Attorney Weddington argued for the plaintiff that the decision to end the pregnancy should be given to the mother right up until birth. The justices agreed this radical view came too close to infanticide. However, the timeline offered by assistant attorney general of Texas, Jay Floyd, that life started at conception, was equally unreasonable to the justices. Justice Blackmun concluded that "for lack of a better place to draw the line," the court could not restrict abortions in the first six months of pregnancy as long as a doctor was willing to perform the procedure.

Here's an excerpt from Justice White's dissent with whom Justice Rehnquist joined:

> *At the heart of the controversy in these cases are those recurring pregnancies that pose no danger whatsoever to the life or health of the mother but are, nevertheless, unwanted for any one or more of a variety of reasons—convenience, family planning, economics, dislike of children... I find nothing in the language or history of the Constitution to support the Court's judgment. The Court simply fashions and announces a new constitutional right for pregnant mother, and, with scarcely any reason or authority for its action, invests the right with sufficient substance to override most existing state abortion statutes. The upshot is that the people and the legislatures of the 50 States are constitutionally disentitled to weigh the relative importance of the*

continued existence and development of the fetus, on the one hand, against a spectrum of possible impacts on the mother, on the other hand. As an exercise of raw judicial power, the Court perhaps has authority to do what it does but in my view its judgment is an improvident and extravagant exercise of the power of judicial review that the Constitution extends to this Court… The Court apparently values the convenience of the pregnant mother more than the continued existence and development of the life or potential life that she carries.

Norma McCorvey's fifteen minutes of fame extended itself when she switched allegiances, becoming an advocate for the pro-life movement. In the summer of 1995, in a Dallas backyard swimming pool in front of a nationally televised audience, McCorvey was baptized. The new Christian gig proved to be a nice payday for the woman who once said regarding her unborn child, "I have this *thing* growing inside of me, and I want to get rid of *it*."

McCorvey was paid to speak out against abortion by several antiabortion groups. The con did a good job convincing everyone she'd found God and how she was thankful that she never did have an abortion. But sadly, the one-time pool hustler had one final trick to play on us suckers who actually think people like that can change.

In her "self-described" deathbed confession in 2017, McCorvey said, "I took their money, and they'd put me out in front of the cameras and tell me what to say… It was all an act. I did it well too. I am a good actress." The classless McCorvey finished her thirty-pieces-of-silver-act-of-betrayal by saying, "If a young woman wants to have an abortion, that's no skin off my ass."

Below is a verse in the Bible written nearly two-thousand years ago by Paul the Apostle that foretold how morality among us would worsen:

But understand this, that in the last days there will come times of difficulty. For people will be lovers

*of themselves, lovers of money, proud, arrogant, abu-
sive, disobedient to their parents, ungrateful, unholy,
heartless, unappeasable, slanderous, without self-control, brutal, not loving good, treacherous, reckless,
swollen with conceit, lovers of pleasure rather than
lovers of God, having the appearance of godliness,
but denying its power. (2 Tim. 3: 1–4 ESV)*

As was the fate of Sodom and Gomorrah, we too will face judgment for our immoral decadence. However, as it says in Matthew
23:36: *"No one knows when that day or time will be. The Son and the
angels in heaven don't know when it will be. Only the Father knows."*

In researching data on abortions, I've concluded it's nearly
impossible to give an accurate number of how many there've been
since the start of Roe v. Wade. Most experts agree that the number of
fetuses terminated since 1973 lies somewhere north of fifty million.
Of that, over one-third of all aborted babies are African American.
Considering this segment makes up only 13 percent of our population but contributes to 35 percent of abortions, I can't help but
wonder exactly when Black lives start to matter?

For those who make the case that abortion is the established law
of the land, I agree. However, this doesn't negate two glaring facts:

1. Slavery was also the law of the land before President Lincoln
    signed his historic executive order, the Emancipation
    Proclamation.
2. The act of abortion is about killing society's most vulnerable.

With their art of deflecting responsibility, the liberal left will
have you believe cops, especially White cops, are a threat to Black
people. Basketball star LeBron James had echoed these sentiments
when he said the way police conduct themselves makes him afraid
to be a Black man in America and that Black people feel "hunted."
I don't know about you, but my heart bleeds for this non-inner-city
kid trapped in his $21-million-dollar Brentwood Park mansion. I
just hope when the *"King"* does go out that whichever car his maj-

esty chooses—Ferrari, Ferrari, Ferrari, Lamborghini Aventador, Rolls-Royce Phantom, Mercedes Benz, Mercedes Benz, Mercedes Benz, Mercedes Benz, Mercedes Benz, or the 1975 Chevy Impala he keeps in the garage for those times he wants to roll into the hood—it doesn't break down.

The life expectancy for a Black man living LeBron James's lifestyle is a tragic seventy-eight years compared to other Black men where homicide is the leading cause of death for this group between the ages of fifteen and thirty-four.

I'm saddened that people who have such a large platform decide to waste it on false narratives. Millions of Black heartbeats were intentionally stopped (*killed*), but it doesn't seem to garner any concern from people like Mr. James or the Democrat Party. Why is that, and why do they fight to keep something that is so blatantly morally wrong?

Fact: there are an estimated ten million different types of species in nature; however, only humans are responsible for killing their unborn while still in the womb.

If one was to investigate the track record of the Democrat Party, it's easy to conclude that they don't care about the Black community. All one has to do is take a look at Democratically controlled inner cities to see how the Jim Crow's Party has utterly failed. While violent crime, systemic corruption, and a failed educational system run rampant through these communities, the left chooses to ignore the problem they've created.

Skeptical? Here's a list starting from 2000 of disgraced mayors and the cities they've failed:

(2000) Milan—Camden, NJ
(2002) Loren-Maltese—Cicero, IL
(2002) Cianci—Providence, RI
(2003) Ganim—Bridgeport, CT
(2004) Russo—Hoboken, NJ
(2005) Onunwor—East Clevland, OH
(2008) Rivera—Passaic, NJ
(2008) James—Newark, NJ

(2009) Dixon—Baltimore, MD
(2009) Cammarano—Hoboken, NJ
(2010) Kangford—Birmingham, AL
(2010) Price—Mandeville, LA
(2011) Elwell—Secaucus, NJ
(2011) Pabey—East Chicago, IN
(2011) Christensen—Port Saint Lucie, FL
(2013) Kilpatrick—Detroit, MI
(2013) Bencivengo—Hamilton, NJ
(2013) Filner—San Diego, CA
(2014) Vela—Progreso, TX
(2014) Cannon—Charlotte, NC
(2014) Nagin—New Orleans, LA
(2014) Mack—Trenton, NJ
(2014) Grace—St. Gabriel, LA
(2014) Borstel—Nogales, AZ
(2014) Robinson—Martin, KY
(2015) Tondreau—North Miami, FL
(2016) Nelson—New Roads, LA
(2017) Harycki—Stillwater, MN
(2017) Aguinaga—South El Monte, CA
(2017) Torres—Paterson, NJ
(2018) Meyer—New Roads, LA
(2018) Barry—Nashville, TN
(2018) Correia—Fall River, MA
(2018) Pawloski—Allentown, PA
(2019) Snyder—Portage, IN
(2019) Jordan—Richardson, TX
(2019) Caraway—Dallas, TX
(2019) Spencer—Reading, PA

Note: All but three went to prison

Margaret Sanger

The term Planned Parenthood has to be one of the most disingenuous market labeling concoctions ever engineered by the scholarly left. I'll assume that since the founders didn't name their very profitable company Planned Abortions (three hundred thousand performed a year) or Planned Eugenics (the direct targeting of the poor and "undesirables"), neither of the more accurate depictions suited their palate.

For those who may not be familiar with eugenics, allow me. The term was first used in 1883 by British biologist Francis Galton when he combined the Greek words of *good* (eu) and *birth* (genos). *Merriam Webster* defines it as "the practice or advocacy of controlled selective breeding of human populations…to improve the population's genetic composition, relating to or fitted for the production of good offspring."

Adolf Hitler and Planned Parent founder Margaret Sanger were big fans of eugenics. Both shared similar ideological thoughts on creating a better society by controlling how humans reproduced. One option the two eugenics proponents believed would help in their cause was sterilizing anyone in the community they deemed should not pass on their genes. As we are all too tragically aware, Hitler took his evil quest for perfection a step further by unleashing his "final solution." During the Holocaust, an estimated six million Jews were put to death, along with an additional five million gypsies, homosexuals, mentally disabled, and Jehovah's Witnesses. The idea was to rid society of what Nazis labeled the undesirables.

Sanger took a different approach by choosing a revolutionary idea regarding reproduction that she termed "birth control." Thought to have been influenced by seeing the toll that eleven childbirths and several miscarriages had on her mother, the outspoken sex educator lobbied the government for a law requiring a permit in order to have children. Unsuccessful in getting the law passed, Sanger decided to open a birth control facility in 1916. In time, the Brooklyn eugenics factory would be more commonly referred to as Planned Parenthood.

Some years later, Sanger became a nurse, married, and moved to Greenwich Village with her husband, William. Similar to today, the free-spirited Manhattan community was filled with left-leaning political radicals, anarchists, and artists looking to change the world. As a nurse, she saw firsthand the brutality of back-alley abortions. She educated the use of contraceptives and hoped for a day when women could control their reproduction with a "magic pill." In one of her less radical quotes, she said, "No woman can call herself free until she can choose consciously whether she will or will not be a mother."

Two things can be true at the same time. Sanger was an advocate for women's rights in obtaining birth control, and she was a racist. Her controversies included the support of sterilization for the mentally impaired and her desire to "exterminate the Negro population" as stated in Sanger's letter to Dr. Clarence Gamble on December 10, 1939.

Let's take a look at some more disturbing quotes by Margaret Sanger:

> But for my view, I believe that there should be no more babies. (1947 interview with John Parsons)

> The most merciful thing that the large family does to one of its infant members is to kill it. (*Women and the New Race*, chapter 5)

> I accepted an invitation to talk to the women's branch of the Ku Klux Klan... In the end, through simple illustrations, I believed I had accomplished my purpose. A dozen invitations to speak to similar groups were proffered. (Sanger's *An Autobiography*)

> Eugenics without birth control seems to us a house builded [sic] upon the sands. It is at the

mercy of the rising stream of the unfit. (Sanger's 1919 Birth Control and Racial Betterment)

The most urgent problem today is how to limit and discourage the over-fertility of the mentally and physically defective. (Sanger's "The Eugenic Value of Birth Control Propaganda," 1921)

Apply a stern and rigid policy of sterilization and segregation to that grade of population whose progeny is tainted, or whose inheritance is such that objectionable traits may be transmitted to offspring.

It [birth control] means the release and cultivation of the better elements in our society, and the gradual suppression, elimination, and eventual extinction, of defective stocks...those *human weeds* which threaten the blooming of the finest flowers of American civilization.

Herr Fuhrer, while spreading his evil propaganda in the Bavarian beer halls in Europe, replaced "American" with "Aryan" and "human weeds" with "Jewish vermin."

Like Hitler, Sanger made no effort to hide her disdain for what they both considered "obstructions" in the way of societal progress. Here's an excerpt from her controversial book *The Pivot of Civilization*:

The most urgent problem of today is how to limit and discourage the over-fertility of the mentally and physically defective...possibly drastic and Spartan methods [infantacide] *may be forced upon American society if it continues complacently to encourage the chance of chaotic breeding that has resulted from our stupid, cruel sentimentalism.*

Sanger's "birth control" crusade was far less about empowering women and more about ridding society of the "feebleminded." She designated classifications according to one's IQ:

- Idiot: 0–25
- Imbecile: 26–50
- Moron: 51–70

The idea was to eliminate feeblemindedness from the human population via birth control or, as she described it, "the very pivot of civilization."

I'm no fan of Margaret Sanger or the organization she created. It's this author's view that Planned Parenthood is nothing more than an abortion factory whose executives have been known to dabble in the enterprising business of illegally selling parts of aborted babies to stem cell research facilities.

Side note: In 2015, while enjoying a glass of Merlot and stuffing her face with some fine cuisine in a trendy Califonia eatery, the National Director for Planned Parenthood, Dr. Deborah Nucatola, took time in between sipping and eating to discuss prices for "fetal parts." Unknown to her at the time, two undercover abortion rights opponents were video recording the conversation. Here's what Dr. Nucatola had to say:

> A lot of people want liver [Nucotola heaves a fork full of food into her mouth before continuing]… So, then you're just kind of cognizant of where you put your graspers. You try to intentionally go above and below the thorax, so that, you know—we've been very good at getting heart, lung, liver, because we know that, so I'm not gonna crush that part. I'm going to basically crush below, I'm gonna crush above, and I'm gonna see if I can get it all intact.

For the record, those body parts the doctor insensitively refers to belong to a living baby inside the womb who's about to be surgically aborted (killed).

In the hidden video, Project Veritas captures Dr. Nucotola cavalierly going over the prices:

"I would throw a number out, I would say it's probably anywhere from $30 to $100 [a specimen]."

After a public campaign denying any wrongdoing by the executives at Planned Parenthood, the company finally admitted under oath in a civil suit that they harvested organs to sell. Even with incriminating undercover video and a confession under oath, there's still no liberal media outcry for a criminal investigation by the Department of Justice.

So, instead of closing the doors once and for all to these mid-evil horror chambers, Planned Parenthood continues to flourish in the Black neighborhoods where Sanger hoped to inflict the most deaths. To bring this full circle, the liberal Dems who champion women's rights and Black Lives Matter turn a blind eye to the systematic extermination of the people they say they care about the most.

Interestingly enough, Margaret Sanger prophesied in one of her writings about the "dead weight of human waste" when it came to those in government and the ones who voted them into office:

> *The danger of recruiting our numbers from the most "fertile stocks" [idiots, imbeciles, and morons] is further emphasized when we recall that in a democracy like that of the United States every man and woman is permitted a vote in the government, and it is the representatives of this grade of intelligence who may destroy our liberties, and who may thus be the most far-reaching peril to the future of civilization... Equality of political power has thus been bestowed upon the lowest elements of our population. We must not be surprised, therefore, at the spectacle of political scandal and graft, of the notorious and universally ridiculed low level [sic]*

*intelligence and flagrant stupidity exhibited by our
legislative bodies. The Congressional Record mirrors
our political imbecility.*

In July of 2020, Planned Parenthood of Greater New York disavowed Margaret Sanger due to her "harmful connections to the eugenics movement." Karen Seltzer, the chair of the New York board, said, "The removal of Margaret Sanger's name from our building is both a necessary and overdue step to reckon with our legacy and acknowledge Planned Parenthood's contribution to historical reproduction harm within communities of color."

To which I reply, "No shit!"

So the question is who put her name on the building and did they not know what every other person who's ever read any of her work knows, which is, she's a female version of Hitler. Also, why had her name stayed on the building for all those decades? Better still, why did the New York City Council in 1993 rename the corner of Mott and Bleecker Streets Margaret Sanger Square?

Here's a shot in the dark. Since Margaret Sanger is beloved by the left, and as long as her dirty little racist secrets stayed out of the limelight, then no one would be any the wiser to her misdeeds. But in 2017, fifty-one years after Sanger's death, a phenomenon ushered in by the left known as "cancel culture" proved to be too much for the eugenics advocate to overcome.

Many people believe that Planned Parenthood is a "good" organization that prevents abortions. Advocates for the company will proudly boast that only 3 percent of their entire business comes from that very procedure. Generally speaking, whenever someone throws numbers around like they're the gospel, maybe dig a little deeper. Yes, the 3 percent number is indeed the clinic's percentage of abortions performed, and there are additional services such as STD treatments, hormone therapy, and dispensing of condoms. However, when each condom given out constitutes a "service," one can start to see that maybe that 3 percent number is a bit skewed. Perhaps a more accurate indicator to look at is the one that shows out of all the operations performed at Planned Parenthood, well over 90 percent are for abortions.

Medical facts from Lifenews.com regarding women who have an abortion:

1. Participants experience over a 100 percent increase in clinical depression and severe issues with self-medicating.
2. The premature birth risk regarding future pregnancies increases by 200 to 360 percent.
3. Compared to women who never had an abortion, the risk of contracting breast cancer increases an incredible 626 percent.

There's no way of measuring the emotional scarring or the level of burden one will carry with them for the rest of their lives. However, those who have had an abortion have significantly higher mental health issues than those who haven't.

There's a mantra out there that if you are against abortion, then you're part of the war on women and their right to choose. Only in today's upside-down world can a person show compassion over killing the innocent and find themselves labeled a misogynist. In all sincerity, this is where I get a bit confused. Allow me to use an example to illustrate my frustration.

Let's say I'm witnessing a guy hitting a woman. What should I do? Obviously, at a minimum, I should call the police. Staying true to my law enforcement background, I think I would probably get more involved than that, especially if I thought a life was in imminent danger. But now I'm being told to ignore the termination of a defenseless life because it's none of my business. So my next question is, when is the fetus considered a life. If it's at birth and not before, women should be allowed to have a legal abortion right up until the fetus is delivered. But that's a bit too squeamish for most, including those on the Supreme Court who believed that late-term abortion was "too close to infanticide." How then does the Supreme Court get to play God and draw an arbitrary line at twenty-four weeks for what is life and what is not? Twenty-four weeks and one day is murder but anything before that falls under privacy? Really?

I've witnessed numerous ultrasounds of unborn babies at different stages. My personal belief is that I'm watching a human life grow inside a womb. So the answer for me is life is at conception. And since it's a violation of moral law to kill another human being, I've concluded that abortion is murder.

In the Bible, when Elizabeth heard Mary's greeting, the *baby* leaped in her womb. Elizabeth exclaimed, "Blessed are you among women, and blessed is the *child* you will bear!"

With words like *baby* and *child* chosen to describe the unborn, I'm confident calling the fetus a life.

A final thought:

I know the taking of an unborn child is as wrong as any injustice there's been throughout history. With each procedure performed, we break the Sixth Commandment and, in doing so, dishonor our Creator. I further understand that if abortions were deemed unlawful today, tomorrow quacks in back alleys would fill the void, putting more lives in danger. So I pray for those who choose to end their pregnancy and for someday our Judeo-Christian society as a whole can view human life as a precious gift and not an inconvenient burden to be so easily discarded. Until that day arrives, it's not for me to pass judgment. However, this in no way means the act of abortion is morally acceptable. It's not!

Knowing I was researching information for this challenging topic, my good friend Wil passed along the following:

Diary of an Unborn Child

October 5:

Today my life began. My parents do not know it yet, but it is I already. And I am to be a girl. I shall have blond hair and blue eyes. Just about everything is settled though, even the fact that I shall love flowers.

October 19:

Some say that I am not a real person yet, that only my mother exists. But I am a real person, just as a small crumb of bread is yet truly bread. My mother is. And I am.

October 23:

My mouth is just beginning to open now. Just think, in a year or so I shall be laughing and later talking. I know what my first word will be: MAMA.

October 25:

My heart began to beat today all by itself. From now on it shall gently beat for the rest of my life without ever stopping to rest! And after many years it will tire. It will stop, and then I shall die.

November 2:

I am growing a bit every day. My arms and legs are beginning to take shape. But I have to wait a long time yet before those little legs will raise me to my mother's arms, before these little arms will be able to gather flowers and embrace my father.

November 12:

It wasn't until today that the doctor told mom that I am living here under her heart. Oh, how happy she must be! Are you happy, mom?

November 25:

My mom and dad are probably thinking about a name for me. But they don't know that I am a little girl. I want to be called Kathy. I am getting so big already.

December 10:

My hair is growing. It is smooth and bright and shiny. I wonder what kind of hair mom has?

December 13:

I am just about able to see. It is dark around me. When mom brings me into the world it will be full of sunshine and flowers. But what I want more than anything is to see my mom. How do you look, mom?

December 24:

I wonder if mom hears the whispering of my heart? Some children come into the world a little sick. But my heart is strong and healthy. It beats so evenly: tup-tup, tup-tup. You'll have a healthy little daughter, mom!

December 28:

Today my mother killed me.
(Anonymous, wol.jw.org g80 5/22 p. 16)

Today we look back on slavery with the universal agreement that it was an abhorrent act against humanity. However, in the mid-1800s, millions of Americans not only supported the practice but were willing to do anything to protect the evil institution. Sound familiar?

Do We Have the Right to Die?

Euthanasia: "The act or practice of killing or permitting the death of hopelessly sick or injured individuals in a relatively painless way for reasons of mercy" (*Merrian-Webster Dictionary*). The word is a combination of two Greek terms, *eu*, meaning "well," and *thanatos*, meaning "death."

I've always found it helpful to research a word in the hope of gaining complete clarity. For example, the colloquial term *senile* is often misconstrued as a diagnosis when in fact, it's a nonmedical observation of someone's physical or mental decline. In the case of the word *euthanasia*, the definition and origin do little to help weigh the morality of such so-called *mercy killings*.

The Constitution writes of "Life, Liberty, and the Pursuit of Happiness." If one's pursuit of happiness is to die, then maybe euthanasia should be protected under the Constitution? Perhaps this is a stretch, but similar to the Bible, it does not explicitly discuss the somewhat nebulous issue. The Good Book speaks of death being swallowed up in victory, the mercy of eternal life, and that to cause death is unacceptable. However, the specific issue of *mercy killing* is not addressed. The general understanding within the Christian faith is there is no reason to believe that life should be "unnecessarily prolonged" during the dying process. In my view, this broad-brush guidance does little toward the controversial right-to-die issue.

Legal

From a legal perspective, I gain no clarity either. After all, under our current system, the killing of an unborn, innocent, defenseless life is permissible but an act of mercy is construed as murder. Under extreme circumstances, wouldn't it stand to reason that an individual should have the *choice* of physician-assisted suicide (PAS)?

In recent years, several countries have legalized human euthanasia. In Switzerland, they allow a physician to provide a lethal elixir, but the patient cannot have any assistance when ingesting the poison. The act of "medical aid in dying" was first allowed in the province of Quebec before becoming legal throughout Canada in 2016. In 1997, the state of Oregon passed the "Death with Dignity Act," allowing physicians to legally prescribe lethal medications to help terminally ill patients end their lives.

Many feel the person responsible for opening the doors to human euthanization in the late twentieth-century was a doctor named Jack Kevorkian. The American pathologist believed so strongly that "dying is not a crime" that he was willing to sacrifice his own freedom to assist over 130 terminally ill patients in ending their lives.

As one might imagine, Kevorkian wasn't without controversy. The American Medical Association believed the abrasive doctor to be a "great threat to the public," and in 1995 claimed he was "a reckless instrument of death."

Regardless if one thinks Kevorkian was dangerous or not, the fact is his "die with dignity" philosophy made the medical field take notice. His critics and supporters alike would agree that because of his advocacy for assisted suicide, doctors became more sympathetic to the terminally ill in severe pain and were more willing to prescribe the necessary medications to help relieve it.

When asked what he was trying to accomplish, the doctor responded by stating, "My ultimate aim is to make euthanasia a positive experience. I'm trying to knock the medical profession into accepting its responsibilities, and those responsibilities include assisting their patients with death."

Medical

Modern medicine has advanced to the point where medical personnel can, under normal conditions, provide palliative care that substantially reduces the suffering of someone with a terminal illness. However, this author fails to understand how this waltz between life and death is acceptable but putting someone out of their misery is a sin?

In preparation for this topic, I interviewed Dr. William Zouzas, formerly of Cabrini Medical Center in New York City. The physician offered a contrarian view to Dr. Kervorkian. He was quick to point out the possible unintended consequences of PAS by stating, "With crippling medical costs, an individual may feel obligated to expedite what they deem the inevitable. They begin to feel guilt over financial hardships or the emotional toll they see it taking on their loved ones, and out of haste, prematurely end their life." There was another issue Dr. Zouzas addressed that could only come from someone who'd taken the Osteopathic Oath. He explained his commitment to healing and swore never to administer poison to anyone who asked. Lastly, the former Massachusetts State high school wrestling champion expressed his concerns for those in the medical field carrying out such physician-assisted suicides, believing that the taking of life would eventually have an emotional toll.

The doctor's candid insight left me with the understanding that, although the medical field can efficiently alleviate terminally ill patients of pain, the moral issue of physician-assisted suicides remains.

Roman Catholic Church

In Joseph V. Sullivan's *The Morality of Mercy Killing*, the bishop argues on behalf of the Catholic Church that to justify mercy killings would violate God's law. Sullivan asserts that to do otherwise may widen the parameters of taking a life and stresses, "You shall not kill."

In Father Francis Jeremiah Connell's *Morals in Politics and Professions*, the Catholic theologian wrote, "No doctor may ever deliberately and directly accelerate death in the case of a dying person... It would be murder to give him a drug with the direct intention of hastening his passage from this world."

Father Connell's view that "it would be murder" to hasten one's death leaves me perplexed since his institution believes "just wars" are acceptable and, last time I checked, people are still getting killed in wars. As for Bishop Sullivan, it should be noted that at the time of his death in 1982, he had several sexual abuse cases pending against him. In 2004, the Roman Catholic Diocese of Baton Rouge settled a lawsuit with one of his victims and promptly removed the disgraced bishop's name from a local high school.

In what appears to be a complete contradiction from the other two clergy members, Pope Pius XII during World War II said, "The removal of pain and consciousness by means of drugs when medical reasons suggest it, is permitted by religion and morality to both doctor and patient even if the use of drugs will shorten life."

If the Catholic Church helped in clarifying euthanasia, please forgive me, but I must've missed it.

I spent many late nights debating doctrine and other Roman Catholic Church practices with my late, learned friend Father Gerald. While sipping Johnny Walker Blue in the upstairs of the Brooklyn-based rectory, the two of us would often square off like an Ali-Frazier heavyweight match. The sides were well established before our snifters clanged: he the defender of norms and me the young, idealistic accusatory.

On one occasion, the topic of "right to die" had found its way into our metaphorical ring. The year was 1985, and the news was consumed about a girl named Karen Ann Quinlan. Julia and Joseph Quinlan's adopted daughter had recently died after being in a coma for the past ten years. She was thirty-one.

In 1975, the attractive twenty-one-year-old brunette fell into a persistent vegetative state after consuming alcohol and tranquilizers. With no hope of recovery, her parents petitioned to have the respirator be disconnected and for their daughter to be allowed to "die with grace and dignity." The case gripped a nation wondering what the right and moral thing to do was.

After a lengthy court battle, the Quinlans were finally permitted to remove the respirator from their daughter but not the feeding tube. Karen survived for the next ten years with zero quality of life in a nursing home in Morris Plains, New Jersey.

Using Scripture, Father Gerald explained how Paul chose to endure all the suffering rather than end his life:

> *If I am to live in the flesh, that means fruit-*
> *ful labor for me. Yet which I shall choose I cannot*

*tell. I am hard-pressed between the two. My desire is
to depart and be with Christ, for that is far better.
But to remain in the flesh is more necessary...*(Phil.
1:22–24)

When done, Father Gerald finished with the go-to non-scrip-
ture, saying, "The Lord works in mysterious ways."

That's where I disagreed with my mentor. I explained to him the
only mystery to me is why anyone would think it was acceptable for
Karen Ann Quinlan to die the way she had. To my surprise, Father
Gerald was more conciliatory toward my words than in opposition.
My pastor explained how the family's priest, Father Trapasso, offered
spiritual and ethical guidance to Karen's devout Catholic parents.
They too had grappled with honoring their faith but also not wanting to see their daughter unnecessarily suffer. Trapasso, at the time,
a member of the clergy at Our Lady of the Lake Church in Mount
Arlington, New Jersey, shared what Pope Pius XII had articulated on
the issue decades earlier. With Father Trapasso's assistance, Mr. And
Mrs. Quinlan concluded that discontinuing the medical equipment
was not the same as taking a life.

Father Gerald believed that Karen's struggles would not go in
vain. When it came to the "right to die" issue, he thought there was
common ground to be had between science and faith.

Masada

The siege of Masada took place late in the first century, around
the time when the Second Temple was destroyed. Jewish rebels
used the flat mountaintop as a refuge against the Roman soldiers.
Thought to be impregnable, the fortress had a single narrow opening nicknamed "The Snake" after its twisting pathway that led to
the summit. The Jewish rebels were able to hold off the Romans for
three years atop of Masada. When defeat was finally imminent, there
looked to be only two choices: surrender and be enslaved or fight to a
certain death against the most powerful army of its day. However, the
group came up with a third choice. The 967 men, women, and chil-

dren decided to die free than live as slaves. The mass suicide demoralized the Roman soldiers, who, after three years in the desert waiting for their day of glory, had it taken away.

One can argue that those at Masada's cunning military maneuver inflicted more damage than if they had fought. But as taught to me as a young child in the Catholic Church, the Catechism declares, *"It is God who remains the sovereign master of life. ... We are stewards, not owners, of the life God has entrusted to us. It is not ours to dispose of."*

As a Christian, I believe that human life is spiritually different than any other living creature, and because of this, it bears the responsibility of respecting God's gift to us. When Jesus spoke of the second greatest commandment being, "Love your neighbor as yourself," He was letting us know that the way to honor Jehovah was by feeding the hungry, clothing the needy, tending to the infirmed, and caring for those most vulnerable. In an ever-growing narcissistic society more concerned with the latest tattoo design, vaping, and nose piercings, I can't help but think of how disappointed our Creator is with the lack of value we've put on human life. But still, God continues to love us. And with all love comes understanding, compassion, and mercy.

In my view, if given a choice to live forever in a world controlled by Satan or die, I'll choose death every time. So if someone has fought the good fight and doesn't feel like fighting anymore, they've not only earned the right to die with dignity but forgiveness as well.

Sexual Orientation

On June 28, 1969, a riot broke out at the Stonewall Inn, a known gay bar in Greenwich Village. The altercation between the police and the gay community sparked several nights of riots and is considered by most historians to be the catalyst that began the gay liberation movement. Around the country, the once-shunned gay community began openly demanding change. Soon after, in 1973, the American Psychiatric Association (APA) removed ego-syntonic homosexuality from the *Diagnostic and Statistical Manual of Mental Disorders* (DSM). The significance was that since the APA no longer considered homosexuality a mental disorder, the road toward equality commenced.

Biblical

Unlike numerous Islamic nations under Sharia law that execute same-sex couples, the United States is a place where one is protected by the Constitution to pursue such happiness without the worry of persecution. That same document affords us, under the First Amendment, the right to exercise religion freely. One's faith and the law of the land are not in opposition to one another. One can still love thy neighbor but disagree with the morality of their lifestyle. Although the Bible makes it clear that "men who submit to homosexual acts...will not inherit God's Kingdom" (1 Cor. 6:9–10 NWT), nowhere in the Scriptures does it condone hate or prejudice due to someone's sexual orientation. The Bible tells us to "be peaceable with all men" (Rom. 12:18), "Love your neighbor as yourself" (Rom. 13:9), and that sex should be between a male and female who are married to one another (Gen. 1:27–28, 2:24).

Simply put, my faith teaches me to reject the immoral conduct, not the people.

In 1 Peter 2:17, the verse teaches us to "honor men of all sorts..." So love, yes—be happy and respectful toward others, absolutely—but don't force a baker to bake the cake for a gay wedding or use the arm of the government to command a Catholic Church to hire an atheist as their bookkeeper.

When the Obama administration imposed a mandate under the Affordable Care Act, forcing Hobby Lobby to cover birth control for their employees, to little surprise, the matter found its way to the Supreme Court. The crux of the case was whether or not the Christian faith owners had the right to refuse coverage for the employees' health benefits plan regarding contraception. An issue that the family felt was an act of abortion and in conflict with their moral beliefs. The Court ruled that the Obama Administration violated the Free Exercise Clause of the First Amendment and the Religious Freedom Restoration Act of 1993 (RFRA).

For the moment, the gay community may have lost the battle, but they were on their way to winning the war.

Side note: At the annual Easter prayer breakfast in April of 2015, President Obama thought it would be an appropriate time to remind us Christians that we haven't always been good. Here's an excerpt from his speech:

> *On Easter, I do reflect on that as a Christian I am supposed to love, and, I have to say that sometimes when I listen to less than loving expressions by Christians, I get concerned.*

I researched any similar remarks that the former president might've said regarding those of the Muslim faith but was unable to ascertain any.

Legal

In the previous ten years as the chief justice, Roberts had never previously read his decision from the bench. However, that changed on June 26, 2015. In what would be yet another Justice Kennedy 5–4 swing decision, the Supreme Court voted that same-sex marriages were protected under the Fourteenth Amendment, paving the way for all fifty states to recognize such unions. The ruling sparked an uncharacteristic scathing dissent from the chief justice. In the historic Obergefell v. Hodges dissent, Roberts lamented:

"If you want to celebrate gay marriage, do it. But don't celebrate the Constitution because the Constitution had nothing to do with this ruling today."

For Roberts, the issue at hand wasn't whether or not marriage should remain historically between a man and a woman, but rather the process in how that decision should be achieved:

> *It is instead about whether, in our democratic republic, that decision should rest with the people acting through their elected representatives, or with*

five lawyers [fellow justices]*who happen to hold commissions authorizing them to resolve legal disputes under the law... The people of the state are free to expand marriage to include same-sex couples, or to retain the historic definition.*

Roberts's opposition to the ruling of same-sex marriage rest on his belief that jurists, like umpires, should be left strictly to calling the "balls and strikes." Instead, judicial activism ruled the day while the duly elected representatives of the people were silenced.

Roberts rhetorically asked his colleagues, "Just who do you think we are?" Concluding that this was "an act of will, not legal judgment."

In both the case of abortions and same-sex marriages, SCOTUS bypassed the will of the people by legislating law from the bench—an act our framers never intended.

Side note: The three branches of government were purposely designed to divide government, and in theory, keep a balance of power. Thus, the United States Constitution was not written to be cherry-picked regardless if a cause is considered virtuous or not. There's a process for making changes, and it does not include bypassing our elected representatives.

The following statement is from a law professor shortly after SCOTUS's ruling in the same-sex case. Mind you, not a millennial law student, but rather, a supposed learned individual in the world of academia. Professor Vladeck's view is what scares the bejesus out of me when it comes to judicial activism and where our country is heading:

> The rhetoric of restraint in the chief justice's dissent is certainly powerful, and in the ordinary case, he's absolutely right that the courts should defer to [the] democratic process. But the whole point of having an independent and unelected judiciary is for days, and cases, like this one. And so, while his dissent today is deeply consistent

with his broader "balls and strikes" judicial philosophy, the real takeaway from today's ruling is
that every once in a while, the [Supreme] Court
is, and is supposed to be, much more than just
an umpire.

Ohhhh, I see. According to Professor V, who also moonlights as
a CNN contributor, if he agrees with the cause, then, by all means,
feel free to urinate all over the United States Constitution. Because,
after all, thanks to Professor V's deep conviction to the law, he'll
abide by the Constitution in an "ordinary case," but when it comes
to the "once in a while" ones that will change the moral fabric of our
nation forever, well, damn the details!

The former mayor of South Bend and Democrat presidential
candidate, Pete Buttigieg, did his own cherry-picking. In this particular case, it wasn't with the so-called archaic Constitution, but
rather with another old, inconvenient relic the godless left despises,
the Bible.

The self-proclaimed deeply religious Christian discussed in a
Rolling Stone interview his view of the Bible by stating: "Any encounter with Scripture includes some process of sorting out what con-
nects you with God versus what simply tells you about the morals
of the times when it was written." The same-sex married politician
explained that since Jesus spoke in "hyperbole and parables," that it
was a "mysterious code," that he felt was "no way that a literal understanding of Scripture can fit into the Bible that I find in my hands."
As difficult and mysterious as Jesus's words are for Buttigieg to understand, somehow, the Tricky Dicky politician could justify abortion
up to the point of birth referencing, of all things, the Bible. In the
same *Rolling Stone* interview with John Gage, Buttigieg attempts to
justify abortion up until birth by saying, "There's so many parts of
the Bible that associate the beginning of life with breath."

In a way, I have to give credit for this guy's creativity. Everything
written in the Bible that conflicts with his lifestyle, he finds a *mystery*;
but when it comes to abortion and collecting the far left's approval,
aka votes, somehow, this sleuth can break the "code."

For the record, the biblical principles offered in the Scriptures don't have an expiration date. Just because humankind's morals have worsened doesn't mean, as some would try to have us believe, the Bible is the problem. We've been warned that evildoers will go from bad to worse (2 Tim. 3:13). It's disgraceful the first attack by those justifying their immoral conduct is to disparage the Bible. Am I supposed to pretend that Jehovah didn't express his displeasure in Leviticus 18:22 when I read that the act of men lying with other men is an abomination? Christianity, the Bible, and the United States Constitution are not the issue. The problem is godless secular bureaucrats telling God-fearing Americans that our faith is wrong and that they're right. Even down to the sanctity of marriage, the left is replacing God's definition with their own.

Just as a reminder, the left won't be satisfied until we worship them and not God. There's no mystery, no secret sauce, no code breakers needed, just the realization that the radical left's quest is to destroy America's Judeo-Christian faith. It's that simple.

So, Pete, have a blast. Swing from chandeliers for all I care, but please stop telling people your version of "Christian ethics" in one breath and that the Bible is outdated in another.

Chapter 5

Donkeys and Elephants

One seldom recognizes the devil when he is putting his hands on your shoulder.

—Albert Speer
Minister of Armaments and Munitions for Nazi Germany

The GOP's elephant is traced back to political cartoonist Thomas Nast. After seeing a drawing in the *New York Herald* that showed an elephant at the edge of a pit with the caption that read, "The Republican vote," Nast decided to incorporate the mammoth descendent into his work at *Harper's Weekly*. Before long, other cartoonists followed suit and began using the elephant as the Republican Party symbol.

The Democrat's donkey has a touch of irony to its origin as well. During the 1828 presidential campaign, the opposition labeled Andrew Jackson a jackass. In what can best be described as "making lemonade out of lemons," Old Hickory himself embraced Shrek's little buddy by having the image of a donkey included in all his campaign posters. The rest, as they say, is history.

So Just How Crazy Is the Left?

There's not a day that goes by that I don't hear or read something that makes me think they're pretty crazy. Ever since Trump won in 2016, celebrities have shown zero self-control when it comes to expressing their hatred. What they call "art," I call pure vitriol.

Just because my plumber can clear a drain like nobody's business doesn't mean I need to know his views on gun control, immigration, abortion, or anything else that doesn't have to do with unclogging the crap from my toilet. Why then do celebs feel it's their calling to enlighten us little people on worldly issues? Whatever their profession might be, making movies, dunking a basketball, or living off the name "Kardashian," God bless them. I hope they make a ton of money for their endeavors. And if these gifted individuals feel it's their civic duty to get involved, be my guest. I'm sure their local city council would very much appreciate their input at the next meeting. But that's not what's going on here. These insecure, egotistical starlets need the bright lights to shine on their self-proclaimed righteousness. Here's the kicker. Let's say tomorrow the Hollywood trend switched to pro-life, securing our borders, and supporting the Second Amendment. All of a sudden, you'd see a flock of stars running to the cameras, carting an AR15 in one hand and a Bible in the other as they sport their crisp new MAGA hat. Why? Because these soulless idiots don't have an original thought of their own. They follow the herd even if it means going off a cliff. Why do you think these self-absorbed prima donnas get tattoos written in Chinese and wear oversize gold crucifixes laid in diamonds around their necks? Do you think it's because nothing says "I Love Jesus" more than having a quote from Buddha written in communist letters across their body? No! It's because they saw it in a rap video, and now this is what the pea brain covets.

In JFK's *Profiles in Courage*, the first-term senator from Massachusetts recounts acts of fortitude by former United States senators when it came to their convictions, even when it flew in the face of conventional wisdom. These individuals could've just as easily gone along to get along but instead took a stand because they felt the cause was more significant than any title or position they might lose.

Kennedy used the word *courage* when describing these fine patriots. Since the following group is anything but, I've decided to subtitle this part of the book *The Cowards*:

"I'm An Artist"

Early on in Trump's presidency, a two-bit has-been hack thought it would be a good career choice for her to do a photoshoot in effigy of the President's bloodied, decapitated head. The last I heard, Ms. Griffin was spinning one of those arrow street signs along Holywood Boulevard that read, "*Free Vapors Ahead.*" Her career choice may have gone up in smoke, but at least she's maintained her artistic integrity. *You go, girl!*

"How Do I Look?"

Jane Fonda, better known by her fellow comrades in Southeast Asia as Hanoi Jane, has been retired from communist propaganda photo-ops for quite some time. However, nothing seems to slow down the "godless wonder women," except perhaps for a dose of senility.

At the height of the pandemic in 2020, the ageless Fonda, almost as ageless as the photo of Hanoi Jane sitting in an antiaircraft gun used to kill American service members, decided God does exist and that He's very generous. Resembling a scene out of the classic 1950 Sunset Boulevard, the Gloria Swanson understudy playfully remarked, "I just think COVID is God's gift to the left." Not done making an ass out of herself in the midst of a deadly virus that at the time had taken over two hundred thousand American lives, Fonda started laughing like a mad scientist before continuing with her disturbing remarks: "That's a terrible thing to say. I think it was a very difficult thing to send down to us, but it has ripped the Band-Aid off who he [Trump] is and what he stands for…"

The only way I can make sense of this thought process is that maybe the female version of Dorian Gray is the normal one and the rest of us little people are crazy. Just kidding, she's nuts!

"I Am God"

Trump-hater Alec Baldwin gave some unsolicited advice to Trump voters: "Just stay home. You know in your heart that he [Trump] is an incompetent idiot and a self-seeking punk. Don't bother voting. Stay home."

I don't know about you, but nothing screams democracy more than staying home and not voting.

I am a little surprised that the actor who was once arrested over a disputed parking space in Manhattan, thrown off an American Airlines flight for refusing to turn off his cell phone, regularly uses photographers as unwitting sparring partners, and left his daughter a voice message that included the fatherly loving phrases, "You're a rude, thoughtless little pig" and "I don't give a damn that you're twelve-years-old or eleven or that you're a child, or your mother is a thoughtless pain in the ass…" would use words like *idiot* and *punk* when describing someone other than himself.

By the way, Mr. "Father of the Year" Baldwin, she was eleven, not twelve, at the time of your little meltdown.

Side note: In the early 1990s, I met Alec Baldwin in a deli in Time Square. I was a young police officer working in Midtown at the time, and Mr. Baldwin was already a well-established actor performing on Broadway in a *Street Car Named Desire*. I was at the counter in the middle of asking the waitress to go waterskiing with me when I heard the sexiest male voice imaginable politely ask, "Excuse me, Officer, where do you water ski around here?" When I turned to see who the idiot was that had interrupted my well-rehearsed dating plans, it was none other than Mr. Baldwin. For the next several minutes, the two of us engaged in a friendly conversation about skiing, the City, and how cute the waitress was. Before leaving, he wished me luck with the girl I'd been trying to get to go out with me all summer and jokingly said that if she turned me down for waterskiing that he knew a good Broadway show I could take her to.

The man I met in the deli that day was smart, charming, and engaging—nothing like the angry person I've previously described. I sincerely pray that whatever anger is festering inside the gifted actor, he addresses the issue before it consumes him.

The following may fall under the *"Who gives a rat's ass" category*, but please indulge me.

My two favorite movie scenes of all time are Jack Nickelson in *A Few Good Men* with his "You can't handle the truth" witness stand testimony and Alec Baldwin's "I am God" in *Malice*.

Here we go. Alec Baldwin, *Malice*, scene 82, take one and... action:

> *I have an MD from Harvard, I am board certified in cardio-thoracic medicine and trauma surgery. I have been awarded citations from seven different medical boards in New England, and I am never, ever sick at sea. So I ask you: When someone goes into that chapel and they fall on their knees and they pray to God that their wife doesn't miscarry, or that their daughter doesn't bleed to death, or that their mother doesn't suffer acute neural trauma from post-operative shock, who do you think they're praying to? Now, go ahead and read your Bible, Dennis, and you go to your church, and with any luck, you might win the annual raffle. But if you're looking for God, he was in operating room number two on November 17th, and he doesn't like to be second-guessed. You ask me if I have a God complex. Let me tell you something: I am God.*

Classic!

Three Idiots

Madonna's "I have thought an awful lot of blowing up the White House" and Johnny Depp's "When was the last time an actor assassinated a president... It's been a while, and maybe it's time," were both received openly to their sycophantic cheering fans. Then there was Cher advocating for institutionalized rape upon the president once Trump was impeached and sent to prison. The often half-dressed entertainer confessed that she'd like to see Trump sent off to the big house and for him to be abused as the *"toy boy of Big Bubba."*

Assuming none of the surgeons' scalpels to Cherilyn's face have penetrated the talented singer's skull, leaving her with permanent brain damage, I'm left to conclude that she too is nuts.

"Blackground"

Sooner or later, if a racist talks or tweets long enough, their genuine underlying hatred toward others will come through. Bette Midler's unveiling came when she tweeted a picture that showed a group of Black men and women at one of Trump's reelection rallies holding up signs, "Blacks for Trump 2020.com." Her tweet read:

"Look, there are African American men in this shot! How much did he [Trump] pay them to be 'blackground'?"

Now I know most people reading this book are exponentially more intelligent than the person who's writing it. So it should come as no surprise when I read Ms. Midler's "blackground" for the first time that I thought it said "background." I couldn't understand what all the fuss was about until I took a second look. The point I'm making here is, I couldn't fathom using a person's race as a pun, so my cerebrum was incapable of registering the classless reference. However, for someone like Midler, who extensively uses the part of the brain known as the putamen—a feature that registers hate, contempt, and disgust—her offensive comment came completely natural.

The songster's racist tweet garnered rebuttals from several prominent African Americans:

Recording artist Joy Will: "Really, Bette? *Really?* You're crazy to insinuate black Americans have absolutely no mind or values of their own and would only support their country & would only support their country @realdonaldtrump for 'money'? SMH you probably think they're all pimps & black women like me are just h***, too?"

Actor Terence K. Williams: "[Trump] did not pay any black people to support him! We can think for ourselves. I never received a check!"

Author Candice Owens: "White Democrats hate that republicans are freeing black people again."

Side note: The feud between Trump and Midler goes back to before he was president. In 2012, the actress was not happy about some of the real estate mogul's projects. Here's a tweet by Midler followed by a "Churchill-esque" response by the Donald.

BM: "Donald Trump architect of the ruination of the West Side, deserves to be held down and his hair cut off or strapped to the roof of the car!"

45: "While @BetteMidler is an extremely unattractive woman, I refuse to say that because I always insist on being politically correct. @BetteMidler talks about my hair, but I'm not allowed to talk about her ugly face or body—so I won't. Is this a double standard?"

Raging Bull

Who will ever forget America's favorite *Taxi Driver*, Robert DeNiro, walking onto the stage of the famed Radio City Music Hall and announcing to the Tony Award audience, "I'm gonna say one thing. Fuck Trump." Bob's fellow narcissistic celebrities raised to their feet as one to applaud the "public service announcement." The bizarre event was reminiscent of the *Hunger Games* scene when the blue-hair host and his audience are so disconnected from reality that they're cheering for the kids who are about to go off and kill each other. Unbelievable!

In a 2016 election campaign video, Bob calls Trump "an idiot, a national disaster, an embarrassment to this country," and then expressed his desire to "punch Trump in the face." In the one-minute ad, an angry Bob goes on a rant about Trump being a dog, a pig, and a mutt. Correct me if I'm wrong, but is it not the left who's always scolding conservatives for referring to the raping, murderous MS-13 members as animals? We're told by the anti-plastic straw hypocrites who fly around in their private jets that this kind of language is racially hateful and how it dehumanizes those "poor misunderstood children."

Note to Mr. DeNiro: Calling Trump crazy is like a patient in Bellevue trying to convince the doctors that he's normal, and they're the ones that need to be committed. Just something you may want to keep in mind the next time you visit the psych ward, Bob.

Cockroaches

John Leguizamo is a Colombian American actor who hates Trump because he feels he's a racist. For this reason, the one-time comedian thought it was acceptable to disparage all those in the Latino community for supporting Trump during the 2020 campaign. In an interview on HBO, the actor said, "Latin people for Republicans are like roaches for Raid." Again I ask, when is the left going to stop dehumanizing people just because they disagree with them?

On a personal note, my wife was born in the same city as Mr. Leguizamo in Bogota, Colombia. In 2016 and 2020, she and a record number of Latino voters proudly cast their ballot for Donald J. Trump for president. Maybe the next time the actor attempts to resuscitate his career, he can do so without insulting millions of his fellow American Latinos in the process.

The Unbiased

The visceral reaction of the left to Trump's presidency was not limited to celebrities. The media had adamantly defended their impartiality while openly labeling the president a racist, xenophobic, bigot, sexist, homophobic, Islamaphobic, and any other phobic they could come up with, so long as it besmirched the reputation of the forty-fifth president.

CNN's host Don Lemon is billed as a *"nonpartisan anchor"* but regularly gives more opinion than news. Lemon defends calling Trump a bigot and racist because, according to the "impartial" anchor, "Those aren't opinions, those are facts." Can anyone imagine Walter Cronkite using these terms when describing the president of the United States and then with a straight face say he wasn't biased? At MSNBC, commentator Rachel Maddow has made her stance as clear as her rival Sean Hannity of Fox. Both are openly at polar opposite ends of the political spectrum, and because of this, I don't take what either has to say as the gospel. But since Don Lemon is trying to come across as Edward R. Murrow, when in reality he's a Democrat operative, I think it's fair game to call him out.

By the way, Mr. Lemon, here are a few things to set the record straight:

A black hole didn't swallow up Flight 370; if robbing a store and assaulting a police officer within twenty minutes is your idea of "another innocent Black man," then you're right to describe Michael Brown as an upstanding citizen; they weren't mostly peaceful protesters; asking Bill Cosby's rape victim why she didn't bite his penis while forced to give oral sex has to be the dumbest, most inappropriate, crudest, insensitive question ever asked on live television. And just curious, are those glasses you occasionally wear real or a prop to try and make you appear less stupid?

Correction: On several occasions, Donald Trump has called Don Lemon "the dumbest man on television." I'm sorry to have to correct you, Mr. President, but with an estimated salary of $4 million a year, Mr. Lemon is the smartest, dumbest person on television. As for the dumbest CEO in the television business, I believe the president and I agree when we say it's the guy signing Lemon's paychecks.

"Yellow Man"

So if Don Lemon isn't the dumbest person on television, who is? Well, that title belongs to Donny Deutsch.

While lecturing America that a third of us are racist, the racist himself used the racial slur "Yellow Man" in one of his early morning rants on MSDNC. Except for the "DNC" part, you just can't make this stuff up.

Donny created his own breaking news when he announced to the world: "One in three Americans are racist. One in three Americans are terrified that this country…is not going to be majority white. That the black man or brown man or the 'yellow man' or woman are going to come and take their jobs and take away their suburbs and scare them."

Donny wasn't finished embarrassing himself. In his later on-air apology for using the racial slur "yellow man," the yellow man himself gave the "*If* I offended anybody" nonsensical non-apology apology. The idiot finished his mea culpa with, "People who know me know where my heart is." Well, Donny, thankfully, since you're not on my speed dial, I'll go as far as to say that I don't know you or where your heart is. But I can tell you what orifice on your anatomy your head is stuck up.

By the way, was anyone curious to know how the dumbest personality on television came up with the scientific algorithm to figure out that exactly one-third of all Americans are racist? It reminds me of the Snapple bottle cap that read, "72.3 percent of all statistics are made up on the spot."

Donny doesn't have any love lost for Trump. On several occasions, the man whose father gifted him a multimillion dollar advertising firm, compared Trump to Hitler and then strongly criticized those Jewish people who supported the president. Once again, if I'm missing something here, please feel free to enlighten me. But if Trump is Hitler, then how come the president had so many Jewish supporters? Also, continuing with the Hitler theme here, why did the Israeli prime minister, who I'm pretty sure is Jewish in a predominately Jewish nation, name the newest town on the Golan Heights Trump Heights. So if Deutsch is correct—and let's face it, why wouldn't he be—then Trump is Hitler and Hitler is Trump, that means Hitler had many Jewish supporters too, and, somewhere in Israel, there's a town named after the Fuhrer. I would've never guessed all of that, but thanks to Mr. Donny Deutsch and his brilliant insight, I've learned something. Thank you, Mr. Yellow Man.

Another thing I learned from Donny was all Trump voters, my wife and I included, are "Nazis."

Well, Donny, you stupid POS, there's a line you shouldn't have crossed. My wife and I aren't Nazis, nor are any of the other 62,000,000 people who voted for Trump in 2016 and the 74,000,000 in 2020. Not everyone who disagrees with your yellow-man ass is a member of one of the evilest groups of people the world has ever seen. I'm just glad I served my country, so little spineless piss ants like yourself have the freedom to enjoy diarrhea of the mouth whenever it pleases you. You're welcome!

In summation, Mr. Donny "Yellow-Man" Deutsch has labeled one-third of the country racist and sixty million plus of us Nazis. It's this hateful, divisive garbage spewed out by morons like Deutsch that show who the real racists are in this country.

Side note: An extraordinary thing occurred after President Trump, the First Lady, and their son contracted the virus in the fall of 2020. Kanye West twitted the following:

"There's a crying need across the board. We need to and will come together in the name of Jesus. I'm praying for President Trump's and Melania's full recovery, just as I would for Joe and Jill Biden if they were stricken, as well as everyone else with COVID-19."

Who would've ever thought the guy who used to sway a bottle of Hennessy whenever he was out in public and the not so proud owner of one of the most awkward onstage encounters in the history of award shows—interrupting Taylor Swift in the middle of her acceptance speech to let the world now he thought Beyonce's video was better—would be the voice of reason. If there's hope for Kanye, there's hope for all of us! Maybe even you, Mr. Yellow Man

The Luv Guv and His Little Brother Fredo

During the height of the Wuhan virus, CNN took it upon themselves to lighten the mood a little with an impromptu Vaudeville act. Well, maybe it wasn't so spontaneous since there were props involved in the Cuomo Brothers comedy show. Although the variety sketch took place while thousands of senior citizens were dying at the hands of an order the governor gave, as far as the dedicated entertaining Cuomo Brothers were concerned, "the show must go on."

With an oversize cotton swab in hand, Fredo jokingly asked his big bro if "this" was the size they needed for his testing, poking fun at the gov's big nose. As the two yukked it up on a split screen, Fredo kept the act going by producing several more swabs, one bigger than the next. This stuff was pure comedic gold. At the time, over forty thousand people in New York State had died from the virus, but that didn't deter the Cuomo Brothers' professional performance. Unfortunately, silly me tuned into CNN that night, hoping the "news anchor" might ask some probing questions to the governor like, "Why, did you issue an order that forced seniors who tested positive for the virus back in nursing homes?" Or "Why didn't you use the hospital ship the president provided, and why did you demand so many ventilators when, in fact, you only needed a small fraction?" Instead, we were treated to a *Laurel and Hardy* skit. As for those mourning their loved ones who tuned in looking for answers, my apologies that those lives that were so precious to you weren't taken more seriously by the people we've entrusted with them. One thing we did get from the probing interview was the governor's new nickname, The Luv Guv.

So how did the Luv Guv handle the utter failure on his watch? Well, he wrote a book, of course. But not just any book. The guy who gave the order that directly impacted the deaths of thousands and refused to take any responsibility wrote a book on "leadership lessons." This would be like Bernie Madoff releasing a book titled "Investing Wisely," right after being indicted for his multibillion dollar Ponzi scheme or the captain of the *Titanic* publishing his memoir, "How to Enjoy Cruising." One can't help but wonder if the Luv Guv is void of any self-awareness?

After President Trump delivered on every one of the Luv Guv's requests, Cuomo went on the *highly sophisticated and newsworthy* Howard Stern show to promote himself and his new book. This would be the same show that broadcasts women having orgasms by sitting on oversize speakers while the host provides *free* physical breast exams. Cuomo decided that it would be during this tasteless venue to announce to Stern's audience that the *Luv Guv* would like to "deck" the president. Only someone who's as egotistical and arrogant as Cuomo could show his appreciation toward the president of the United States by threatening to assault the man who bailed his ass out.

As far as I'm concerned, nothing illustrates leadership better than threatening violence, accepting zero responsibility, writing a book that should be in Barnes and Noble's fiction section, and then doing a spot on the Howard Stern show to praise oneself. All this as the pandemic raged and people were dying. *Way to go, Luv Guv!*

By the way, in case anyone was wondering, the Luv Guv's skit on the radio show was a solo—sorry, Fredo. But I do think it's only fair since I've castrated his brother's leadership skills that I should give Fredo equal time.

Dear Fredo,

> *First, let's begin with your nickname Luv Guv—oops, sorry, wrong Cuomo—it's Fredo.*
>
> *In my old neighborhood in Brooklyn, only one of two nicknames stuck, great ones like The Hammer, The Pope, Bruiser, and Ice or the ones that would get under somebody's skin. Take a wild guess which category yours falls under? I'll give you a hint, your not the Pope, Fredo.*

It didn't help the CNN news anchor that a video went viral (August 12, 2019) of Fredo going berserk over someone calling him, of all things, Fredo. It might help if Fredo read his brother's book on *leadership skills*, and if that doesn't seem to do the trick, he could try this one: sticks and stones may break my bones, but words will… well, you get the idea.

As for Fredo's altercation, it all started when some wiseguys started teasing him by calling him, well, Fredo. The following is officially how every catfight starts in New York:

WISEGUY: Hey, Fredo! What's up?
FREDO: Punk ass bitches from the right call me Fredo. My name is
    Chris Cuomo. I'm an anchor on CNN.
WISEGUY: I thought that was your name.
FREDO: That's like the N-word for us.
WISEGUY: I don't want any problems.
FREDO: You're going to have a big fuckin' problem.
WISEGUY: What are you going to do about it?
FREDO: I'll fuckin' ruin your shit. I'll fucking throw you down these
    stairs.

Of course, like 99 percent of these stupid hissy fits, each guy was restrained by their respective friends and life when on in obscurity for the "Wiseguy." But Fredo wasn't so lucky. Remember that thing about being an "anchor on CNN," well, that makes him a celebrity, and the Internet loves when celebrities screw up. Of course, to justify his steroid-induced rage, the White guy tried going to the race card. *Sorry, Fredo, but you can't compare your name to the N-word. Nice try!* Just kidding, that was not a nice try. It was a pitiful attempt on Fredo's part to play the victim card. For a kid that was born with a silver spoon in his mouth and a gold rectal thermometer permanently stuck up his ass, you'd think he'd know better not to say something so asinine.

I think Donald Trump Jr. summed it up best when he Tweeted: *"Hey @Chris Cuomo, take it from me, 'Fredo' isn't the N-word for Italians, it just means you're the dumb brother."*

For Fredo, his temper tantrums didn't lighten up any after contracting the Wuhan virus. Fortunately, he made a full recovery but not before going berserk on one of his neighbors. The situation occurred when an older gentleman had the audacity to ask "Chris" why he was outside of his house while he was sick. Unlike the first confrontation, this incident wasn't caught on video. So we're left with two versions of the story. To no surprise, at least not to me, the neighbor accused Fredo of being aggressive and agitated when confronted. The interesting point here is that regardless of what exactly transpired, Fredo told his viewers that he was quarantined in his Hampton's basement the entirety of his illness, which was clearly not true.

Fredo's lack of candor is nothing new. For months in 2020, he pounded his CNN desk, demanding us little people to wear our masks. During that time, maskless Fredo photos emerged of him out in public, enjoying a nice stogie. Then there was Fredo's run-in with the management's office to the Manhattan apartment he rents. The letter in part read:

> You have been observed entering and exiting the building and riding the elevator without the required face coverings. Even though staff members have asked you to comply with this requirement, you have refused to do so. This is a violation of the Executive Order, building policy, and places other residents and our staff at risk.

There are no exceptions to this rule, and you are required to comply.

Merriam-Webster's definition of *hypocrisy*:
"A person who puts on a false appearance of virtue…a person who acts in contradiction to his or her stated beliefs or feelings…" aka a "Fredo."

I want to share one final thought on the Cuomo brothers. When it came to the pandemic, these two bozos were part of a conga line of public personalities and officials who followed the hypocrisy of the "do as thee, not as me" mantra. I compare them to the Sunday churchgoer who waves their finger at everyone else during the week, but because they sat through a ninety-minute sermon, they somehow feel exempt from following the rules. I dedicate this next verse to the high and mighty:

> *Thou hypocrite, first cast out the beam out of thine own eye; and then shalt thou see clearly to cast out the mote out of thy brother's eye. (Matt. 7:5)*

Katha Pollitt

Now and again, I may say something out loud that, after hearing it, I wish I could take back. I don't think I'm alone in this self-loathing condemnation. I'm sure we've all said something that has come out the wrong way and wished we could somehow hit rewind. One of those regrettable occasions for me was when I was invited to a ritzy party on a Manhattan rooftop. Everyone was dressed beautifully, but there was one glamourous young lady who stood out from all the rest. She was wearing a long elegant emerald-colored dress with a wide-brimmed white Victorian-style hat. Upon introduction, I complimented the young socialite on her attire and then asked how the weather was this time of year at Buckingham Palace. As soon as the words left my lips, I knew my attempt at extending a compliment with humor was a bad idea. As for the young lady, she gave me a warranted glare, took a sip from her flute champagne glass, and continued on her way.

Due to my lack of a filter between my cerebrum and mouth, I've taken the prudent measures of never going to cocktail parties again or opening a social media account. I'm guessing there are many people out there who would still be employed if they'd followed similar advice.

Then, there are those who throw caution to the wind and unapologetically say or publish whatever outlandish, disgusting thing pops into their head. Allow me to introduce journalist Katha Pollitt.

Pollitt, a writer for the left-leaning publication *The Nation*, wrote in an article during the 2020 presidential campaign; and I quote, *"I would vote for Joe Biden if he boiled babies and ate them. He wasn't my candidate, but taking back the White House is that important."*

If there were ever a poster child for "Trump Derangement Syndrom," this female's handsome mug would no doubt find its place upon it along with her deranged, inhumane metaphor of "boiled babies."

Pollitt is the quintessential leftist living in an alternate universe that sees no harm in her words. I'll even bet she tested the morally repugnant "boiled babies" line at one of her upper-eastside cocktail parties to entertain her equally disturbing sycophant friends. To appreciate how disgusting her comment is, one should be aware that Politt is an ultra-pro abortionist. I'm sure this revelation comes as no surprise to anyone after reading her infanticide appetizer recipe. So it wasn't by chance that the so-called feminist chose babies and not cats, dogs, or rats. After all, in her demented world, a baby has less value.

At the time of writing this, Pollitt is still employed and apology-free. In fairness, the author of the essay, "Why I Hate Family Values," may not have time for an apology. It seems that the God critic herself is very busy writing poems on the New and Old Testaments. You just can't make this stuff up.

The Wuhan Prophet

In 2018, the atheist Bill Mahr of HBO began praying for a recession. After two years, the minority owner of the New York Mets finally had his godless god's prayers answered when over thirty-five million people lost their jobs due to the Wuhan virus. And why might you ask, would someone who owns a part of "America's pastime" want to have all these people suffer? The incredulous reasoning was so Donald Trump wouldn't be reelected. *Hey, Bill, have you ever heard the one about the bathwater and baby?* Well, here's a new idiom compliments of Bill Mahr, or as I like to refer to him as *the Wuhan Prophet*: *let's destroy millions of lives because I don't like the fat orange hair guy occupying the White House.*

Emergency side note: In case you're impressed with my perfect grammar, don't be. I pay $99 a year for a program that will remain nameless. Thankfully, the company doesn't charge by the mistake; otherwise, this poor writer would be even more poorer. Here's a good example of how the program works. When I previously typed in the words "more poorer," a notification popped up from my $99 app telling me I'm an idiot. Well, not in those exact words, but it did recommend for me to consider changing it to the "appropriate comparative form" (whatever the hell that means). Now that you're as much of an expert on this software as I am, I want to share something that just happened, and I'm not joking.

In the previous paragraph, I referred to the pandemic as the "Wuhan virus," and this is what popped up on my computer screen:

"Phrases like wuhan flu can encourage bias and misinformation. Try using the official name used by the World Health Organization."

WTF, are you kidding me? More left political correct nonsense. And for the record, for the entire month of February in 2020, CNN called it the Wuhan virus before they changed course and decided to report that anyone who uses the term is a racist.

So back to my app. Where do you think my $99 tech gadget company is headquartered? Ding! Ding! Ding! If you said the home of left-wing Crazy Nancy (aka San Francisco), you're a winner.

I hadn't planned on writing about the WHO, but now that I've been *commanded* by Big Brother to watch my p's and q's, let's see where this graft-ridden rabbit hole leads us.

The World Health Organization

In 2017, Dr. Tedros was the first nonmedical doctor elected as WHO's director general in their seventy-two-year history. After his handling of the Wuhan virus, I'm guessing that maybe the organization will think twice about doing that again. After the far-left politician secured his $260,000-a-year position at WHO, his first act was the attempted appointment of Zimbabwe president Robert Mugabe as a goodwill ambassador. The ninety-three-year-old Mugabe nomination raised eyebrows in the international community since, under his watch, the country's health-care system was an utter failure. According to the *Times UK*, the attempted appointment was a triangular agreement between China, Mugabe, and Tedros. Under international pressure, Tedros withdrew Mugabe's nomination.

This wasn't the first time one could see a Tedros-China connection.

When Tedros was foreign minister in Ethiopia, China committed tens of millions of dollars to the country compared to only $345,000 for the previous decade combined. All of a sudden, China got very generous whenever Tedros was around. According to *Washington Post* reporter Frida Ghitis, "China worked tirelessly behind the scenes to help Tedros defeat the United Kingdom candidate for the WHO job… Tedros's victory was also a victory for Bejing…"

I can't say Dr. Tedros was a puppet of China. However, I question how a health minister in Ethiopia with a track record of covering up cholera epidemics was at the helm during the worst pandemic in modern history? Equally concerning was that the very country the director general should've been investigating for a global outbreak was the same commie POS helping him with his career. I'm sure in no way this conflict clouded Tedros's judgment, right? After all, if someone like FBI agent Peter Strzok could keep a "professional" unbiased position toward Trump, even though he believed his supporters smelled like Walmart and that Trump should lose the election "one hundred million to zero," why then shouldn't we think Tedros did everything in his power as head of the WHO to protect the globe and not just China's interest? Or, and I'm just spitballing here, Tedros and his cronies were beholden to China and maybe that's why WHO was willing to take at face value when told the virus wasn't transmittable from person to person. After all, one doesn't want to bite the hand that's been feeding, clothing, five-star hotel lodging, and cha-chinging money into their graft-ridden coffers now, does one?

How this POS Tedros and corruptible bandits of buddies are not in front of an international tribunal is beyond me. The fact that he's part of the global leftist machine probably helps. But like I said, I'm just spitballing here.

In an article written in the *National Review* back in the summer of 2017, nearly three years before the outbreak, Jeff Stier published his piece titled: "Stop Funding WHO Until It Cleans Up Its Act." In the article, which I highly recommend reading, Stier sounds the alarm bells for "taxpayers, members of Congress, and the Trump administration, regarding the new director-general [Tedros]." Stier predicts the "condemnation of the administration's plan for steep cuts in funding…" The reporter explains that "tough love" may be precisely what is needed to clean up the scandal-plagued World Health Organization. Below is an excerpt from Stier's article. I remind the reader that this was written in 2017, several years before the pandemic crisis of 2020:

> *Global public health is indeed, critical to American interests at home and abroad, and the U.S. government is the largest contributor to WHO's approximately $2 billion budget. However, like other U.N. subsidiaries, WHO is plagued by persistent wasteful spending, utter disregard for transparency, pervasive incompetence, and failure to adhere to even basic democratic standards. None of these problems are new, but they are worsening* [ain't that the truth], *and the latest developments underscore the need for tough love in the form of responsible stewardship of our largess.*

Stier goes on to describe a few of the irregular spending practices along with some unsolicited self-praise Tedros threw in for good measure:

> *The AP obtained documents showing that WHO "routinely has spent about $200 million a year on travel expenses, more than what it doles out to fight some of the biggest problems in public health, including AIDS, tuberculosis and malaria combined..." Without a hint of irony, Tedros proclaimed that "this election* [2017 director-general] *has been unprecedented in that it brought transparency to the organization, and even greater legitimacy to the director-general."*

Stier concludes the article by questioning WHO's ongoing "malfeasance" at the expense of US taxpayers and the world's poorest people. Too bad the powers that be were once again looking out for their own interests instead of doing their jobs.

Black History

In the winter of 1988, I was completing my first year as a police officer in New York City. Still considered a rookie with hardly any seniority, I was at the mercy of the squad sergeant to where I'd be spending my nine-hour shift. That particular winter had to be the coldest on record. Temperatures were dipping into single digits regularly throughout the month of February. Any assignment other than a heated squad car was brutal.

At muster, the sergeant barked out, "Simpson, 1 PP." I had enough time on the job to know all the regular assignments, but I had never heard of "1 PP" before. As it turned out, 1 PP was short for One Police Plaza, the fourteen-story brick building in lower Manhattan that housed the NYPD's headquarters.

Upon my arrival, I reported to the shift supervisor. He informed me that my assignment was securing an exhibition on the second floor. He pointed in the direction where it was to be held and instructed me that there'd be several local elementary schools passing through during the day on field trips. After making my way upstairs, I walked around the hall to see what the presentation entailed. The theme was Black History Month. Displayed on the walls were life-sized posters of historical African American figures with a brief bio. I made my way around the circular room and began to read their stories one by one. I recognized some prominent individuals like Fredrick Douglass, George Washington Carver, and abolitionist Harriet Tubman. But what stood out to me the most was how many African Americans on display I'd never heard of before.

I was nearly done going through the exhibit when the first class from PS 19 arrived. My job had nothing to do with instructing the students on Black history. Fortunately, at least for the children's sake, that assignment was left to the exhibit curator and their teacher. My responsibility was more ceremonious. I guess the brass at headquarters thought it would be a nice idea to have someone in uniform standing there so the students could see a real cop while at One Police Plaza. For me, I was just happy to be out of the cold and inside a warm building.

Before the morning was over, the students pulled me into their field trip by asking who I felt was the most influential African American. I was less interested in what I thought, so without answering, I returned the question back to the group of students by asking, "Who do you think?" As the children began to yell out names, I could hear the ones I mentioned previously, along with Martin Luther King Jr., Benjamin "Pap" Singleton, Rosa Parks, Muhammad Ali, Jackie Robinson, and so on. Toward the back of the group, I heard one of the students yell out, "Hiram Revels." I knew I had never heard of the name before and quickly realized that it must've been one of the displays I didn't get to yet. I scouted out the young scholar and asked him who Hiram Revels was.

"He was the first African American elected into Congress," the PS 19 student proudly responded.

When the group of students departed, I made my way to Mr. Revels's bio. There it was, "1870 Washington, D.C., Hiram Revels was sworn in as the first Black man elected into Congress as the Senator from the Magnolia State of Mississippi." I was dumbfounded. How was it that I never heard of this person before?

Later that day, I went to the New York Public Library on Forty-Second Street and Fifth Avenue and began my research project, my version of the world wide web back in the day.

Hiram Rhodes Revels was born a free man in Fayetville, North Carolina. He was a minister in the African Methodist Episcopal Church, an educator, and, yes, the first African American elected to the United States Senate.

What I found out next made me realize just how fractured our country was during the reconstruction period. The Democrats in the Senate initially blocked the duly-elected Mr. Revels from taking his oath. Their bad faith legal argument was that the Constitution mandated senators to have been citizens for at least nine years. The Dems stated that since the Republican Revels had obtained his citizenship four years earlier in the 1866 Civil Rights Act (Fourteenth Amendment), he was not eligible. To help bolster their argument, the Democrat Party of White Southern men went as far as to cite the disastrous 1857 Supreme Court decision in the Dred Scott case that ruled Blacks weren't citizens. It took two days of arguments, but eventually, Revels and his fellow Republicans were able to prevail.

I learned a lot that day, and thanks to one student shouting out Hiram Revels's name, I had a newfound thirst to know more. For starters, why was he a Republican and not a Democrat? After all, wasn't the Democrat Party always more supportive of the minority cause than the Republicans? As for me, my research project was just getting started.

The Republican Party elected an African American forty-five times to Congress before the first Black Democrat won office in 1937. That's sixty-seven years after Revels won his congressional seat. The Democrat who won was Arthur Mitchell. The four-term representative from Illinois was the son of parents born into slavery. Mitchell started as a Republican, but like many African Americans during this period, switched parties in favor of Democrat president Roosevelt's New Deal policies. What happened next can only be described as the greatest exodus since Moses took a left turn in the desert.

Over the past 83 years, there have been 20 instances where an African American was elected to Congress as a Republican compared to 845 by their Democrat counterpart. To put this in perspective, if we were talking about a sporting event, the score at the end of the first half would've been Republicans, 45; Democrats, 1. However, there was still another half to play. In the second half (1937 to present), the Democrats roared back to go ahead 845 seats to the Republican's 20.

The final tally (so far): Democrats, 846; Republicans, 46

Back in my old neighborhood, we'd call that an old-fashioned butt whipping.

If one takes the time to research the Democrat Party's history, it's difficult, at least for me, to comprehend how they consistently garner 90 percent of the African American vote. Let's take Maxine Waters, the Democrat congresswoman representing the Forty-Third Congressional District, for example. The politician has been in public service for over forty years, thirty of which have been at her current gig. Interestingly, although Maxine is a representative of the people in her district, she chooses to live outside the area in a six-million-dollar mansion. Meanwhile, her constituents, those would be the people who pay her salary to afford that sweet crib of hers, have seen crime spike, education drop, and sidewalks in Inglewood that resemble more Fallujah than America. Sadly, this is not the exception for democratically controlled inner cities but the norm.

In 2016, presidential candidate Donald Trump posed a question to the Black community that no other Republican thought of asking before: "What the hell do you have to lose?" The question itself shed light on the Democrat Party's complacent attitude toward their most loyalist of constituents. Although Trump only garnered 8 percent of the African American vote in 2016, it opened up some to see that their support was being taken for granted. Whether that was the reason or a case of a terrible candidate in Hillary Clinton, the fact remains that 4.4 million Obama voters stayed home, more than a third of them Black. Four years later, President Trump did better in every Black community except for the four that cost him the election: Detroit, Atlanta, Philadelphia, and Milwaukee.

The Democrat Legacy

Since the Republicans are well-known as the Party of Lincoln, I thought it would be only fair to research who the Dems consider their standard-bearer. Instead of finding one, I discovered an ominous history that looks to be tragically repeating itself. The political thirst for power that divides our nation today is the same ruthless behavior used by Southern Democrats to preserve slavery leading to America's bloodiest war.

- Before the Civil War, Southern Democrat men backed by the law would patrol for runaway slaves. After the North's victory and the slaves' emancipation, these men continued their work surreptitiously. They went from capturing and returning slaves for the owners to a clandestine intimidation campaign. Wearing hoods and white robes, the newly formed group known as the Ku Klux Klan harassed and, on many occasions, killed Republican leaders and voters, Black and White.

   Note no 1: According to the Archives at Tuskegee Institute, between 1882 and 1964, there were 4,742 lynchings: 3,445 Blacks and 1,297 Whites.

   Note no. 2: Nathan Bedford Forrest was not only Forrest Gump's great-great-granddaddy, but he was also the first Grand Wizard of the KKK and a proud Democrat.

- The poll tax, a literary test, and the grandfather clause (a law that stipulated a man would only be allowed to vote if his ancestor voted before 1867) were all strategies used by the Democratic Party to suppress the Black vote.

- The Dred Scott case, which deemed slaves property, and the infamous Plessey v. Ferguson ruling that brought the Jim Crow segregation laws were compliments of the Democrat Party.

- The twenty-eighth president of the United States, Woodrow Wilson (D), arguably the most racist commander in chief in history, saw segregation flourish throughout the federal government under his presidency. When civil rights activist Willian Monroe Trotter questioned Wilson as to why his federal agencies were expanding the segregation practices, Wilson remarked that he viewed the move as a benefit to Blacks, saying, "Were seeking, not to put the Negro employees at a disadvantage but, to make arrangements which would prevent any kind of friction between the White employees and the Negro employees." Trotter, feeling betrayed due to Wilson's previous assurances to the contrary, sternly told the president that the Jim Crow policy in federal buildings was degrading to Black employees. Wilson was furious with Trotter's "tone" and promptly threw him out of the Oval Office.

  Trotter wasn't the only African American shown the door. During Wilson's administration, he terminated all the Blacks appointed by his predecessor, President Theodore Roosevelt.

  Presidential trivia: Thanks to Woodrow Wilson's choice in movies, the answer to today's *Final Jeopardy* is "The First Film Screened in the White House." The question, sadly, is "What is Death of a Nation?" The alternate acceptable response is, "What is the Best KKK Recruiting Film of All-Time?"

- After the 1936 Olympics in Berlin, Franklin Delano Roosevelt (D) invited the Olympic team to the White House. Only the White participants were extended the honor, which meant that four-time gold medalist winner Jesse Owens, and the other seventeen Black athletes, were snubbed. African American Olympian John Woodruff, the winner of the gold medal in the eight hundred-meter race, said in a 1996 interview, "There was very definitely a special feeling in winning the gold medal and being a Black man. We destroyed his [Hitler's] master-race theory when-ever we won those gold medals." Silver medalist winner in the two hundred-meter dash Mack Robinson, the older brother of future baseball Hall of Famer Jackie Robinson, said that representing his country in Berlin was an honor of a lifetime. Future congressman Ralph Metcalfe won gold in the 4x100-meter and silver in the 100-meter relay. These were just a few of the African American Olympians not invited to FDR's Democrat "White" House.

Note: FDR was not the only head of state to reject the company of Black athletes. When the Hitler Youth repre-sentative suggested to Adolf Hitler to take a photo with the victorious Jesse Owens, the chancellor of Germany replied, "The Americans ought to be ashamed of themselves for let-ting their medals be won by Negroes. I myself would never shake hands with one of them."

- The Civil Rights Act of 1960 that outlawed the discrimi-natory poll tax was filibustered by 18 Democrats for 125 hours. Not one Republican senator opposed the bill.

- The Civil Rights Act of 1964 was nearly derailed by a fil-ibustering Democrat faction hoping to kill the bill. If not for the minority support of the Republican Party, the bill would've never passed.

- President Lyndon B. Johnson (D) was a racist who regu-larly used the N-word in private and was well-known for his bigotry-laden statements to fellow senators. In Ronald Kessler's book, *Inside the White House: The Hidden Lives of the Modern Presidents and the Secrets of the World's Most Powerful Institution*, the author recounts the day LBJ signed the welfare programs of the Great Society into law aboard Air Force One. Present during the signing were two gover-nors and a steward by the name of Ronald M. MacMillan. As LBJ was signing the document, MacMillian claims that

Johnson looked over at the two governors and said, "I'll have them n——s voting Democrat for two hundred years."

Only those present and God know for sure if the president said these offensive words or not. However, many African Americans, including Shelby Steele, the author of *White Guilt*, and Thomas Sowell, *Black Rednecks and White Liberals*, agree that the Great Society policies have done nothing but destroy the Black family unit. Harvard Professor Paul Peterson credits the program with "actively discouraging marriages." The numbers overwhelmingly support their concerns. With Black birth illegitimacy jumping from 20 percent in 1960 to 77 percent by 2017, and incarceration soaring from 1,313 per 100,000 Blacks in 1960 to 4,347 per 100,000 in 2010 (according to Pew Research Center), it's clear LBJ's "Great Society," and the Democrat platform has been a disaster for inner-city America.

By the way, it's been nearly sixty years. When exactly are we going to see the fruits of this Great Society?

- Legal immigration has been the backbone of our nation. Except for the Native American Indians, our existence in America comes via "huddled masses yearning to breathe free." So there's no reasonable person who says immigration is wrong, but the Democrats' proposed open-borders policy is ludicrous. My father would often say if they were all lawyers flooding in from Mexico, Congress would have our immigration problem solved in ten minutes. The truth is that the people coming here illegally put a strain on taxpayers' resources, hurting all of us. But the ones who feel it the most are those lesser-skilled American workers who are now forced to compete with undocumented workers, pushing wages ever lower. This is yet another democrat policy that flies in the face of wanting to help the Black community. For a Party that constantly reminded the American people during Trump's administration that "nobody is above the law," they conveniently forget that the nearly fifteen million immigrants who have come here illegally are currently breaking the law.

- The Democrat Party has taken the African American vote for granted for a long time. A perfect example of this was when former vice president Joe Biden (D), in an interview during the 2020 campaign, said, "If you have a problem figuring out whether you're for me or Trump, then you ain't black." Of course, the left brushes a comment like that away by saying, "What he meant to say was…fill in the blank." However, the problem for Biden is that he has a list of these fill-in-the-blank moments. For example, in 1977, when Biden opposed public schools' desegregation in Delaware, he argued that he didn't want his kids to grow up in a "racial jungle." Or the time Biden authored the 1994 crime bill that led to the mass incarceration of young Black men, warning that these "predators are too sociopathic to rehabilitate."

  Maybe Biden and his cronies on the left can explain away these "gaffes," but there's one comment by the former vice president that gives insight into his heart condition, otherwise known as racism. This is Biden in 2007 describing then-candidate for president Barack Obama:

  "I mean you got the first mainstream African American who is articulate and bright and clean and nice-looking guy. I mean, that's a storybook, man."

  Biden later went to the catch-all damage control phrase: "My comment was taken out of context." However, for some reason, he still felt it was necessary to apologize to Obama and, in an interview, said he shouldn't have used the word "clean" but rather "fresh." You just can't make this stuff up.

- In my view, it's been the policies set forth by the Democrat Party that have done the greatest harm to the African American communities. Senator Ted Cruz believes the next most significant civil rights issue for this century will be school choice and that once again, the Dems will be on the wrong side of history.

In Zelman v. Simmons-Harris (2002), the court ruled 5–4 to uphold the Ohio program, which awarded school vouchers to public, private, and religious schools. The majority opinion on the Court claimed the case did not violate the First Amendment's establishment clause.

The latest assault against school choice by the Dems illustrates another example of how the libs would rather keep the status quo of broken down, underachieving schools in predominately Black neighborhoods than give these families a *choice*. For a party big on *choice*, one would think they'd love the idea of allowing the people who are affected the most to decide what's best for their family's education.

So as politicians like senator Elizabeth Warren call to end private school choice programs, even though the policy overwhelmingly serves low-income families, one has to ask the question, why? I'd hate to think the Democrat Party is more beholden to the teacher's unions than their own constituents. Still, I find it challenging to come up with any other reasonable explanation for this travesty.

In other less shocking news, Senator Warren was caught fibbing about sending her son Alex to public schools when in fact, he attended a costly private school. Once again, the "do as thee, not as me" hypocrisy continues to flow in Washington with no end in sight.

The Republican Party

In 1854, anti-slavery Democrats and some other political factions decided to break away from the pro-slavery Democrat Party to establish what we know today as the Republican Party. The catalyst behind the move was the unwanted expansion of slavery into the American territories led by the Kansas-Nebraska Act.

Four years earlier, in 1850, the Democrat Congress passed the Fugitive Slave Law, which forced northerners to return escaped slaves. An obvious pitfall to the newly passed law was the human smuggling created between the Southern-seeking slave hunters and free Blacks living in the North. The Democrat-led policies were making life so unbearable that eventually, tens of thousands of free African Americans were forced to flee into Canada.

Two years after coming into existence, the newly formed Republicans issued its inaugural presidential party platform. Out of the nine components addressed, six of them were on Black equality and civil rights.

The contrast between the two parties was clear. The Republicans were doing everything in their power to abolish slavery. While on the Democrat side, lifelong bachelor and presidential candidate James Buchanan's ominous forecast of the "unhappiness of the people" signaled his party's support of the Southern states' rights to continue business as usual when it came to the abhorrent institution. Buchanan's fearmongering to the North and wink of the eye to the South paid off when he was sworn in as the fifteenth president of the United States.

Four years later, the Republican Party put forth as their presidential nominee: a self-taught lawyer from Illinois named Abraham Lincoln. The platform remained similar to the previous presidential election. Added were talking points on the disastrous Dred Scott decision (1857) along with a reaffirmation to end slavery and win civil rights for Blacks.

Lincoln's opponent, Senator Stephen Douglass, also from Illinois, championed the Fugitive Slave Law and the Dred Scott decision, policies strongly supported by the Dems. Southern Democrats' choice for president was clear. If Douglass were to lose and the anti-slavery platform of the Republican Party headed by Lincoln was to win, they'd secede from the Union. From the time Lincoln won the election in November of 1860 to his swearing-in on March 4, 1861, seven Southern states had already broken away. Six weeks after Lincoln's inauguration, the Confederate troops fired on Fort Sumter in Charleston, South Carolina. Although this began the Civil War, it did not distract Lincoln's quest to liberate the slaves.

A year later, slavery was abolished in Washington, D. C.; and a year after that, on January 1, 1863, President Abraham Lincoln issued the Emancipation Proclamation declaring all persons held as slaves "hence forward shall be free."

The Republican Congress wasted little time passing bills protecting and securing equality under the law for the four million newly emancipated African Americans. Included in the process was the Senate passing Bills 99 and 145, which protected Blacks equal access throughout the judicial system and ensured anyone serving in the military would receive equal pay, equipment, uniform, arms, and medical attention, regardless if they were Black or White.

In the "Reconstruction" period following the Civil War, the Republican-controlled government passed the Thirteenth, Fourteenth, and Fifteenth Amendments, which extended legal and civil rights to those previously enslaved. The ratification of these three amendments by the former Confederate states was a condition set forth by the Union before the rebels could regain federal representation. Although all states that seceded from the Union signed unto the ratification, this did not stop the Southern Democrats from doing all they could to undermine the new laws.

Three-Fifths

From 1820 to the mid-1850s, the democratically-controlled Congress undid many of the provisions set forth by our framers limiting slavery. Laws that prevented slavery into federal territories and the barbaric practice of slave trading were cast aside. It seems that the Democrats, then and now, play one of two ways. When they're in power, they change all the laws that are inconvenient toward their agenda. When they're out of power, they threaten to blow everything up unless they get their way. In 1860, it led to the Civil War. The question is, where will it lead to next time when these unyielding bureaucrats declare armageddon?

In 1860, the Dems' line in the sand was slavery. Today it's abortion. I'm just making an observation here, but doesn't this party's moral compass continuously seem to be a bit off?

Fact check: Historians are quick to point out that our founders viewed slaves as less than human, citing the Three-Fifths Clause found in Article 1, Section 2 of the US Constitution. I'm willing to take this one step further by stating that slave owners didn't even view them as human but rather property. Just as a quick reminder, it was the idiots sitting on the Supreme Court who reaffirmed that slaves were indeed property in the 1857 Dred Scott case, deserving of zero rights.

So we have racist slave owners, racist jurists, and racist Founding Fathers, right? Well, before the race-baiters claim victory upon this victimization, let's clarify the role of our Founders and this supposed subhuman Three-Fifths Clause.

Yes, most of our Founding Fathers were slave owners. At least one, Thomas Jefferson, had six children with his *property*, Sally Hemings. I don't care if these Founders were the *nicest* slave owners in all the world. To me, that's like saying the terrorists on 9/11 allowed complimentary beverage service before crashing the planes. An abomination is still an abomination. However, it's important to point out that many of our framers were adamantly opposed to slavery. For example, Franklin, Rush, Hamilton, and John Jay greatly supported the growing aboli-tionists' cause, and it's from this movement we have the Three-Fifths Clause. Does that mean the people who despised the institution of slavery viewed Blacks as less human? Of course not. The Three-Fifths Clause referred to representation, not a person's worth. The abolition-ist knew if the South were allowed to count all their slaves, they'd have more pro-slavery representatives in Congress, hence, more power.

The irony here is that the plantation owners who never con-sidered slaves anything but property now wanted them to be fully counted as people. To offset this, the North facetiously proposed to tally up all their property—horses, cattle, and the rest of their live-stock—for congressional representation. In the end, the two sides agreed to the "Three-Fifths" *compromise*.

The sad part today is some leaders wish to manipulate the mean-ing of the Three-Fifths Clause. Race-baiters such as Al Sharpton and the disgraced New York City politician Charlie Rengel would instead like to stoke the flames of hate by suggesting that our Constitution considers Blacks only three-fifths of a human. Here's some rhetoric by people who sadly knew better, but for personal gain, wish to keep our country divided:

Congressman Rengel: "I wasn't even considered three-fifths of a guy."

Sharpton: "Any black, at any age at any stage, was three-fifths of a human."

Chicago's Mayor Lightfoot: "The Constitution didn't even recognize me as a human being when it was first ratified."

This race-baiting nonsense by anyone should be considered misleading and divisive. However, the fact that it comes from leaders in the Black community crying "victim" makes it downright disgraceful!

Worthy of a Statue

Allow me to preface that I believe George Washington is the greatest American to have ever lived, and without his services, we are not the nation we are today. However, the fact remains our Founding Father was a slave owner. This from a man who said of slavery: "There is not a man living who wishes more sincerely than I do to see a plan adopted for the abolition of it."

My view on Washington having been a slave owner is similar to my stance on those choosing to have an abortion: it's not for me to judge the individual. In both cases, I'll leave judgment to a higher authority. As for Washington's service to his country, it's unparalleled and worthy of statues.

Chapter 6

Racism

Darkness cannot drive out darkness; only light can do that.
Hate cannot drive out hate; only love can do that.

—Martin Luther King Jr.

H old on, boys and girls. The bald, old, White, fat, opinionated guy, BOWFOG, will attempt to dive into the issue of racism in America. It's not too often you get to watch someone drive off a cliff, so you may want to pay close attention. One slight slip of my tongue, or in this case, keyboard, and my reputation for the rest of my life will be exiled somewhere between Adolf "you know who" and anyone who donates to the RNC.

However, before taking my foot off the emergency brake, allow me to state a few facts:

1. I'm not Black. Remember, I'm a BOWFOG.
2. Racism, anytime, anywhere, by anyone, is abhorrent to me.
3. To the best of my knowledge, none of my ancestors were slaves or slave owners. Both sets of my grandparents immigrated to the States during the Great Depression-era of the 1930s.
4. If one is unsure if their words or actions are of a bigoted nature, it might be a good idea to stop and think of how others, especially the targeted group, may construe such behavior.

5. Disparaging any person or group of people because of their race, skin color, religious beliefs, or sexual orientation for whatever nonsensical reasoning one may have to spread their hate disgusts me.

Allow me to amplify point no. 5 a bit.

Back in 1987, I was in the NYC police academy. During a training film session, my class watched a thirty-minute film on racism and discrimination. Bill Cosby used a comedy routine in the documentary to discuss what he hated about every ethnic group. The idea was to show how ridiculous the notion was to stereotype an entire group of people. Cosby did not hold back, going after every race, including his own. Understandably, my fellow cadets and I found the social science lesson for the day quite amusing. After all, this was Bill Cosby, the cool Jell-O gelatin pudding Cosby, and not the old, blind rapist one. Since I don't wish to offend any group, I won't repeat the dialogue in its entirety. However, the film served its purpose to illustrate just how absurd and ignorant stereotypes can be.

Here's a sample:

Cosby: "I hate (blank). Everyone knows they're cheap. Oh, and those (blanks). They can't drive worth a shit. Don't even get me started with them (blanks). Those people are a bunch of drunks."

Point of order: Before moving forward, can we all agree that this rhetoric is wrong and hurtful? It would be inappropriate regardless of who's the instigator or the victim. So if we can agree that it's wrong to disparage any one group, I hope you find the following as disturbing as I do.

Below is a transcript that aired during a podcast on August 27, 2020. The DNC was coming off their convention while the RNC was just getting started with theirs. Riots had been breaking out throughout the summer in several urban cities under cover of protests. Although the statistics do not support the argument that police shootings of unarmed Blacks are rampant, this didn't stop domestic terrorist groups from taking advantage of weak, local Democrat leaders by burning, looting, and killing at an alarming rate. Sadly, instead of our leaders helping to calm the violence, some felt it necessary to inflame an already volatile situation.

I will not divulge who said the following until the end. However, it won't be hard to figure out who the person is as one moves further along in the text. Politics aside, I implore everyone to read the following with the premise, what if the colors of the people mentioned were reversed? There may be some who believe the interview is perfectly acceptable. I'm not of that opinion. In fact, I find the manner in which this person so easily labeled an entire group of people ("White America" and "White folks") to be intentionally hostile, divisive, and deplorable:

> *Where I am just a Black woman, I notice that* White folks *don't even see me. They're not even looking at me. I'm standing there with two little black girls another Black female adult—they're in soccer uniforms, and a White woman cuts right in front of us to order. Like she didn't even see us. I can tell you a number of stories like that when I've been completely incognito during the eight years in the White House walking the dogs on the canal. People will come up and pet my dogs but will not look me in the eye. They don't know it's me. And what White folks don't understand is, it's like that. That is so telling of how* White America *views people who are not like them.* (Former First Lady Michelle Obama)

I take umbrage with the former First Lady on several accounts. Firstly, since 73 percent of America is White—that's approximately 240 million people—and Mrs. Obama is claiming "White folk" don't see her, then can someone please explain to me how it was that "White folk" were able to find her husband's name on the ballot twice when it came time to vote for the first-ever Black president? If I didn't know better, I might think the former First Lady was trying to divide our country. Or, at a minimum, conducting a little race baiting.

Secondly, I find her story to be more convenient than truthful. We're supposed to believe that the most identifiable woman in the world—surrounded by secret service, her daughters, and a dog that was on the cover of *People* magazine—wasn't recognized because she was "incognito" on her ice cream run? Unless she has pictures of herself dressed up as a rodeo clown licking an ice cream cone, I'm calling bullshit on this one.

Finally, we're led to believe that a "White folk" came up and petted her dog, but her annoyance is that they didn't look the First Lady in the eye?

Note to Michelle:

If the person were indeed a White racist, as you're leading us to believe, they wouldn't have bothered to come anywhere near a Black woman to pet her dog. I have no doubt your fans have great reverence for you and accept whatever nonsense you feed them; however, since I'm not one of them, maybe in the future, you can try pitching a more convincing story to fit your victim's narrative.

One would think with an education from Harvard Law and Princeton that the former First Lady could come up with something more respectful than "White folks" when describing people who look similar to me (Bowfogs). Like Joe Biden's "C'mon, man" tell when annoyed, Michelle's use of the "White folks" seems to follow with a bit of aggression. For example, in a 2019 interview at the Obama Foundation Summit, Mrs. Obama spoke of the traumatic "White flight" experiences as a child growing up in Chicago. Here's a portion of the interview:

"As we moved in, White folks moved out because they were afraid of what our families represented... I want to remind White folks that y'all [sic] were running from us. And you're still running."

After a nervous chuckle and a quick darting of the eyes to see how her ridiculous words were received, the First Lady continued by discussing the judgment she felt by her new neighbors.

"You know this when you're young. You know when people are running from you. And you can see it... One by one, they [White folks] packed their bags, and they ran from us."

I have to say that I'm surprised the Obama's purchased an $8 million house in Washington, D. C., with neighbors like Jared Kushner (White), his wife Ivanka (White), and Jeff Bezos (White). I would've thought Michelle was too traumatized to go through another "White flight," but this woman is brave. Why do I say this, you ask? Well, not long after dropping $8 cha-chings in D. C., the former First Lady summoned the courage to drop another $12 million in, of all places, the Blanca-de-Blanca Martha's Vineyard. I can picture the scene of all those White crackers—excuse me, I mean White folks—running for the ferry screaming louder than Paul Revere, "The Blacks are coming! The Blacks are coming!" I'm surprised the chaotic scene didn't make it on the six o'clock news. Or, and I'm just shooting in the dark here, there wasn't any "White flight" on Martha's Vinyard or D. C.

Staying with this alternate universe theory of the Dems, something I like to call reality, maybe those "White folks" who moved away from that city block in Chicago where the former First Lady grew up departed for the same reason she and George Jefferson did: it was time to "movin' on up to the east side to a deluxe apartment in the sky because they finally got a piece of the pie," and not because, as Mrs. Obama viscerally put it, due to "y'all White folks" running from Black people.

Side note no. 1: In my extensive research of the Obamas and their real estate holdings, which are numerous, I was unable to uncover any purchases of a home on the same block Michelle Obama grew up on or anywhere within the zip code of her old neighborhood. I don't know if this term exists yet, but can this be construed as "Black flight"?

Side note no. 2: When I was young, I'll never forget asking my father about a sign I saw while we were on one of our summer road trips. It read: *No dogs or Jews allowed.* That was the first time I learned about racism and the ignorance that accompanies it. My dad took the time to explain that some people, for no good reason, didn't like anyone different from themselves. The thought of living in such a big world with such a narrow view seemed very sad and lonely to me. As I was exposed to more of the world, the easier it became to spot this disgraceful practice. In my opinion, the only thing worse than racism is those people who make false claims of racism to further an agenda—did I hear someone say Jussie Smollett? There's enough discrimination in the world. There's no need to create where none exists.

The Three Spiritual Stooges

Jeremiah Wright had been a pastor emeritus at Trinity United Church of Christ in Chicago for nearly four decades. If not for a freshman senator from Illinois by the name of Barack Obama deciding to throw his hat in the ring to run for the presidency, most of us would've never heard of the blaspheming preacher who said, "Not God bless America, God damn America." To say that Wright came with some controversial luggage for the presidential hopeful would be like saying water is wet. Barack already had enough issues to overcome in trying to be the first African American to become president. The last thing he needed was to be associated with a radical reverend who chanted, "White folks greed runs a world in need." So when tapes appeared of Barack's long-time spiritual leader spewing hate from the pulpit, the future president quickly distanced himself from the racist Reverend Wright. Claiming the Sergeant Schultz defense of, "I see nothing, I hear nothing," Barack explained that he never heard the pastor say any of the statements that are "so contrary to my own life and beliefs."

Interestingly enough though, in Obama's 1995 memoir, *Dreams of My Father*, he recounts Wright's "The Audacity of Hope" sermon:

> *It is this world, a world where cruise ships throw away more food in a day than most residents of Port-au-Prince see in a year, where* White folk's *greed runs a world in need, apartheid in one hemisphere, apathy in another hemisphere.*

At least now we know where Barack and Michelle picked up that "*White folks*" talk.

It's almost unbelievable that Barack and his wife, in all the years they attended Wright's sermons, never heard any *other* remarks that would've raised an eyebrow or two. I'm going to have to assume further that the Obamas canceled their subscription to the church's *Trumpet Newsmagazine* before the publication had awarded their "Man of the Year" to Louis Farrakhan, someone Wright described as "a man of greatness."

As the Nation of Islam leader, the anti-semitic Farrakhan has targeted Jews, White people, and the LGBT community. Farrakhan argues that Judaism is a "deceptive lie" and "theological error." In a 2018 speech, the "man of greatness" who regularly referred to the Jewish people as "the satanic Jew," told his loyal followers, "When they talk about Farrakhan, call me a hater... Call me an anti-Semite. Stop it. I'm not anti-Semite; I'm anti-termite."

When then-presidential candidate Obama was asked about the Wright-Farrakhan connection, he explained that he and the minister sometimes disagreed, and Farrakhan is one of those instances.

Call me fussy, but if I found out my "spiritual advisor" was chilling with the likes of a POS Louis Farrakhan, I'd immediately find myself a new source to fill my daily dose of holy consumption. However, and I'm just shooting in the dark here, maybe the Obamas shared Wright's ideological views, and the only reason Barack denounced the reverend was that he knew if he didn't, it would hurt him politically. One thing I do know is if I were sitting in one of the pews listening to Wright for twenty years, there's a good chance I'd be saying "White folks" in the same tone as Michelle so freely does.

Barack Obama has had some "interesting" spiritual friends over the years. We had him doing a photo op with the likes of Louis Farrakhan (a photo that was conveniently buried until after he was elected president) and attending a church that spewed more hate than hope. But we're not done. One reverend visited the White House during Barack's presidency more than any other, and that was Al Sharpton.

I've been around long enough to see Al trade in his jogging suit for an Amonte and his gold medallion for a microphone. Regardless of his new waist size, once a con, always a con. Many consider his

National Action Center nothing more than a conduit for the "shake-down artist" himself to extort money from corporations or risk facing unruly protestors at their doorsteps. Make no mistake, racism is big business, and nobody knows this better than anti-Semite Sharpton.

Over the years, Sharpton has used incendiary language to promote violence and hate. He's often been accused of referring to people of the Jewish faith as "bloodsucking Jews, Jew bastards, White interlopers, and diamond merchants." At a 2019 congressional hearing, Florida representative Matt Gaetz asked Sharpton if he ever said, *"If the Jews want to get it on, tell them to pin their yarmulkes back and come over to my house."* Sharpton responded that he was directing the comment at one Jewish man and not all Jews. According to Al's demented logic, if the racial epithet is directed at one person and not a group, it shouldn't count as racism. You just can't make this stuff up.

There's more light on the dark side of the moon than Sharpton's shady past. For starters, there's the infamous Tawana Brawley case that would've sent any other human being back into the hole they came out of, but not Fat Al. Sharpton helped perpetuate the most disgraceful reverse discrimination case in history when a fifteen-year-old Black girl cried wolf. The allegations were nothing but a hoax that included accusing a White assistant district attorney of being part of a gang rape. It didn't take long for the girl's story to fall apart. But Al did his best to continue his media attack on the innocent Dutchess County ADA Steven Pagones. In a civil suit, Sharpton was found guilty of defamation and ordered to pay Pagones $65,000.

Sharpton's legal woes continued with numerous arrests for tax evasion and fraud. Somehow the former FBI informant kept skating through the legal system with only short stints in the joint. It's a mystery with such an impressive resume why more presidents didn't tap Fat Al before Barack did?

There's a buddy of mine from my old neighborhood in Brooklyn named Bobby. He's one of these guys that makes life harder for himself by always picking the wrong woman to marry. After the first marriage, I felt sorry for my friend's woes. At the end of the second, I began wondering if maybe Bobby wasn't more to blame for his "bad luck." When he filed for his third divorce, I was convinced my friend was responsible for his misery and not the other three women. My thinking was anyone can make a mistake, maybe even two. But three of the same types of errors can no longer be considered bad luck but rather a trend.

With that in mind, I have to question why President Obama associated himself with not one, not two, but three spiritual advisors who were all anti-Semite, anti-America, and anti-White? It's no wonder the former president gave the Islamic Republic of Iran billions of dollars while treating our closest ally in the region worse than any other president since the inception of the state of Israel.

Words Matter

It was the nineteenth anniversary of 9/11 when I found myself at my kitchen counter looking at an article written by South Florida's *New Pelican* editor, Michael d'Oliveira. Ordinarily, I would've been watching the news that Friday morning, but as I'd done every year on the anniversary of 9/11, I chose to keep my television off.

There were two prayers I still had to make that morning: one at 8:46 and the other at 9:02. So, while I waited for Alexa's automated female voice to kindly remind me, I began reading Mike's column. I already had a pretty good idea of what the piece was about since Mike sought my "okay" for the article a few weeks earlier. His story was about me and my experience down at the *pile* following 9/11. Giving him the green light to write the piece was the easy part. However, bringing myself to reading it was a different story. I'd grown weary of anything related to the tragic events surrounding 9/11. But I knew Mike put a lot of time into the piece, going as far as to read my memoir. So I figured if he could get through 304 pages of my indecipherable madness, I could bring myself to reading his one-page article on one of the darkest days in American history. (Article: "I Knew I Had to Get Myself to Ground Zero," page 312)

I didn't get past the first paragraph before my eyes began to well, and by the third, I was officially in need of some Kleenex. A lot of emotions and memories that I'd locked away had come racing back. Eventually, I was able to get through the article. I sent Mike a "thank you" text and told him how appreciative I was for keeping the memory of those who are no longer with us alive.

Later that day, when my wife came home, I showed her the article and then warned her that I might not be my usual cheerful, cantankerous self. She laughed and then, as she always does, gave me a big hug.

That night I did something I'd never done before. I read my memoir, *The Blue Pawn*. I know that sounds a bit odd since I wrote the damn thing, but as it was, once the book was published, I never sat down and read it from cover to cover. I was all too aware of the reason why. It was the same one behind my apprehension to read Mike's article.

As I read through the book, I was reminded all too often of the brave officers I had the privilege of working with who perished in the line of duty. I described my former coworker Anthony Dwyer's agonizing death when pushed from a rooftop in Times Square. Then there was my neighborhood buddy Jimmy Riches. Jimmy had recently transferred over from the NYPD to the New York City Fire Department. His firehouse was the closest to the Twin Towers, which meant Jimmy and his company were the first of the first responders to enter the buildings on that sunny autumn morning. It took over six months until Jimmy's body was recovered by his father, Battalion Chief Jim Riches. The chief went to the pile every day, literally nearly working himself to death until he finally found his son.

The story I tell toward the end of the book was about Officers Rafael Ramos and Wenjian Liu. A few days before Christmas in 2014, the two patrolmen were sitting in their police cruiser when a cowardly thug consumed with evil opened fire on the defenseless officers. Two of New York's Finest were no more.

The tragedy was similar to another senseless murder that occurred twenty-five years earlier. The officer was my friend Edward Byrne. Eddie and I did our rookie time together in Midtown Manhattan back in 1987. When it was time to receive our permanent assignments, Eddie was transferred to one of the city's most dangerous precincts. He was only there a few weeks when he found himself sitting in a squad car guarding a witness's house on an overnight shift. That's when three cowardly thugs consumed with evil opened fire on the defenseless Eddie, killing him instantly.

The difference between Eddie's death and Officers Ramos and Liu was the motive. Eddie was killed over drugs, greed, and power, whereas Ramos and Liu were killed strictly because of their uniform.

Here's an excerpt from *The Blue Pawn* where I warned of an ominous, deadly trend I saw coming:

> *As 2014 came to a close, I couldn't help but wonder if this latest tragedy* [Officers Ramos and Liu] *was an anomaly or something far worse, an opening for other delusional copycat offenders to act out their demented fantasies.*
>
> *There was a new organization* [BLM] *stoking the flames by using several disturbing chants at their rallies, such as:*
>
> *"PIGS IN A BLANKET, FRY'EM UP LIKE BACON"*
>
> *"WHAT DO WE WANT? Dead Cops! WHEN DO WE WANT IT? NOW!"*

By the time I finally put the book down, I was emotionally spent. I said a prayer to God thanking Him for all His blessings, asked Him to look over our brave first responders, and then went to sleep.

The next evening on September 12, 2020, news broke that two officers had been shot in what appeared to be an ambush attack. A nearby security camera had caught the entire deplorable act. Sadly, it was the same old story: a cowardly thug consumed with evil opening fire on two defenseless officers.

One would think there would've been outrage against the African American male who pulled the trigger, but instead, it seemed that some found the horrific act amusing. Immediately after the officers were shot, another African American man who happened to be on the block at the time of the shooting laughed as he live-streamed the tragic occurrence.

It only grew worse from there.

That night so-called protesters blocked the entrance to the hospital where the officers were fighting for their lives, chanting,

"Fuck the pigs."

"We hope you die mother fuckers."

"I hope the bitch dies," referring to the thirty-one-year-old female officer.

When a reporter questioned a Black Lives Matter activist about what his thoughts were regarding the shooting of two police officers, his response was telling, "This is a good start."

Have we lost our minds? Is this how a civilized society acts? Or is this how a Marxist revolution begins?

What Is BLM?

Following the George Zimmerman acquittal in the Trevon Martin case in 2013, a thirty-two-year-old African American woman from San Francisco and future cofounder of the BLM movement, Alicia Garza, posted on Facebook "Our lives Matter." Fellow cofounder of BLM Patrisse Cullors resent Alicia's post with the "#Black Lives Matter."

Garza explains in her book, *The Purpose of Power*, how an encounter with the police at seventeen in her upper-middle-class northern California neighborhood made her conscious of the inequality in the justice system. She writes:

"One night… I'd taken my mother's car to study with a friend, which really meant that we were meeting up to smoke weed…"

Garza goes on to explain how she was terrified to see the red-and-blue lights in the rearview mirror, but after the police officer pulled her over and discovered the marijuana, he let her off with just a warning. Alicia admits she was given a second chance but then voiced her concern that if she, a young woman of color, had been caught in a worse neighborhood with the same amount of marijuana, she would've been arrested. The self-proclaimed civil rights activist believes that the criminal justice system treats some people differently than others. Because of this, she calls for the dismantling of the "system" that, as she explains, "Is designed to criminalize Black people, designed to criminalize poor people, people of color and other oppressed people."

Alicia stressed the importance of "reimagining of what it looks like to have dignified communities where we are not patrolling [them] with guns and tanks."

This author wasn't aware that communities in the United States were "patrolling" their streets using tanks. So I'm assuming Alicia's statement is more about taking guns away from the police than her concern over Abrams M1A2s rolling down Lombard Street. Furthermore, I'm a little confused that the person who came up with "Black Lives Matter" doesn't seem overly concern with all the Black-on-Black gun violence in places like Chicago and other inner-city communities. I guess I just need to "reimagine" a safer Southside, and somehow it will magically occur. Or maybe I can borrow Obama's magic wand.

So Who Are the Founders of BLM?

According to cofounder Patrisse Cullers, she, along with Alicia Garza, are "trained Marxists." In her book, *When They Call You a Terrorist: A Black Lives Matter Memoir*, Cullers defends her support for her Marxist ideology. In fact, on the BLM website, the group shares thoughts on their utopia commune:

> *We disrupt the Western-prescribed nuclear family structure requirements by supporting each other as extended families and "villages" that collectively care for one another...*

So with an agenda to defund the police, seek reparations, and a goal to systematically dismantle the family unit, government, and capitalism, Black Lives Matter tapped into corporate America's deep appeasement pockets to help further their cause.

So who manages all that money?

It might be interesting to learn that a group known as Thousand Currents is the administrative arm behind BLM's money. And behind

Thousand Currents is a communist convicted terrorist by the name of Susan Rosenberg. That would be the same Susan Rosenberg who had her sentence commuted by President Clinton on his last day in office.

In 1985, Rosenberg was sentenced to fifty-eight years in prison after she was convicted of criminal possession of 640 pounds of explosives, a cache of illegal weapons, manuals on terrorism, and fake IDs. She was also strongly suspected of being involved in an armored Brinks robbery where two police officers and a security guard were killed. Adding to her lawless resume, the convicted terrorist Rosenberg was affiliated with several communist organizations during her criminal career, which spanned over three decades.

With such an asset to the American way of life, I can't imagine why Bubba waited until his last day to pardon the commie POS. Rumor has it that the soon-to-be-former president nearly forgot to sign the pardon on his way out of the White House. In fairness to Bubba, he might've been a little distracted since it was his last day at work, and the flight to Pedophile Island was about to take off.

On the Thousand Currents web page, they show a lovely picture of a smiling Susan Rosenberg followed by her very long title: *"Human and Prisoner Rights Advocate and Writer Thousand Currents Vice Chair of the Board of Directors."* Imagine having to repeat that at cocktail parties. I know how important titles are, but one would think it would've been a lot easier to go with the shorter version of *Vice Commie POS.*

In her beautifully written bio, she states that she's a "human rights and prisoners rights advocate, adjunct professor, communications consultant, award-winning writer, public speaker, and a formerly incarcerated person." That last one, *"incarcerated person,"* must've given her a lot of street cred. Unfortunately, the part about being a communist terrorist was nowhere to be found in the bio. I guess with a sixteen-word title before her name, there wasn't much room left for such inconsequential details. Oh, well.

So, as we connect the dots to this well-oiled terrorist machine known as BLM, there's still one more player who needs to be introduced.

Her "slave name" was Joanne Chesimard, but today, she's more commonly known by her West African name of Assata Shakur, the late rap singer Tupac Shakur's aunt. However, I've decided to address her by what she really is, a "cop killer."

In 1973, cop killer Shakur, along with two accomplices, murdered New Jersey State Trooper Werner Foerster in cold blood, leaving him to die on the New Jersey Turnpike. The cop killer was a member of the Black Liberation Army at the time of the police slaying. Inexplicably, the cop killer escaped from prison in 1979 and then fled to Cuba, where the communist regime gave her political asylum.

The notorious Black Liberation Army that cop killer Shakur was so proud to be a member of was responsible for killing ten police officers and injuring numerous more during the 1970s. One of the officers murdered at the hands of BLA was NYPD's Joseph Piagentini. He was shot thirteen times by multiple handguns as he begged for his life. In case you're having a difficult time picturing what these terrorists were like, start with a soulless vessel consumed with evil and then go from there.

The Black Liberation Army supported the May 19 Communist Organization, the Weather Underground, and other revolutionary Marxist groups. During that time, a friendship bloomed between two terrorists, cop killer Shakur and the Vice Commie, Rosenberg.

Although the convicted murderer is hiding in Cuba, cop killer Shakur's influence on the BLM movement and the founders is profound. She is considered a "political inspiration" and a "symbol of resistance" by those involved in the Black Lives Movement. Demonstraters at organized BLM events have adopted the words of the exiled terrorist in what is known as the Assata Chant:

"It is our duty to win. We must love each other and respect each other. We have nothing to lose but our chains."

I'll have to assume all that "love" and "respect" they call for doesn't include the men and women in blue who are regularly harassed, spat on, and assaulted by BLM at their rallies.

So, instead of BLM's Alicia Garza condemning cop killer Shakur, the cofounder has been embraced with open arms by the

Marxist terrorist. Here's an excerpt from a piece written by Garza titled "A Herstory of the #BlackLivesMatterMovement":

> When I use Assata's powerful demand in my organizing work, I always begin by sharing where it comes from, sharing about Assata's significance to the Black Liberation Movement, what its political purpose and message is, and why it's important in our context.

What does all this say about an organization whose founders are Marxist, inspired by a cop killer, and financially in bed with a convicted terrorist? To me, if it talks like a commie, kills like a commie, tears down statues like a commie, and preaches hate like a commie, maybe, just maybe, it's an f—ing commie. Oh, in case anyone forgot, communists hate the American way of life, despise individual liberties, and are godless. Besides that, I hear they're real pieces of sunshine.

So to all the idiots out there donating to this revolution in hopes of easing their guilt created over "White privilege," I have some abandoned pet rocks for sale that were imported from the northern hemisphere continent of a planet known as Earth. All donations go to saving as many of these homeless rocks as humanly possible. For anyone interested, please take a twenty, no make it a fifty, better yet, let's go all out, and use a crisp one-hundred-dollar bill; roll down the window to whatever vehicle stupid White people are driving these days; and proceed to throw it out. The best part is the rock somehow magically finds its new owner. There's no limit to how many donations one can make toward the homeless rocks, so feel free to keep on throwing as many *Benjamins* out the window as the heart desires.

During an interview with KUSI Newsroom in 2020, the retired NYPD police commissioner and my former boss, Bernie Kerik, posed himself the question, "What is Black Lives Matter?" His answer: "They're a radical left-wing revolutionary group that wants the overthrow of this government. They're not really about Black lives. They're not concerned with Black lives because if they were, they'd be in Chicago marching every night, they'd be in Baltimore, they'd be in Cleveland, they'd be in Milwaukee or Minnesota, or I can give you twenty other cities that are run by Democrats in this country that have the highest crime rate, the highest violence rate, and the highest murder rates."

The Race Card

Senator Joseph McCarthy labeled anyone who disagreed with his "Red Scare" propaganda as a communist. It was a convenient tactic that worked for a while until brave men stood up to the bully. Today we are experiencing a new *scare* in the form of being labeled a *racist*.

As a society, we have chosen to ignore calling out blatantly racist Blacks who commit violent crimes against non-Blacks in fear of such a stigma. Without hesitation, news outlets use terms like "White Cop Shoots Black Teen" along the bottom of their screen (known as a chyron). However, when it comes to Black teens assaulting defenseless Orthodox Jews in Brooklyn (please, feel free to Google) or countless other Black-on-White violent crimes, the media either doesn't cover the story or, if they do, omit the race of the assailant(s) and victim(s).

In a February 4, 2021 article by Dion Lim, the local news reporter chronicled a "skyrocketing number of hate crimes" against Oakland's Chinatown residents. In a four-second news video posted with the story, one can see a Black man violently push an elderly Asian American man from behind, causing the ninety-one-year-old senior to fall to the ground. The unprovoked, senseless attack took place in broad daylight in front of the Asian Resource Center. In the article, Lim repeatedly refers to the assailant as the "male suspect." Since the video clearly shows a Black man committing a racist hate crime, I can't for the life of me understand why she omitted the assailant's race in the article.

When *Honey, I Shrunk the Kids* star Rick Moranis was punched in the face by a Black man in front of his Central Park apartment house on October 1, 2020, race was nowhere to be found in the story or chyron. I'm just shooting in the dark here, but if a muscular White teen went up to a sixty-seven-year-old Black senior citizen who weighed 130 pounds soaking wet and stood five feet six with lift insoles, and, without provocation, let loose with a roundhouse to the Black person's face, I'm guessing the media might've found room in the article to mention race.

The point here is when we have a corrupt press that pushes White racism and White privilege but ignores other stories that don't fit their "victim" narrative, it's no wonder why race relations in this country appear worse than they are.

A perfect example of media bias was never more exposed than when a sixteen-year-old Catholic high school student was caught on camera smiling. *How dare he!* Leave it to the liberal media to fall all over themselves when they thought they had a racist White MAGA-hat-wearing teen "discriminating" against an American Indian. As it turned out, Nicholas Sandmann did nothing wrong, but those in the press desperately wanting the racism narrative to be true ran the story before getting all the facts. The mainstream media had a field day until a full-length video exposed that Sandmann was not the instigator but the victim. The poor kid stood there motionless as some deranged idiot approached him with a drum and started pounding it inches from his face. Even after all the facts were out, *Today* show host Savannah Guthrie in an exclusive interview with Sandmann, tried turning the tables on the poor youngster by asking loaded questions like:

"Do you feel from this experience that you owe anybody an apology?"

"Do you see your own fault in any way?"

However, the sixteen-year-old held his own by responding to the disingenuous host that he had every right to be standing where he was.

On a separate note to Ms. Guthrie:

The next time I'm in NYC, I'll be sure to bring my drum to NBC Studios and bang it inches from your face. When I'm done, I hope the "experience" will inspire you to want to apologize to me. If that's too much to ask, then hopefully, you can reflect inward to see if you're at fault in any way.

It was in Martin Luther King Jr.'s *"I Have a Dream"* speech that he so eloquently spoke the famous words:

"I look to a day when people will not be judged by the color of their skin, but by the content of their character."

I lived that dream while serving in the United States Army. There were no Black or White soldiers, just red-blooded American men and women who took an oath to defend the Constitution of the United States against all enemies, foreign and domestic.

When I was in basic training at Fort Jackson, South Carolina, I was assigned to Delta Company. My drill instructor was the toughest SOB I ever met. From top to bottom, Drill Sergeant Peters was more of a soldier than I could ever hope to be. He was there before reveille to kick our butts out of bed in the morning and was the last to leave, yelling, "Lights out!" on his way out the barrack's door. Outside of my father, the Alabama decedent of slaves with a voice that could make the earth shake is the male role model I've respected most in my life.

Drill Sergeant Peters retired as one of the most decorated instructors in United States Army history. He earned all his accolades, not because of the color of his skin but the content of his character.

D. I. Peters is *"the best of the best!"*

My dream is the day when we no longer identify people by gender or race but by what we are, Americans.

John Brown and Susan B. Anthony

When it came to ending the institution of slavery, nineteenth-century abolitionist John Brown believed God chose him to carry out the "divine mission." The deeply religious, impatient Brown would not be satisfied until all slaves were freed. Obsessed with succeeding, Brown devised a daring plan to arm the slaves in their revolt by capturing the United States armory at Harpers Ferry, Virginia. Brown took control of the arsenal for a short time but eventually was overwhelmed by military forces and captured.

For many, John Brown is considered a hero who helped spark the Civil War. Frederick Douglass patriotically compared Brown with "Give me liberty or give me death" Patrick Henry. Douglass said, "Henry loved liberty for the rich and the great. Brown loved liberty for the poor and the weak."

At Brown's ensuing trial, a soldier held captive inside the armory testified as a witness to the insurrection. In reading the transcript of the soldier's testimony, I was amazed by what I discovered next. The brave soldier approached John Brown and informed him that one of his men was severely injured and desperately needed medical attention. The noncommissioned officer went on to say that he gave his word from one Christian to another that if Brown let him take the injured soldier to the nearby hotel for treatment, he would return. John Brown agreed. The sergeant then left the armory with the wounded soldier and, shortly after, returned as promised.

I'm still left wondering which man showed the most honor that day. How about we call it tie.

Note: In the name of righteous justice, Brown would order his men to abduct slave owners in the middle of the night from their homes, have them dragged into the woods where their bodies would be hacked into pieces. Whether one believes John Brown was a martyr who helped free the slaves or a vigilante terrorist who took the law into his own hands, I pray that we can all agree there's no justification at any time for playing Whac-A-Mole to Big Daddy's torso with an ax.

A family side note: The Great Fire Fiasco of 1976

I recall when my father poured a gallon of gasoline on the side of the house because we had an "issue" with carpenter ants around our wooden foundation. Yes, my father achieved his goal of killing the pesky wood-eating insects, but at the same time, he found him and his family homeless for a few days while repairs were being done. Please, don't think less of my father for his unique exterminating skills. In fairness, I never did see another unwanted living creature crawling around our house again.

His demise, along with many other men throughout history, was that he fell victim to the dangerous, intoxicating combination of overkill and unbridled power. The formula goes something like this: one match, a gallon of gasoline, an obsession to kill, topped off with a self-righteous indignation justifying the cause.

Unlike my father and John Brown, Susan B. Anthony took a drastically different approach when battling to achieve her goal of voting rights for women. Knowing she'd be arrested for unlawfully voting, the fifty-two-year-old political activist cast her vote in the 1872 presidential election between Ulysses S. Grant and Horace Greeley. Horace who, you ask? The only thing worth noting about Mr. Horace is that in 1869, *Harper's Weekly* declared him "the most perfect Yankee the country has ever produced." Of course, poor Horace would lose even this distinction by the middle of the next century when a young kid from Martinez, Califonia, named Joe DiMaggio, aka the Yankee Clipper, was crowned as the greatest Yankee ever! Sorry, Horace. However, I will give Horace an honorable mention for coming up with the phrase, "Go west, young man."

Getting back to the suffrage movement.

Susan B. Anthony was subsequently arrested, tried, and convicted—all by men. After being told to sit down and be quiet by the often short-tempered Judge Ward Hunt, the judge immediately told Anthony to stand back up so he could sentence her. So, on a stifling June day in a packed upstate New York courthouse, all eyes were now fixated on the judge. After clearing his throat as to make full use of his pitch, no doubt so the reporters standing in the back of the courtroom could hear him without difficulty, the Honorable Judge Hunt announced, "Having been found guilty by a jury of your peers for knowingly and willingly casting an unlawful ballot, you are sentenced to pay a one-hundred-dollar fine, plus court costs."

Anthony wasted little time telling the judge what she thought of his decision.

"May it please Your Honor. I'll never pay a dollar of your unjust penalty. I shall earnestly and persistently continue to urge all women to the practical recognition of the old revolutionary maxim that *the resistance to tyranny is obedience to God.*"

Susan B. Anthony never did pay the fine. The judge strategically added in the sentence that Anthony was allowed to be released before having to pay the court fees. Hunt's move eliminated any chance of Anthony filing an appeal and, in the process, hoped to stop her from garnering any additional national attention for the suffrage movement. However, due to Anthony's persistence, the court case's political damage set the path for the later ratification of the Nineteenth Amendment and women's right to vote. All accomplished without a single shot fired.

When expressing his opposition to the Fugitive Slave Law in 1851, Ralph Waldo Emmerson wrote, "An immoral law makes it a man's duty to break it at every hazard." As our splintered country moves forward, I pray we can learn to resolve our differences in a way that reflects the peaceful values of a Martin Luther King Jr., Mahatma Gandhi, and Susan B. Anthony, and not a fanatic like John Brown.

Chapter 7

The Death of Journalism
1791–2020

The tyranny of a prince in an oligarchy is not so dangerous to the public welfare as the apathy of a citizen in a democracy.

—*French Philospher Montesquieu*

The *Washington Post's* signature slogan is "Democracy Dies in Darkness." Assuming for a moment that the publication is an advocate for democracy, how then does the paper explain their historic blackout in 2020 on three of the biggest corruption scandals in modern political history?

1. *The Russian Hoax*
2. *Hunter's Laptop*
3. *Election Fraud*

When the same institution wanted to believe Trump colluded with our enemy, the endless parade of "unnamed sources" and stories based more on speculation than fact never seemed to cease. However, once Special Counsel Robert Mueller's report showed Trump and his campaign had not colluded with the Russians in the 2016 election, these same pit bull reporters at the *Washington Post* who were accepting Pulitzers for their participation in the hoax, unapologetically moved on to the next hit job: Ukraine!

In what has to be a twist of irony, there actually was a campaign in the 2016 election that did conspire with the Russians, but because it was coming from their comrades on the left, the morally corrupt media chose to look the other way. In my opinion, this type of omission of truth is more dangerous to our republic than the reporting of known erroneous stories. Ironically, it's the *Washington Post* with their trademark slogan that has forewarned us of what will become of our democracy if it stays in the dark—it dies!

Mueller

A hundred years from now, the *Final Jeopardy* answer will be: *"Home of the popular paska (Easter bread), as well as, this country that was in the middle of the 2020 impeachment of American president Donald J. Trump."*

I can promise unless Ken "The Genius" Jennings is still alive, all three brainiac contestants will say, "What is Russia?" That's when the latest cyborg model of Alex Trebek turns with a computer-generated grin and responds, "Sorry, but we were looking for Ukraine." For the next few minutes, a debate breaks out on stage as to whether or not Ukraine was even a country in 2020, and what the hell is paska?

Mueller spent nearly two years and over $48 million on Russia, Russia, Russia and found that the entire Russian-Trump collusion saga was a hoax. However, not all was lost. During that period, has-beens like Carl Bernstein, who swore the story was "bigger than Watergate," made good money on CNN promising that the "president will be impeached" and that "we are seeing evidence of a conspiracy." Day after day Bernstein assured the left mob that Trump's days were numbered. It was sad to see the legendary *Washington Post* investigative journalist quest for one final shot at glory. There'd be no "deep throat," clandestine meetings in dark parking garages, or famous actors portraying him on the big screen. Like Shakespeare's character Shylock in *The Merchant of Venice*, Bernstein's crusade against the president came across as an old man seeking vengeance, not the truth.

Side note: Can someone please do me a favor and tell Carl that he's an annoying little man who was played by an equally irritating little man (Dustin Hoffman). Maybe at the same time, someone can let Carl know that Watergate was fifty years ago, and there have been two generations since who really don't give a rat's ass. And if anyone thinks I'm picking on Carl and Dustin because the two eighty-year-olds have great hair and that I'm jealous, well, they'd be right!

The story, or should I say, what should've been the story once Mueller finished his report was that Trump and his campaign, although stupid beyond belief, did not conspire with the Russians. However, faster than Imelda Marcos moving through Manolo Blahnik in New York City, the press—who'd been beating the impeachment drum every day since January 20, 2017—shamelessly moved on to the next story.

"Washington, We Have a Problem"

More than one-third of House Democrats boycotted Trump's inauguration. The Democrat Party all but assured its constituents Trump would be thrown out of the White House before he finished unpacking. Former Secretary of State Clinton, Trump's opponent in 2016, labeled Trump "an illegitimate president." Keeping with the sore loser theme, Michigan Rep. Rashida Tlaib, or who I like to think of as our generation's Margaret Thatcher, Eleanor Roosevelt, and Jacqueline Bouvier Kennedy all rolled into one, declared with grace and dignity on the night of her swearing-in ceremony in front of her two preteen sons that her first order of business was to go to Washington and then "We're gonna impeach the motherfucker!" Next on Capitol Hill beating the *"Impeach 45"* drum was political hack Maxine Waters, who said:

> As I have stated time and time again, Donald Trump is a dangerous and dishonorable man. He has no respect for our Constitution or the rule of law. It is past time that Congress fulfills its constitutional duty to impeach him.

But there was one itty-bitty problem for the bloodthirsty Dems. Trump was clean, well, as clean as a guy can be after allegedly having an affair with a porn star. The fact remained that after a $48 million witch hunt, the Dems still had nothing on Trump. The clock was ticking. After all, a promise is a promise, and this was one the libs desperately wanted to keep. So, with the left in panic mode, Judiciary Chairman Jerry "The Human Gnome" Nadler wanted Trump charged with obstruction. I want to take a second for that to sink in. The gnome wanted to bring articles of impeachment against a duly elected president because he *felt* there was enough evidence to do so, although there was no underlying crime. Yes, legally, that was an option since the Dems controlled the House of Representatives. But after two years of nonsense, thanks to a six-foot-eight clown posing as an FBI director (James Comey) who purposely leaked documents to tripwire the hoax, members of Nadler's own party could see it was a losing move so told the little man to cool it. Then through the powers of godless intervention, the Dems atheist prayers were answered. A whistleblower came forward with a transcript that clearly showed Trump was asking for a quid pro quo from Ukrainian president Volodymyr Zelensky. Here's the transcript that indicates the "this for that" exchange:

> I said, no, I'm not going to—or, we're not going to give you the billion dollars. They said you have no authority. You're not the president. The president said—I said, call him. I said, I'm telling you, you're not getting the billion dollars. I said, you're not getting the billion. I'm going to be leaving here in, I think it was about six hours. If the prosecutor is not fired, you're not getting the money. *Well, son of a bitch. He got fired.*

Clearly, the exchange shows a quid pro quo and possibly borders on a "Tony and Vinny" extortion operation. But what do I know about the law? Oh, and apparently, I know even less about the origin of the previous quote. It seems I credited the wrong person with the quid pro quo. That was Vice President Biden bragging about the Tony Soprano move and not Trump. My apologies, but I'm going to have to ask everyone to ignore that quid pro quo, just like the press did, as I attempt for a second time to show what was worthy of President Trump's first impeachment? Here's the most explosive part of the phone call between President Trump and President Zelensky that took place on July 25, 2019:

45: Biden went around bragging that he stopped the prosecution, so if you can look into it… It sounds horrible to me… Whatever you can do, it's very important that you do it if that's possible.
PRESIDENT Z: "Yes, it is very important for me and everything you just mentioned.

Well, leave it to Washington for a whistleblower to come forward who didn't actually listen in on the conversation but was outraged nonetheless. In the whistleblower's complaint, he writes, "I have received information from multiple US government officials that the president of the United States is using the power of his office to solicit interference from a foreign country in the 2020 US election." The whistleblower then made a curious declaration that Trump "repeatedly pressured the president of Ukraine…about eight times." I say curious because unless Trump released the transcript, there was no way of knowing if this was true or not. Since it would be unprecedented and doubtful that Trump would make available the transcript to the phone conversation, the appearance of impropriety would hang in the air. However, for the Dems, as they had been doing ever since Trump came down the escalator in 2015, they miscalculated the fat orange-hair guy again. By releasing the transcript, Trump showed that the whistleblower was intentionally misleading. Not to worry. The Dems quickly dressed up a round-face Charlie Brown lookalike in Lt. Col. Alexander Vindman to give the impeachment proceedings a sense of legitimacy. After all, according to the Dems, you have to believe all women when it comes to sexual misconduct cases and anyone in a military uniform, meaning au revoir to due process and that innocent-until-proven-guilty nonsense. To anyone who remotely believes this thought process makes sense, I pray that it won't take being the victim of false charges to come to appreciate the legal system we have in this great nation.

Thanks to an innocuous phone call, a secondhand whistleblower, and Joe Biden's *alleged* misdeeds, Trump was now in the Dems crosshairs. But more importantly, for the bias press, they could now refocus their attention on bashing Trump on something other than Russia. In fact, by the time the Ukrainian gift in the form of a phone call arrived, the press wanted nothing more to do with looking into Russia, bogus FISA warrants, and the Biden family's multimillion dollar overseas racketeering interests. *Come to think of it, that phone call was about as fortuitous to the Dems as was that virus that Jane "Hanoi" Fonda referred to as "God's gift to the left."* Now I don't mean to get into conspiracy-theory mode here, but please indulge me in a few hypotheticals: what if Mueller reported in two months what took him two years that there wasn't any collusion? What if there wasn't any Ukrainian phone call to fall back on to impeach the president? And what if China along with billionaire George Soros's heavy investments into the Wuhan-based biotech company WuXi didn't start World War III in the form of a biological virus? I ask, what would the Dems have done during Trump's administration? It's my brain's tinfoil-wrapped opinion that the trifecta of all three made for a very convenient way to undermine Trump, expand the global net of socialism, and create lots of shade for years of abuse and corruption that went all the way from our intelligence agencies to the Obamas, Bidens, and Clintons.

Get Trump!

When the Democrat chair of the Judicial Committee, Nadler, remarked, "We cannot rely on an election to solve our problems," it further illustrated the desperation in not wanting to leave it up to the American people to decide their next leader. Instead, the Dems took matters into their own hands by impeaching Trump with a presidential election less than ten months away.

House Speaker Nancy Pelosi, who pledged she'd never put our country through an impeachment process unless she had overwhelming bipartisan support, took the occasion to get her hair done and have commemorative pens made. You just can't make this stuff up. Senate Majority leader Mitch McConnell was not impressed with Pelosi's glossy-black pens, which she had her signature emblazoned in gold and "literally came in on silver platters." McConnell remarked, "This final display neatly distilled the House's entire process into one perfect visual. It was a transparently partisan performance from beginning to end."

I only wish Pelosi would've saved one of those pens to… I don't know…maybe sign some meaningful legislation that could've benefited the American people during her stint as Speaker, or better yet, her resignation!

So what was the *Washington Post*'s response to the keepsake extravaganza:

"*PELOSI WAS RIGHT TO HAND OUT IMPEACHMENT SOUVENIR PENS*" *(January 21, 2020).*

The disconnected story reminded me of the *Washington Post*'s very first headline all the way back in AD 33:

"*PONTIUS PILATE WAS RIGHT TO HAND OUT CRUCIFIXION SOUVENIRS.*"

Let's not act surprised. Remember, this was the same publication that wrote in Soleimani's obituary how the murderous Iranian general liked poetry and walks along moonlit beaches. But somehow, the *Post* ran out of room in the piece to squeeze in the *trivial* fact that Soleimani was a terrorist who was responsible for killing thousands of American soldiers. The obit was reminiscent of Adolf Hitler's back on April 30, 1945:

"*CHANCELLOR OF THE GERMAN REICH, A DOG LOVER, AND ASPIRING ARTIST, QUIETLY DIED TODAY IN THE BASEMENT OF HIS ESTATE, ONE DAY AFTER MARRYING HIS LONG TIME LOVE EVA BROWN.*"

It just goes to show, marriage isn't for everyone.

It's amazing how this publication can always find silver linings for deadly, brutal terrorists and dictators but can never seem to find a nice thing to say about a Republican.

As for the rest of the press, except for a few conservative outlets, their interest in the Russian collusion story *mysteriously* dried up. It wasn't like there weren't any meaty stories. I, for one, would love to know more about the disgraced former FBI lawyer Kevin Clinesmith.

For the record, the document that opened the floodgates to continue spying on Carter Page—which, let's not kid ourselves, really meant spying on Trump—came down to one little felonious switcheroo by a dirty FBI lawyer named Kevin Clinesmith. This would be the same Kevin Clinesmith who sent an email the night of Trump's 2016 victory, "Viva the resistance." For Clinesmith, "Long live the revolution" meant completely discarding the American people's trust and abusing his government position. The Trump hater so much wanted the fat orange-hair guy out of office that he altered a crucial email in the Russia inquiry. He changed the content of an email from "Carter Page was a source for the Central Intelligence Agency" to "Carter page was not…" Thanks to Clienesmith's lack of integrity, his actions enabled the surveillance to continue, eventually giving birth to the Russia hoax.

So what does a disgraced FBI lawyer who cost the American taxpayers tens of millions of dollars, created chaos for the Trump administration, and tried to oust a duly elected president get when he's caught? How about a year of probation. According to presiding US District Judge James Boasberg, he felt the defendant had suffered enough by losing his job and dealing with the public's scrutiny over the incident. I'll leave it up to you, the reader, to decide whether or not justice was served.

My apologies in advance for using the "shoe on the other foot" argument, but let's face it, if Clinesmith were a conservative lawyer changing the wording on a Democrat's document, the press would let us know where he attended kindergarten, what movies he likes to watch on Netflix, and who were his buddies at the FBI. That last one really has me curious. And who knows, maybe with some digging, we can discover who's the bigger liar, McCabe or Comey, and what exactly was that "insurance policy" discussed in Andy's office with Peter Strzok and Lisa Page. And just as a quick reminder, this was all done with one purpose in mind: to overthrow a duly elected president. But still, the press struggled to find a story worthy of their time. To be fair, there was one person the media wanted an explanation from, and that was Congressman Adam Schiff.

For two years, Schiff took the opposite approach of businessman Donald Trump's under-promise, over-deliver philosophy by going with the disastrous combination of the over-promise, under-deliver methodology. Some may take the slimy politician's words a step further and extrapolate Schiff's over-promising rhetoric as lying.

Schiff swore to any camera and microphone that he could find that there was "more than circumstantial evidence" of collusion between the Trump campaign and the Russians. Now that Mueller came back with a big goose egg against Trump and newly declassified documents showed the Intelligence Committee's chairman was either a liar, an idiot, or both, Schiff now had some explaining to do. So how did the snake slither out of his lies? Well, he first acknowledged Inspector General Horowitz's report that showed seventeen "significant errors or omissions" by the FBI (all going against Trump) while obtaining the FISA applications. Then, in a performance worthy of an Oscar nod, he claimed that had he known, he "would have called out the FBI." If anyone is waiting for the media's follow-up question about where's the evidence he promised, I suggest not holding your breath.

I'll never understand how Trump withstood all the pressure he was under while he was president. As if the job wasn't challenging enough, the forty-fifth president of the United States had to deal with a hostile press, a lunatic Speaker of the House, an unwarranted impeachment, attacks on his children, and a previous administration (Obama) doing everything in their power to undermine his presidency before it ever started. Mind you, part of that *undermining* was the unleashing and weaponization of government agencies, mainly the FBI, DOJ, and the IRS. In case there's any doubt about how high up the ladder the operation went, let's not forget disgraced FBI agent Peter Strzok's text to his mistress Lisa Page: "POTUS [President Obama] wants to know everything we're doing."

So the obvious question is, why did Obama and his cronies do everything in their powers to try and sabotage a duly elected president? The answer to this question is relatively a simple one, but it still may shock most Americans. The guy with the charming smile, easygoing personality, and as Biden described: "I mean, you've got the first sort of mainstream African American who is articulate and bright and clean and a nice-looking guy," is anything but clean. Obama's use of the intelligence agencies was right out of the Soviet's Secret Police playbook of "you bring me the man, I'll find you the crime."

Here's some examples:

-   James Rosen of Fox News was secretly monitored during the Obama administration because he wouldn't reveal his source on a story regarding North Korea in 2009. Obama suspected the source, or as he put it, "the leak" came from inside the White House.
-   Under Obama's watch, the IRS aggressively targeted conservative organizations.
-   Trump and Hillary were both accused of conspiring with the Russians. There was zero evidence when it came to Trump and a mountain of evidence against Hillary. Can you guess which campaign was investigated and surveilled?

Obama's "if you like your doctor, you can keep your doctor" and his promise about health-care premiums going down $2,500 is right up there with a used-car salesman telling their next victim that the vehicle was driven by a little old lady going to and from church on Sundays. In my view, no president lied in office more than Obama. Unfortunately, instead of the press doing their job, they committed the cardinal sin when it comes to journalism: they chose sides.

As a reminder, during the campaign in 2016, Trump made the charge that Trump Tower and his campaign were under surveillance. The media scoffed at the allegations and called Trump paranoid. As it turned out, he was right, and they were wrong. And what was the press's response once it was discovered that Obama and his minions were acting like Stalin and the KGB—crickets again!

Kevin Clinesmith's involvement in this entire charade cannot be overstated. The FBI lawyer was tasked with finding out if Carter Page previously worked for the CIA. Whatever information he received from the agency was to be forwarded to the FISA Court to help the judge in his decision. If the answer were yes to Page's past involvement with the CIA, then getting a FISA warrant to continue surveillance would've been highly unlikely under the circumstances. If the answer was no, the answer Clinesmith illegally inserted, then the spying could continue on the Trump campaign. Clinesmith, in the spirit of *viva the resistance*, changed the document; and as they say, the rest is history.

So how did the FBI *almost* get away with "Crossfire Hurricane," the code name given to the Russian investigation?

Firstly, it should be noted that if Hillary Clinton won, all of these dark little secrets would've stayed in the closet. But since that wasn't the case, what we needed now was someone willing to get their hands dirty and start doing some digging. Enter Congressman Devine Nunes.

If there was a hero other than Donald J. Trump throughout the Russian hoax, it was Congressman Devine Nunes. Early on, the House Intelligence Committee chairman smelled something that wasn't kosher and began peeling back the Russian onion. What he discovered was worse than he could've imagined. And since he went poking where he wasn't welcomed, the character assassination by the media commenced. The allegations were ruthless. The congressman was accused of renting a yacht to use with his buddies for a day of partying with prostitutes and cocaine use—or what Bill Clinton called happy hour at the governor's mansion in Little Rock. The conveniently timed story was released in May of 2018, nearly three years after the alleged incident. However, it's an open secret in Washington that when it comes to a smear campaign with the goal being to seek and destroy an enemy's reputation, there's no such thing as a statute of limitations.

Since Nunes wasn't at the alleged party in question, the publication was served a $150 million defamation suit compliments of the congressman. Sadly, since the story's goal was to divert the public's attention away from the investigation of corruption into the Russian hoax, the media was temporarily successful in redirecting the public's focus on the shiny object off to the side. Once again, the objectives had nothing to do with journalism and everything to do with protecting the media's agenda. Thanks to a new phenomenon known as "Trump derangement syndrome," the rudderless press was sailing through their profession with their moral compass nowhere to be found.

One good thing to come from the Nunes smear campaign was that it signaled to the congressman that for the powers that be to pull out the heavy trifecta of the yacht, cocaine, and prostitutes, he must've been getting closer to the truth.

The congressman's attention was now focused on a document known as the Steele dossier. This would be the same dossier that FBI Deputy Director Andrew McCabe testified under oath that without it, they wouldn't have been able to acquire any of the FISA warrants used to spy on the Trump campaign. Nunes wanted to know who paid for the dossier and, equally significant, why the greatest investigatory agency in the world used an unverified document to predicate an investigation?

Finding out who flipped the bill for the dossier was as easy as following the money. Since Christopher Steele, the author of the document, was being paid by the FBI, it was time to see where the money trail led. The first domino to fall was the connection between Steele and the company that represented him, Fusion GPS. Nunes then subpoenaed the bank involved in the financial records for the payment transactions. The statements showed a money trail that connected the Democratic National Committee (aka Hillary Clinton) to the law firm Perkins Coie, who paid Fusion GPS, who then paid their employees, Christopher Steele and Nellie Ohr.

Who's Nellie Ohr, and what did she get paid to do?

Nellie Ohr is the wife of once high-ranking DOJ prosecutor Bruce Ohr. While Nellie worked for Fusion GPS on "Trump-Russia research," she conveniently passed along to her husband some intelligence she had gathered on Trump and some of his associates. On July 31, 2016, Nellie, Bruce, and Christopher Steele met at the Mayflower Hotel in Washington. At the meeting, Steele addressed some serious concerns regarding Trump to Bruce and hoped the DOJ or FBI could help. The next day, Bruce Ohr brought the newly acquired Steele dossier to then-deputy FBI director Andrew McCabe, and the Russian collusion hoax was hatched.

In case the maze was a little twisted, allow me to simplify, connecting the dots:

The DNC (Clinton) hired the law firm Perkins Coie—they hired Fusion GPS for the sole purpose of digging up dirt on a political opponent (Trump)—Fusion GPS hired Christopher Steele to collect the dirt and Nellie Ohr to facilitate his dirt through a backdoor channel at the DOJ, her husband, Bruce Ohr. Four years, four illegal wiretaps, one sacrificial lamb (Carter Page), one dirty lawyer (Clinesmith), several corrupt FBI agents, one senile special counsel (Mueller), and the waste of $48 million in American tax dollars later, everyone would find out that it was all a bunch of bullshit. Any questions?

So as Hillary Clinton and the press were crucifying Trump for allegedly conspiring with a foreign nation to influence an election's outcome, Hillary was conspiring with a foreign nation to influence the outcome of an election. Again, nothing but crickets from the media.

The irony, if one can call it that, is when Nunes released his redacted version of the Russian investigation's events in a memo, Schiff countered with his own version, completely contradicting the chairman's. One of them had to be lying. Take a wild guess who the press decided to believe and who they labeled a "Russian agent" (MSNBC political analyst John Heilemann, January 30, 2018).

Heilemann took his bogus "Russian agent" character assassination of Nunes a step further by saying, "Doesn't his behavior speak of that, though? I mean, I'm not the first person who's raised this. He's behaving like someone who's been compromised, and there are people in the intelligence community and others with great expertise in this area who look at him and say, 'That guys been compromised.'"

Side note: I'm still looking for someone to tell me what the hell it is that my wife brought home from her pottery class. *So, Heilemann, if you or your "people" can let me know via these amazing superpowers you guys possess, I'd appreciate you letting me know.*

For Washington opinion reporters Greg Sargent and Paul Waldman, they definitively knew which memo was the real deal and which one was written on toilet paper. Here's the title of one of their articles shortly after the release of the two memos. I hope it's not too tricky to figure out who they were rooting against: *"The Nunes Memo Is Out. It's a Joke and a Sham."*

Here's *Washington Post's* Greg Sargent again putting nails in Nunes's coffin in an article the following day: *"Devin Nunes's Laughable Spin to Protect Trump Crashes and Burns."*

It took nearly two years, but when the unredacted version of the FISA warrants was finally released, it showed who the honorable man was and who was nothing but a "sack of schiff."

In case anyone was wondering, all these clowns that generously call themselves "political experts" are still employed at their respective organizations without ever having to apologize for their slanted words. Worse than the lack of apology was the hypocritical silence these men and women in the press clung to in lieu of criticizing Schiff for his unethical behavior. But then again, who has time for apologies and reporting the truth when there was still so much work to be done by these cowards to rid the nation of that chubby orange-hair guy.

It's this author's opinion that the actions of those involved in hatching and perpetuating the Russian hoax constitute an act of treason. In case one was wondering if the term might be too harsh, allow me to offer the only crime defined in the United States Constitution:

Article III, Section 3
Clause 1

> *Treason against the United States, shall consist only in levying War against them, or in adhering to their Enemies, giving them Aid and Comfort. No Person shall be convicted of Treason unless on the same overt Act, or on Confession in open Court.*

Clause 2

> *The Congress shall have Power to declare the Punishment of Treason, but no Attainder of Treason shall work Corruption of Blood, or Forfeiture except during the Life of the Person attainted.*

Now, I'm sure many hotshot lawyers out there would argue that spying on a presidential candidate, and later president, does not fall under the article previously listed. However, when one adds in the intent to overthrow the executive branch of the United States government by individuals who solemnly swore to support and defend the Constitution against all enemies, foreign and domestic, and freely bear true faith and allegiance, then the enemy is clear and the "War" at hand is over control of Article II of the United States Constitution. Make no mistake, the powers that be in Washington, aided by a corrupt press, attempted a coup d'etat against a duly elected president. Although it is highly unlikely, every person responsible should be charged, tried, and, if convicted, face the appropriate sentencing.

Hunter

From all accounts, Robert Hunter Biden is an idiot. In 2014, while his father was sitting vice president and a heartbeat away from being the commander-in-chief, Hunter was booted from the United States Navy Reserve for testing positive for cocaine use. His "punishment" was a lucrative seat on the board of a known corrupt Ukrainian energy company named Burisma. In my opinion, that in itself should've been worthy of some digging by the media, but all we heard were crickets…again. The same could be said for Hunter's dealings with communist China and a Russian mayor's wife who forked over $3.5 million to the VP's son for reasons that still have not been explained. Evidently, for the *Washington Post*, not only does democracy die in darkness, but so does anything that may be embarrassing, perhaps even criminal, for the Democrat Party.

To say I was frustrated by the lack of transparency during the 2020 presidential election from the Democrat nominee would be putting it mildly. The former vice president hardly interacted with the press, and when he did, the reporters were handpicked with hard-hitting questions like "What flavor is your ice cream cone?" and "Why do you think Trump is bad for America?" Questions regarding his proposed $4 trillion tax hike, his opposition early on to Trump's travel ban on China, or anything that resembled a probing journalist digging for the truth were all missing in action. But then pay dirt hit. A laptop owned by Hunter Biden was left at a repair shop in Delaware that, if authentic, had incriminating content on the Bidens. We're talking about emails that directly contradicted the former Vice President's claim that he knew "nothing" of Hunter's overseas business dealings and how he never spoke to his son about Burisma. The smoking gun came in the form of a thank-you email found on Hunter's hard drive from a top executive at the energy company named Vadym Pozharskyi. The associate expressed his appreciation for Hunter coordinating an in-person meeting with his father, then vice president Joe Biden. Finally, Uncle Joe would be forced to answer some questions, right? The first and obvious question to ask "Creepy Joe" was why he sniffs women's hair so much. *Okay, maybe that shouldn't be the first question, but boy, what's up with that?* So, one would think the first query by reporters who attended Journalism 101 would be, "Excuse me, Mr. Vice President, did you ever meet with Vadym Pozharskyi?"

There are three possible responses Creepy Corrupt Joe could've given:

1. "Yes."
2. "No."
3. "I'm not going to answer that because if I do, it will be the headline for all the papers tomorrow."

For the record, no. 3 was Joe's go-to response on the campaign trail whenever he was asked whether or not he would "pack" the Supreme Court. Of course, it would've been nice for him to tell the American people his intentions before the election regarding changing our republic fundamentally, but for the former VP, he didn't want to make headlines, WTF! Say what you want about Trump, but he would at least answer the questions asked by the press and not act like the Cowardly Lion from the *Wizard of Oz.*

So getting back to which answer Joe gave. Well, sorry, but it was a trick question since the leftist sycophant reporters never asked a single question about the contents found on the laptop. Allow me to point out from the time the *New York Post* broke the story in mid-October to election day that there were still several weeks left in the campaign and a scheduled national debate. Yet the former vice president was never forced to answer a single question on the matter. The print and news media outlets all received the same unwritten *memo* to circle the wagons and protect the Democrat nominee.

At an ABC "News" town hall that aired amid the laptop firestorm, moderator George "The Clintons' Piss Boy" Stephanopoulos asked nothing regarding the damning allegations published in the *New York Post. Great journalism, George. Now go rub Hillary's bunions!*

However, there was one poor bastard who didn't receive the unwritten memo and, for a nanosecond, remembered he was still a journalist. The news reporter was CBS's Bo Erickson. He dared to ask the Democrat heir to the throne a question that wasn't on Biden's cheat sheet.

REPORTER: Mr. Biden, what is your response to the *New York Post* story about your son, sir?

BIDEN: I know [sic] you'd ask it. I have no response. It's another smear campaign right up your alley. Those are the questions you always ask.

I guess, hell hath no fury than a busted politician.

Biden's vitriol response to what should've been a softball question if the allegations were a farce was far from his campaign's prepared remarks they gave just two days before. In the earlier statement, Biden's presidential campaign gave the vanilla response by explaining the former vice president "carried out official US policy toward Ukraine and engaged in no wrongdoing."

Please forgive me, but I'm about to express myself like Andrew Cuomo and talk to everyone like they're stupid and I'm smart. In case anyone has forgotten what he sounds like, it's a monotone pitch drenched in self-righteousness. Here are a few of his classic examples:

"People, if you don't eat the cheesecake, your ass wouldn't be so huge."

"Who cares [if they] *died in the hospital, died in a nursing home. They died."*

"Let's try not to be obnoxious and offensive in your tone because you're 100 percent wrong."

Reminder, the following are my words but Andrew's superiority tone:

People, are we stupid. Do we not see what's going on here. Are we supposed to believe it's all one big unbelievable coincidence that the Vice President's loser son was able to secure all these lucrative deals in the same places where Joe was heading our foreign policy? And, if the laptop wasn't authentic, and it was all another Russia, Russia, Russia conspiracy, then why hadn't we heard from Hiden' Hunter?

But at least Joe came prepared for the final presidential debate when Trump pushed the "laptop from hell" narrative. The former VP didn't miss a beat by stating, "Fifty former national intelligence folks who said that what he's [Trump] accusing me of is a Russian plan." The nonsensical remark prompted Trump to retort, "You mean the laptop is now another Russia, Russia, Russia hoax… You have to be kidding."

It's funny how fifty idiots signed some bogus piece of paper to discredit the laptop, but all that had to be done was for one Hunter Biden to come forward and say, *"It's not mine. You can put that in my crack pipe and smoke it."* Instead, we have Brennan and Clapper, the world's number one and number two dumbest "intelligence" personnel in American history, respectfully, assuring the nation that this was all Russian disinformation.

Here are a few questions to mull over regarding our pair of Inspector Clouseau(s):

Question no. 1: How accurate were Brennan and Clapper regarding the last Russian (Clinton) disinformation campaign?
Question no. 2: Do either of these idiots still have any credibility left after being caught lying to Congress?
Question no. 3: Does anyone besides Republicans go to jail anymore for perjury? Just asking!

Where the Hell Is Hunter?

For the record, that's me who's asking that question. I'm directing it at Republicans Ron Johnson and Chuck Grassley, members of the Senate Committee on Homeland Security and Government Affairs. I fail to understand how these two Republican senators could investigate the corruption swirling around the VP and his son regarding Burisma and not subpoena Hunter to testify in front of their committee. Just as a reminder, *Frick* and *Frack* had subpoena powers in 2020 but remarkably never could get around sending one to Hunter.

A few months before the 2020 election, an eighty-seven-page report summing up the Senate's investigation into Joe Biden's *"possible"* conflict of interest while he was the vice president produced no damning evidence. Senator Johnson warned before the report was issued there'd be no surprises, saying that there was a "misconception on the part of the public that there would be [a smoking gun]."

Now call me an idiot, but wouldn't it have made sense to request Hunter Biden to testify in front of the investigating committee before closing the investigation? Since I never made detective like my father or finished law school like my niece, I'll have to assume smarter people than yours truly know the answer to this mystery. But here's my low-IQ shot in the dark. What if the little clique known as the United States Senate wanted to protect a former member of their ranks (former Senator Joe Biden) in the remote possibility that they may find a family member of their own under investigation one day? In politics, it's known as the "I'll scratch your back if you'll scratch my corrupt sorry ass and leave my son alone back" policy.

Fast-forward a few weeks. New revelations of a laptop containing damning materials of Hunter and his foreign dealings are brought to light thanks to Rudy Giuliani, the *New York Post*, and a computer repair store owner named John Paul Mac Isaac. *If* the computer is Hunter's, and *if* the hard drive material is authentic, I would think Johnson and Grassley may have wanted to call Hunter in to ask him a few questions under oath.

Before anyone starts yelling, "It's not fair to go after the family members of our leaders," I'd like to remind everyone that Trump Jr.,

Eric, and Ivanka, were all dragged in front of committees for zero proof of any wrongdoing while their father was in office.

In the middle of this firestorm, and just a few weeks before the 2020 election, Senator Johnson joined Maria Bartiromo on her Sunday morning show to discuss the latest Hunter Biden case developments. The Fontbonne Hall alum, and fellow Brooklynite, asked the senator a question I'd been yearning to know the answer to: "Why haven't you subpoenaed Hunter Biden"? For the next ninety seconds, Johnson did a Peter Strzok impersonation and gave a terrific answer to a question that was never asked (God bless you, Trey Gowdy). Johnson went off in so many different directions to avoid answering that by the time he was done, the audience not only didn't have an answer to a very legitimate question, but most Americans had forgotten what was initially asked. Thankfully, I was not one of them. So while sitting at my kitchen table, I decided to take over the interview for the Fox host by inserting my own question and answer:

QUESTION: *Why were the Republican Senators refusing to do their job and bring this scum of the earth Hunter in for questioning?*
ANSWER: Except for one or two senators, the upper chamber of Congress is comprised of a bunch of spineless cowards.

JOURNALISM

RIP

DECEMBER 15, 1791

OCTOBER 14, 2020

Not all of our framers were in favor of the Bill of Rights. Hamilton openly opposed the idea by arguing that the Constitution already included what amounted to a bill of rights. In an essay regarding the issue, he explained:

> *For why declare that things shall not be done which there is no power to do? Why for instance, should it be said, that the liberty of the press shall*

> *not be restrained, when no power is given by which*
> *restrictions may be imposed.*

However, there was strong opposition against Hamilton and in favor of guarantees when it came to freedom of speech, press, religion, and privacy. The military occupation at the hands of the despotic English monarchy produced the motivation, while James Madison provided the words. The creation was in line with Thomas Jefferson's philosophy:

> *A bill of rights is what the people are enti-*
> *tled to against every government on earth, general*
> *or particular, and what no just government should*
> *refuse, or rest on inference.*

Like France's political philosopher Tocqueville, Jefferson felt strongly that the press was America's centurion when it came to democracy and our liberties. Jefferson believed so strongly about an open and free press that he said: *"Were it left to me to decide whether we should have a government without newspapers or newspapers without a government, I should not hesitate a moment to prefer the latter."* When it came to the First Amendment, Washington echoed Jefferson's observation when he said: *"If freedom of speech is taken away, then dumb and silent we may be led, like sheep to the slaughter."*

Jefferson, who was much maligned by the newspapers in his day, never once wavered in his beliefs regarding their importance to our society. Madison acknowledged the difficulty in attempting to regulate the industry. He said that any attempt to control the abuses by newspapers could destroy its purpose and the gains provided by such an instrument. Madison explained:

To the press alone, checkered as it is with abuses, the world is indebted for all the triumphs which have been gained by reason and humanity over error and oppression.

Today's press has a critical role to play when it comes to the health of our republic. This is why I'm appalled at the institution as a whole for its dereliction of duty. And before anyone starts to think that I'm some MAGA-wearing Trump diehard, I'm not. Allow me to disclose my true feelings about "45."

Donald Trump has an ego the size of Texas. He stiffed personal friends who worked on his defunct Taj Mahal in Atlantic City and other properties throughout NYC. Trump's company still owes one of them $250,000 for architectural services. He says stupid things, can be crude, and, on occasion, has shown to be disrespectful toward women. Personally, I think he's a self-centered, narcissistic opportunist whose timing was perfect in 2016. And, as bad of a person as I believe he is, I voted for him in 2016 and 2020. Why? Three reasons. The first two should be self-explanatory: Crooked Hillary and Creepy Joe. But allow me to borrow Alexander Hamilton's thought process when he was forced to choose between the lesser of two evils.

When Thomas Jefferson and Aaron Burr tied the 1800 presidential election, Hamilton found himself in a unique position. He had enough political clout in Congress to help push one of the men over the finish line. One problem, Hamilton wasn't a big fan of either. Jefferson was his political enemy who he disagreed with on nearly every major issue of the day while Burr was a man he saw unfit to hold the highest office. Hamilton decided that Jefferson was "by far not so dangerous a man" compared to Burr. Hamilton said, *"I'd rather have a president with the wrong principles than a president who had no principles."* My sentiments exactly when it comes to Joe and Hillary.

As for my third reason:

I have no desire to have a beer with Trump, and I'm pretty confident he has no desire to have one with me (regardless of the fact that neither one of us drink). I would never leave my wife alone with him anywhere at any time. However, in 2016, I wasn't looking for a drinking buddy or someone to entertain my wife. I was looking for someone who might actually want to do what's in America's best interest and not Iran, China, or Russia's. So, even though I'm not Black, I took the "Donald's" advice when he rhetorically asked the African American community, *"What the hell do you have to lose."*

The best way to describe 45 is he's the Rodney Dangerfield of politics. Let's face the fact that he was never going to be accepted by the elite into their blue blood swamp. However, as long as he contributed big bucks into their campaign coffers, they tolerated him and even attended his weddings, but they were never going to respect the orange-hair billionaire as one of their own. The second 45 crossed over into the political arena, Trump's friends in the media and politics like Rosie O'Donnell, Joe and Mika Scarborough, Oprah, and the Clintons went from attending Trump's galas and social events to persona non grata. I guess the moral of the story is if one wants to find out who their friends are, they should go into politics.

In my view, Trump never received a fair shake from the press. Even when he had several monumental accomplishments, somehow, those entrusted in reporting the news either buried them or omitted the story altogether. Unfortunately, giving credit where credit is due is not part of the winning formula when it comes to trying to oust a president.

Since the press is still reluctant to give the chubby orange-hair guy any credit due to a possible 2024 presidential bid, I'll do it for them. Here are some of Trump's accomplishments during his presidency:

- Signed Right-To-Try legislation for those terminally ill needing a miracle.
- Signed the VA Choice Act and VA Accountability Act. Being a veteran, I'm grateful that Trump could do what people like the late senator from Arizona John McCain never were able to accomplish.
- Imposed a travel restriction on China early on during the Wuhan virus when no one thought it was necessary.
- Strengthen our military and "encouraged" NATO to hold up to their obligation of 2 percent GDP spending on its military. Our allies increased their spending to $69 billion more since 2016.
- Appointed three Supreme Court justices and filled more seats on the circuit court than any other president in history.
- The USA became energy independent during Trump's presidency while CO_2 emissions fell nearly 3 percent. In

2018, the US became the largest producer of crude oil in the world.

- Reduced our troops in harm's way and kept us out of any new wars.
- Unlike three of his predecessors, Trump kept his campaign promise by moving the US Embassy to Jerusalem.
- Negotiated a new trade deal with Mexico and Canada.
- Was able to raise the GDP to 4.2 percent when Obama scoffed at the idea in 2016, sarcastically asking: "What magic wand do you [Trump] have?"
- Signed the criminal justice reform bill, the First Step Act. For someone who has been labeled a White supremacist by many in the media, this one act alone benefited numerous African Americans.
- Secured billions of dollars in aid to farmers due to unfair trade retaliation by China and other countries.
- Negotiated the release of twelve prisoners being held by our adversaries in China, North Korea, and Iran.
- *Poverty rates under the Trump administration for Hispanics and African Americans were the lowest in recorded history.
- *Orchestrated "Operation Warp Speed," which helped expedite and facilitate a vaccine for the Wuhan virus in record time.
- *Facilitated two historic Middle East treaties between Israel and their Arab neighbors.

*It's this author's opinion that these three accomplishments—minority prosperity, Operation Warp Speed, and the Abraham Accords—will go down in history as some of the most outstanding achievements by a sitting president in US history.

So how did the press respond to these great accomplishments:

- NBC News (8/23/2020): "Trump didn't build a great economy. He inherited it."
- *The Washington Post* (9/15/2020): "The mirage of Trump's 'peace' deals'"

- *The Washington Post* (9/21/2020): "The UAE-Bahrain-Israel accords are a big step—in the wrong direction"
- *The New York Times* (9/15/2020): "Inside Trump's Failure: The Rush to Abandon Leadership Role on the Virus"
- MSNBC (10/23/2020): "Trump is an 'epidemiological menace'"
- Business Insider (9/29/2020): "Trump's Middle East accord is the illusion of peace"
- CNN (8/14/2020): "Israel-UAE agreement a meek version of the historic Mideast deal Trump pledged"
- *The New York Times* (10/23/2020): "Trump's Economy Was Never So Great"
- *Forbes* (2/19/2020): "No President Trump, Obama's Economic Recovery Was Not a Con Job"
- *The Daily Beast* (3/8/2020): "Trump's 'Spectacular Economy' Was Far Better for the Middle Class Under Obama"
- NBC News (7/22/2020): "Biden says Trump is first racist US president"
- *Mother Jones* (7/7/2020): "Donald Trump Listens to His Gut, and It's the Gut of a Racist"
- CNN (12/13/2020): "Trump engages in self-sabotage ahead of historic vaccine rollout"

And what exactly was the "self-sabotage" CNN was referencing? The media mogul accused the American president that because he was questioning the outcome of the election, he was spreading "election disinformation" and "distracting Americans from [his] great accomplishment." For the record, that's about as close as CNN has ever complimented the president, even if it was a left-handed one.

One gets the idea that no matter what Trump did during his presidency, he would never garner praise from the reporters. Now don't get me wrong. I don't believe that's their job, but nor do I think they should be looking to undermine 45's position simply because they don't like him or his policies. I would think that the idea is to have an objective press that can report the news and allow the rest of us to digest it so we may come to our own conclusions.

Unfortunately, that's a risk "fake news" isn't willing to take. Instead, they find every imperfection they can with their metaphoric jeweler's loupe so they can undersell the good and hammer the flaws. And when all else fails, they ask loaded questions like "Have you stopped beating your wife." Case in point, here's Chris "The Snake" Wallace as the moderator in the 2016 Presidential Debate:

"Mr. Trump…you've repeatedly disavowed him [David Duke, a former member of the KKK] since then, but I'd like to go deeper than that. What are your views on the Ku Klux Klan and the White supremacist?"

Here's Chris "The Senile Snake" Wallace as the moderator in the 2020 Presidential Debate asking virtually the same question he asked four years earlier:

"Are you willing tonight to condemn White supremacist and militia groups and to say that they need to stand down and not add to the violence in a number of these cities as we saw in Kenosha and as we've seen in Portland?"

Unless you were visiting a different planet during the spring and summer of 2020, it was obvious to all watching that the leftist radical groups Antifa and BLM were causing 99 percent of all the chaos in major cities around the nation. Night after night, I watched as these Marxist groups illegally rioted, set cities ablaze, looted, killed, raped, and in the American city of Seattle, took over six square blocks for weeks for what the liberal mayor deemed to be action toward a "summer of love." As for the mainstream media's coverage of the rioting, they viewed it as "mostly peaceful protestors." *You just can't make this stuff up.*

For Chris Wallace, he wasn't done hammering home the Democrat talking points. During the 2020 debate, Wallace asked a question that implied the rioting was coming from both the Democrat and Republican-run cities:

The Snake: There has been a dramatic increase in homicides in America this summer particularly, and you [Trump] often blame that on Democratic mayors and Democratic governors. But in fact, there have been equivalent spikes in Republican-led cities, like Tulsa and Fort Worth. So the question is, is this really…a party issue.

Allow me to answer this one:

No, Chris, there's no difference between Democrat cities and Republican. In fact, Chicago, Los Angeles, Detroit, New York, Philadelphia, Atlanta, Milwaukee, and D. C., are just as safe as places like Lafayette, Knoxville, Chattanooga, Scottsdale, and a host of other American cities labeled as conservative. Just last weekend, when fifty-three people were being shot and eight killed in Chicago, a John Deere tractor was stolen from a farmer by some kids using it for a joy ride down Courtland Green Street in Woodlands, Texas. Equivalent? Hell, the two cities are nearly identical. And remember when all that looting was going on in those Democrat-run cities— windows smashed, flat-screen TVs loaded into the back of vans, and buildings set ablaze. Well, an eerily similar occurrence happened in the conservative city of Racine, Wisconsin. A lady was reprimanded at a local Piggly Wiggly for helping herself to too many of those complimentary sugar packets.

Chris, if the best you could come up with is stretching the meaning of the word *equivalent* to fit your ludicrous narrative, along with the regurgitation of *race-baiting* questions, I think, perhaps, it's time for you to cancel your monthly supply of Grecian Formula and hang up the mic.

So, as the left had their *summer of love*, did Joe Biden get asked by the Snake Wallace to condemn Antifa and BLM? Was the former vice president asked why his running mate, Kamala Harris, raised money to bail out "protestors" in Minnesota? Or was Uncle Joe asked about any of his numerous racist remarks about Blacks or how one "cannot go to a 7-Eleven or a Dunkin Donuts unless you have a slight Indian accent"? The answers: *Hell no! Hell no! And…hell no!*

Then there was that "plagiarism thing" committed by Mr. American Values himself that inexplicably was forgotten all about by the press during the 2020 campaign. But somehow, when Wallace was preparing the debate questions, the best he could do was replay an *oldie but goodie* question on White supremacy for Trump but conveniently forgot to add anything remotely probing as to whether Biden condemned the acts of Antifa and BLM.

Journalism wasn't dead yet. But let's face it, it wasn't like Edward R. Murrow and Walter Cronkite were walking into the newsroom any time soon.

Today we're stuck with presidential moderators like The Snake Wallace and C-SPAN's Steve "I've Been Hacked Again" Scully, who, if you recall, was suspended for conspiring with a former Trump aide and then was caught lying about it. The idiot used the Anthony Weiner defense of "my computer was hacked" but soon realized his coverup would invite the FBI to ask a few questions, so he finally came clean. Just another fine example of the unbiased, high-ethical standards found in American journalism today—not! So as for journalism itself, it was on life support with the left inscribing DNR (do not resuscitate) across the First Amendment. However, at the time of the first debate (Tuesday, September 29, 2020), how was anyone to know that in a little over two weeks, thanks to Twitter, Facebook, and virtually every news outlet across the nation, the plug would be pulled on journalism for good. The official cause of death was censorship brought on by a willingness to conspire against the United States Constitution.

A final point regarding the 2020 presidential debates:

As was the case with Chris "The Snake" Wallace in his disastrous debate performance, moderator Kristen Welker failed to ask either candidate a single question on foreign policy. It should've come as no surprise since Trump had numerous accomplishments in this area while Joe had decades of being on the wrong side of history. In my view, this was yet another way to protect Biden but was a disservice to the American people. Since anytime a nation starts to get complacent enough not to ask a single question about what's going on around the globe, one would think that's usually right around the time the dirty diaper hits the fan.

Here's my 2024 *prediction*: I don't know who the candidates will be nor the moderators, but I can assure everyone that after four years of a Biden-Harris administration (or according to Joe, Harris-Biden administration), the 2024 debates will have numerous foreign policy questions.

Murder at Forty-Eighth and Avenue of the Americas

On October 14, 2020, the *New York Post* dropped what could very well go down as the biggest "October Surprise" in modern political history. Hunter's laptop and all the allegedly incriminating material found inside was exposed in an article written by reporters Emma-Jo Morris and Gabrielle Fonrouge. The story was titled *"Smoking-Gun Email Reveals How Hunter Biden Introduced Ukrainian Businessman to VP Dad."*

Like any October surprise, the twilight-hour dumping of the story right before the election is meant to create maximum damage to his or her political opponent. *I guess all is fair in love, war, and politics.* For Trump, his surprise in 2016 came at the hands of Hillary Clinton. The release of the classless *Access Hollywood* audiotape of him describing his disgusting exploits with unsuspecting women was a bombshell. Trump was already struggling with suburban housewives, and this well-timed hit job looked like it would finish the poor bastard off. Well, not so fast. We all know the outcome of the 2016 election. So it's fair to say there are no guarantees of a victory simply because you have the goods on your opponent.

Mudslinging and politics is nothing new in our republic. To this day, the 1800 presidential campaign between Jefferson and Adams is considered one of the ugliest in history. The openly-biased newspapers ran articles like a battering ram daily in an attempt to disparage the opposing candidate. In 1880, the New York *Truth* published a letter thought to be written by James Garfield that stated the "Chinese problem" (referring to immigrants as cheap labor) wasn't really a problem. Understandably, workers were outraged and felt threatened with the prospect of an influx of foreign workers pouring into the country. It's believed the letter (which was later proven to be a fake) had cost Garfield the election. In 1872, Henry Kissinger gave the "peace at hand" speech regarding the Vietnam War two weeks before the election in 1972. In 2000, the surprise was the release of George Bush's drunk driving arrest that took place years earlier.

So what is the duty of the press when it comes to reporting on these October surprises? For Garfield, I think he would've appreciated a little more digging by the New York *Truth* before they published the letter. There's no way to quantify the effects such a dishonest act had on his campaign, but I think we can all agree that it didn't help. I believe it's the publication's responsibility to do its due diligence to authenticate any material before releasing such sensitive information. In my view, if a good faith effort was made to confirm the story and all indications showed the material to be accurate as well as newsworthy, then I believe it would be a dereliction of duty not to publish the article.

For the *New York Post*, the oldest newspaper in the nation with the fourth largest publication, they put their reputation on the line and stood by publishing the Hunter Biden laptop story. It's important to distinguish between the "Hunter laptop" and the fallout that proceeded. The laptop was the October surprise, but the censorship was the story.

So in broad daylight and without a shot being fired, the First Amendment's remnants laid in a chalk outline in front of the *New York Post* headquarters on Forty-Eighth and Sixth. The godless culprits were a complicit press corps and out-of-control tech giants.

The Press Cover-Up

The only stories run by MSNBC, CNN, the *Washington Post*, and the *New York Times* were all to discredit the *New York Post* story. These prostitutes of the First Amendment should take whatever plastic press credentials they've been issued and burn them. Collectively, they decided that the ends justify the means. Allow me to put it another way: they hate Trump more than they love America.

CNN immediately dispatched *Mr. Integrity* himself, James Clapper, to discredit the *Post*'s laptop story by saying that it was "textbook Soviet Russian tradecraft." *My apologies to Jane Brady*, but one last time: *Russia, Russia, Russia.* Enough already. Mind you, neither Hunter nor Joe came out to deny that the laptop was the eldest son's, but somehow Clapper was able to ascertain through some magical porthole he has that it was once again the *Russians.*

Hey, Clapper, I'm still trying to figure out what my wife brought home from that pottery class of hers. I was hoping since you can make definitive determinations without seeing things, that you could do me a favor and text me what the hell it is. Thanks!

Here's Clapper's classic line of crap that aired on *The View* in 2020 after being asked about Trump calling him a "lying machine":

MEGHAN McCAIN: The president tweeted about you that Clapper is a lying machine that now works for fake news CNN. What's your reaction?

CLAPPER: Oh, the president is calling me a lying machine. Well... okay. [The remark garners a chuckle from the liberal New York City audience]... The remark stems from an exchange I had with Senator Wyden...about a security program. He was asking me about one thing, and I was thinking about another. So I made a mistake, but I didn't lie.

McCAIN: What your referencing...is James Snowden blowing the whistle on the NSA illegally spying, and in 2013 when you were asked about it, you said no. So that is a lie.

CLAPPER: [Raises his right index finger in a sign of assertion] No, that isn't a lie. I'm sorry, that isn't a lie. I was thinking about something else—another program. I could get into all the *technical details* about [it]. He was asking about the metadata program, and the *euphemistic way* he asked about it, I didn't *break the code*.

Clapper goes on for another minute or so with some technical babble stuff and then has the nerve to get facetious by finishing with, "I've been trotting up the Hill testifying for twenty to twenty-five years, dozens of hearings, hundreds of questions, and I've always tried to answer them straight. But gee, just for a change of pace, I think I'll lie on this one question, and by the way, do it on live television in front of one of my oversight committees. Really? No. I made a mistake."

To which the BS meter rang: "Ding, ding, ding, we have a winner!"

So what were all those *"technical details"* and *"euphemistic"* babble that confused our highest *intelligence* official to the point that he failed to *"break"* Senator Wyden's *"code"*? Now please forgive me, because I'm about to get all high-tech in my writing skills here. I would love to dummy it down for you simple-minded people, but in fairness to Mr. Clapper, I think it's only appropriate to present the Q and A between Wyden and himself precisely how it transpired during the hearing that took place on March 13, 2013. Again, I apologize if the following goes over anyone's head. Trust me. I had to read the senator's question a dozen times before breaking the code that confounded Clapper.

SENATOR WYDEN: I was wondering to see if you can give me a yes or no answer to the question: does the NSA collect any type of data at all on millions or hundreds of millions of Americans?

DIRECTOR OF NATIONAL INTELLIGENCE JAMES CLAPPER: No, sir.

Of course, thanks to whistleblower Edward Snowden and his leaking of classified information, we now know that James Robert Clapper is a liar. Or, in fairness, maybe he legitimately has difficulties decoding yes and no questions.

A final point regarding the visceral *View*. Leave it to Joy Behar to screech in immediately after Clapper finished his rendition of "my dog ate my homework" to remind the audience that "Trump lies nine times a day according to the *New York Times*."

Nice pivot, Joy, and thank you for your contribution to our society. Now if you really want to perform a public service, can you please rip out your vocal cords before you annoy another human being.

Wow! My apologies. That was a bit harsh. I think I might be turning into a Democrat.

Twitter to the Rescue

It's been said that Representative James Clyburn is the one who resuscitated Biden's campaign in the South Carolina primary. Maybe that's true, but it was Jack Dorsey who saved the VP's ass. Like Bruce Wayne responding to the Bat-Signal, Dorsey and his minions at Twitter came to Biden's rescue.

Some believe that Twitter's censoring of the *New York Post* brought more exposure to the story than it would've otherwise. To what I say nonsense. The story was huge regardless. The only thing Twitter did by playing the communist censorship card was provide shade to a desperate senile old man. Instead of the news cycle being exclusively about Hunter, the media now had another angle to play while still pretending to be journalists.

On October 18, 2020, columnist Miranda Devine of the *New York Post* wrote an op-ed on the step-by-step timeline regarding Hunter Biden and his infamous laptop from hell. The piece was straightforward, starting with how they came into possession of the hard drive and everything that proceeded. Devine finished her detailed work with an interesting observation:

> The [*New York*] *Post* has been transparent about the provenance of the material we have published. We stand by our reporting and the authenticity of the material. It's hard to believe the rest of America's media does not want to know the full story about a man running for president.

Leading the parade of the see no evil, hear no evil, speak no evil mantras were Twitter billionaire snowflake CEO Jack Dorsey and Facebook's Mark Zuckerberg. After what was perceived to be an unfair advantage when it came to social media use by the Trump campaign in 2016, algorithms were now designed to flag and censor posts. Similar to the "Surgeon General's Warning" found on a pack of cigarettes, Twitter posted the following if anyone tried accessing the *New York Post* after the release of the Hunter Biden laptop story:

> *Warning: this link may be unsafe*
> *…nypost.com2020/10/14email-reveals-how hunter-biden-introduced-ukrainian-biz-manto dad/…*
> *The link you are trying to access has been identified by Twitter or our partners as being potentially spammy or unsafe, in accordance with Twitter's url*

policy. This link could fall into any one of the below categories:

- malicious links that could steal personal information or *harm electronic devices*
- spammy links that mislead people or *disrupt* their experience
- violent or misleading content that could lead to *real-world-harm*
- certain categories of content that, if posted directly on Twitter, are a violation of the *Twitter Rules*
- *I'm Jack Dorsey, and I'm one weird mother…*

I don't know about anyone else, but if I read that apocalyptic warning (except for that last one that must've been inserted via a computer hack), I'd unplug my laptop and hide in the bathtub. After all, that dangerous *New York Post* isn't following *the Twitter rules*, so they must be either trying to harm my computer or brain or end the world.

As for the more polished Zuckerberg, he champions the First Amendment at congressional hearings regarding the importance of free speech and how his company is not a publisher. The Facebook CEO states that he doesn't seek to be an "arbiter of truth." However, his words and his company's actions weren't on the same page when Facebook decided to join Twitter in censoring the *New York Post* article.

Let's compare Patrick Henry and Voltaire to Dorsey and Zuckerberg:

"Give me liberty, or give me death!" said patriot Patrick Henry at the Second Virginia Convention in 1775. The words became a rallying cry for the newly forming nation.

"I disapprove of what you say, but I will defend to the death your right to say it." Attributed to Francois-Marie Arouet, or better known as Voltaire. On several occasions, the French Enlightenment thinker Voltaire was imprisoned for his outspoken beliefs on tolerance toward

different religions and speech. The quote describes just how deeply Voltaire believed in the importance of freedom of speech.

Mark Zuckerberg: *"I don't think it's right for a private company to censor politicians."*

Jack Dorsey: *"I love espadrilles. And this glass of wine. And the word 'asperity.'"*

Note: I went back fifteen years to find something interesting that Jack Dorsey said, and trust me, that previous quote was about as good as it gets.

During a speech in 2019 in New York City, nearly a year to the date before Twitter took the unprecedented action of removing the feed to the *New York Post* story from its site, Dorsey said the following regarding freedom of speech:

"We talk a lot about speech and expression, and we don't talk about reach enough, and we don't talk about amplification."

Mr. Dorsey, who the hell elected you and put you in charge of what the media are allowed to report. Oops, my apologies Senator Cruz, I nearly forgot you already used that line when you tore a new ass into the nose-ring billionaire. Let's try this again. Mr. Dorsey, can you please explain how shutting down the Twitter feed to a major US publication is in the best interest of freedom of speech, and furthermore, how the hell does it jive with your wanting more "reach" and "amplification"?

Allow me to answer this one for the weird wonder boy. It doesn't jive because Mr. Dorsey and the rest of his idiots at Twitter despise the right and embrace the Marxist left. That's why the only tweets to be flagged were directed at one side of the political aisle.

Once Twitter implemented their new "rules," the leftist at Twitter had a field day censoring POTUS. Here's an example. When Trump posted a tweet regarding that mail-in ballots would result in a "rigged election," Twitter flagged the POTUS tweet by attaching that its content "violated its civic integrity policy." Mind you that the tech giant allows Iran's Ayatollah Khamenei to tweet freely about calling for the genocide of the Israeli people, but Trump's tweets get flagged. Allow me to share the *genius* behind Twitter's reasoning for the double-standard:

"The elimination of Israel is nothing more than foreign policy saber-rattling..."

To further explain why the Iranian dictator's tweets are not blocked, the Twitter spokesperson said that the Ayatollah's tweets fall under the category of *"commentary on political issues of the day"* while Trump's could *"inspire harm."*

I don't know how much the spokesperson for Twitter makes, but I think I speak for everyone when I say anyone who can pull crap out of the air like that deserves a raise.

While we're on the topic of Twitter employees, please allow me to introduce Yoel Roth, head of site integrity. What exactly does Mr. Roth do? Well, he's in charge of policing the tweets. And how does one get to be "head of site integrity" at the big tech company, you ask? Well, apparently, sending a tweet calling the Trump team *"actual Nazis in the White House"* seems to go a long way in securing an executive position at Twitter that has the word *integrity* in its title. In fairness to Mr. Roth, he never liked Trump from the beginning. Going all the way back to election night of 2016, Roth tweeted: *"I'm just saying, we fly over those states that voted for a racist tangerine for a reason."* And if you think Mr. Roth cooled things off with the highly inappropriate comparisons to Nazis, well, here's a tweet by the smug elitist referring to White House counselor Kellyanne Conway: *"Today on Meet the Press, we're speaking with Joseph Goebbels about the first one hundred days..."*

Now, with employees like that, why would anyone think there might be some bias at Twitter?

We're Still Looking for Hunter

Prior to his laptop screwup, Hunter opened up about his addiction and the pain it had caused him and his family in *a Harper's Bazaar* interview:

"I was in the darkness... You don't get rid of it. You figure out how to deal with it."

For Hunter, dealing with *it* meant making lots of money through his father's connections, getting a stripper pregnant, and having an affair with his late brother's widow. Now, for the record, two out of three of the previously mentioned occurrences mean very little to me. However, when the son of a vice president is making millions for doing nothing from countries that his father is the lead rep on, I would think maybe, and I'm just shooting in the dark here, but just maybe one of these millennial hotshots with a graduate degree from some fancy place like Northwestern University's Medill School could do something that remotely resembles what we used to call journalism. But that's just some crazy BOWFOG talk.

Instead, the press writes fluff stories about how Joe Biden is a great family man. Well, I guess if being a good family man is providing your son, your brothers, and your sister cushy jobs that pay millions for doing nothing at the taxpayer's expense, then I'd have to agree. All I was hoping for was that maybe the press would do a little homework and ask a few questions. Perhaps Hunter Biden is more than qualified to run a 1.5 billion-dollar hedge fund out of China, and his skills on the Burisma board in Ukraine were second to none, but would it have killed a reporter to have asked Joe why his son was doing business with countries he himself had political influence over?

To illustrate just how skewed the *fake news* is toward the chubby orange-hair guy, the *Washington Times* reported in the summer of 2020 that the President's negative press coverage was an astounding 95 percent negative on major broadcast networks. At first, I was shocked that Trump garnered even 5 percent positive press until it was revealed in the study that it wasn't as much positive as it was neutral. The same study showed Biden received 67 percent positive evaluative statements from the same ABC, CBS, and NBC news outlets. Okay, allow me to put on my Mr. Sarcasm hat:

I guess the press couldn't find any negative stories to run on a senile seventy-seven-year-old presidential candidate that's been in politics for forty-seven years, has millions of dollars' worth of properties, been wrong on every major foreign and domestic decision he's ever been involved with (FYI, he was against killing Bin Laden and his '87 and '94 crime bills disproportionately incarcerated blacks as compared to whites) and has a son that gift-wrapped a Pulitzer for any reporter willing to write about all the misdeeds on the Biden syndicate. Instead, we get, "Joe, what flavor is your ice cream today?"

To summarize, Trump looks and acts like a buffoon but had policies to strengthen America and get things done. In contrast, aviator sunglass-wearing Biden has the porcelain veneers smile and politician-charm but is entirely void of any substance. The American people, along with a few van loads of ballots marked for Biden, have spoken and have chosen the empty vessel over Rodney Dangerfield. It's that simple.

One point on the 2020 election and for those of you who think it was stolen: of course, the election was fixed, but it doesn't matter. The Republicans could've worked on election reform at any time but chose not to. So don't start crying that it wasn't fair. Guess what? Life isn't fair, and Democrats cheat better than Republicans. If either of these two facts comes as a shock, it's time to remove the tinfoil from your head and come back to reality.

Note: I'm not big into social media. The only reason I opened a Facebook account in 2018 was to promote my first book... I sold six copies before shutting it down. I was told by people smarter than me that I should at least belong to Twitter. I can proudly say that I've never tweeted or retweeted in all the years I've had an account. So why keep the Twitter account? Two reasons: Firstly, the only contact I have in the media world uses the Twitter messaging platform to correspond with me. The second is to follow Dinesh. Here's how the filmmaker described the 2020 election in 140-characters or less:

Dinesh D'Souza @ DineshDSouza

> *The Supreme Court doesn't want to look at fraud. The DOJ is MIA. The media tacitly supports the fraud while publicly pretending there is none. The GOP knew this was coming but didn't do anything to stop it. Does it follow then that the bad guys are going to get away with it?*

I know it's a rhetorical question, but since Mr. D'Souza went through all the trouble of sending that tweet on my birthday (December 16, 2020), I feel it's only fair to respond with the tragically obvious one-word answer: *yes!*

Coup d'état Deux

For the second time in four years, a coup attempt was perpetrated against the land's highest office. Tragically and against all rules of law, the second time was successful. How could such an event happen in America? Well, instead of the use of FISA warrants mixed in with corrupt government officials to carry out the misdeeds, the modus operandi was cloaked in mail-in-ballots and—yes, you guessed it—more corrupt government officials.

The argument by the Democrats going into the 2020 election was simple: *"There's never been any proof that mail-in ballots aren't secure."*

Of course, anyone who wanted every legal vote to count would understand via an ounce of common sense that a mass mailing out of nearly one hundred million ballots would create at a minimum an accountability issue and, more likely than not, mass fraud. The libs who thrive on chaos and unaccountability found the perfect vessel in mail-in ballots. In conflating the secure absentee ballots with the mass dumping of millions of filings to everyone listed on the voter roll, dead or alive, the left was able to make the convincing argument that the hemlock was safe to drink.

However, leading up to the 2020 election, those who hadn't blindly drunk the crap the left was doling out tried voicing their concerns. One way to bring some rational acceptance that mass mail-in ballots were a disaster waiting to happen, Trump officials began citing the 2005 bipartisan report by the Federal Election Reform Commission, cochaired by former president Jimmy Carter and former secretary of state James Baker. In the report, the commission concluded that *"mail-in voting is fraught with the risk of fraud and coercion."* Those in favor of the mail-in ballots were quick to correct Carter's earlier view by explaining that he was in favor of expanding the program and that he had been urging federal and state governments to do so. Those same advocates failed to mention in the same May of 2020 statement by the former president that he suggested to "provide adequate funding as quickly as possible to allow for the additional planning, preparation, equipment, and public messaging that will be required." There was nothing to suggest that even the most inept president in history (Carter) thought it was a good idea to send out one hundred million ballots and hope for the best.

If anyone thinks there weren't any significant issues by states dumping ballots in the mail at an unprecedented rate, please feel free to shed light on the following questions and anomalies:

- For only the second time in history, a candidate won the presidential election without winning Ohio or Florida (both states going to Trump). Coincidentally or not, the previously mentioned states had safeguards in place for voter fraud in the 2020 election, and neither state needed to stop the count during the election evening and restart again.
- Why was the counting stopped in several critical states at approximately the same time? Note: the president was significantly leading in four of those states (GA, PA, MI, WI) before the interruption and, by morning, mysteriously found himself trailing.
- Why were windows boarded up in Detroit to prevent observers from witnessing the counting?
- Why were dead people, out-of-state residents, and felons allowed to vote?
- How did a Republican incumbent lose the White House, but the party gained significant seats in the House and lose only two seats in the Senate?
- How can more people vote in a county than there were registered?
- Then there's the statistical anomaly regarding the eighteen out of the nineteen bellwether counties that historically

indicate the eventual winner going for Trump. I guess that makes it eighteen out of twenty now.

- How was it that Biden underperformed with African Americans everywhere in the United States except for four key swing cities: Atlanta, GA; Detroit, MI; Philadelphia, PA; and Milwaukee, WI?
- Coincidentally or not, all four states stopped their count the night before with Trump leading, and all four had significant irregularities with their election process.
- Why weren't signatures authenticated on mail-in ballots?
- And finally, how was it that hundreds of thousands of mail-in ballots were processed without a crease?

I like to call this last point "the obvious."

The reason detectives are good at what they do is not because they're geniuses but because dishonest people are stupid. Take George W. Bush for an example. Let's face it, "W" is not exactly the brightest bulb on the Christmas tree but because of his daddy and the Republican machine, he became president.

In 2004, Dan Rather and *60 Minutes* broke a story that George W. Bush's National Guard service was a sham. The piece described how Bush received a cushy assignment in a Texas unit via a political favor, along with documentation that showed an unauthorized absence for over a year during 1972–1973. *If true*, leave it to Bush to scam his way into a sweet stateside gig like the 147th Fighter-Interceptor Group as boys his age were getting blown to smithereens in Vietnam, and he still couldn't do the minimum of showing up once a month. Unbelievable!

The Killian document, as it was referred to, was used to corroborate the story. Unfortunately for CBS, Rather, and four executives who were dismissed over the fiasco, the papers in question turned out to be bogus. The smoking gun, if you will, was in the document itself. The reasoning behind why it couldn't have been genuine was the print on the memos did not match the typewriter lettering used in the early 1970s and was more in line with Microsoft Word. Something that didn't exist at the time.

Sadly, the damage to Rather's otherwise remarkable career had taken a severe blow. Less than two years after airing the National Guard story, the newsman's forty-four years at CBS came to an acrimonious end.

On a personal note, I had the pleasure of meeting Dan Rather on several occasions. We were first introduced to one another by a mutual friend, Father Tim, who was a frequent guest at the West Fifty-Seventh Street CBS studio. At the time, I was a police officer in the nearby Midtown North Precinct. Over the years, while I was in my police uniform, I had the distinct privilege of meeting numerous celebrities, politicians, and athletes. Throughout that time, nobody was more gracious and respectful toward me and the uniform I wore than Mr. Rather. Thank you, sir.

So what do George W. Bush, Dan Rather, and non-creased ballots have to do with one another?

A few years after the National Guard story, I was watching a documentary on the 1972 Republican National Convention. The camera was scanning the crowd and stopped on the Bush family. There was George senior, the matriarch of the family Barbara, and long behold, there was a George W. sighting. I began to chuckle at his hippie hairstyle when I realized Rather's report was right all along. Having served in the Army Reserve myself, I can tell you there is no way one can get their hair to grow over their ears. The reason is simple. With drill every four weeks, and the mandatory inspection of uniform, boots, and grooming taking place at each, there's no way one's hair can grow that long in between drill appearances unless one wasn't attending. *Bingo!* There it was in plain sight for everyone to see. The idiot forgot to at least look like a soldier while he was busy drinking and snorting in West Texas. And those uncreased mail-in ballots—*how the hell did people put their ballot in the envelope without folding them? Bingo again!* Those ballots, hundreds of thousands, never saw the inside of an envelope because they never arrived via the postal system. So if they weren't delivered via the postal system, which is the law, how then did they magically appear at the voting stations in Detroit, Atlanta, Milwaukee, and Philadelphia so crisp and clean? Well, maybe those poll workers used Obama's magic wand. Or, and

I'm just shooting in the dark here, some dishonest individuals running several key polling locations cheated.

A Final Thought on Journalism

Starting with my first book, I like to start every chapter with the commonly-used practice of providing a quote. I use the technique to set the tone for what's to come. For the first time, I'd like to end with a few quotes. Each of which should give us pause when it comes to where this nation is going with our precious First Amendment.

> *Our Republic and its press will rise or fall together.* (Newspaper crusader Joseph Pulitzer)

> *The Revolution will be complete when the language is perfect.* (From George Orwell's dystopian novella "*1984.*")

In the spirit of late Supreme Court Justice Louis D. Brandeis of "more speech, not enforced silence," this author declares that journalism's death will not come from reporting a false story but rather the story that never gets told.

Chapter 8

Judeo-Christian Values
and the Bible

*God writes the gospel not in the Bible alone, but
on trees and flowers and clouds and stars.*

—Martin Luther

Each year, over ten million tourists flock to the Louvre Museum in Paris to see some of history's most renowned pieces of artwork. In 1984, Chinese-American architect I. M. Pei was commissioned to modernize the entranceway to the world's largest museum. Pie's seventy-foot tall iconic glass and steel pyramid (Pyramide du Louvre) is what now stands in its place.

As tourists make their way around the twelfth-century fortress, they begin to take in classics like the rare Greek marble statue *The Winged Victory of Samothrace* and portraits such as the *Coronation of Napolean* and, of course, *The Mona Lisa*. However, in one part of the museum, there is a curious black stone pillar erected over seven feet tall. It's doubtful anyone would mistake the work for a da Vinci or Michelangelo, but its significance is still worthy of belonging among the classics. The piece I'm referring to is the Code of Hammurabi. Inscribed on the single, four-ton slab of black stone stele are 282 laws and punishments that King Hammurabi (reign 1792–1750 BC) enacted on his Babylonian subjects. The brutally strict code of justice outlined various standards depending if an individual was a landowner, freedmen, or slave. The concept of all men being equal under the law, leniency, and rehabilitation for offenders wasn't exactly in vogue with a king who punished those found guilty by removing body parts—eyes, hands, breasts, etc. Proving one's guilt or innocents would rely less on evidence and more on their swimming ability. It was common practice to have the accused pushed into the Euphrates River. If the individual returned safely to shore, they were innocent; if not, they were deemed guilty, as well as dead.

The Law

In 1 Timothy 1:9, it states, *"The law is not made for a righteous man, but for the lawless and disobedient."* In essence, the scripture means to protect the good and punish the bad. Unfortunately, as lawmakers pass bills to help protect the evildoers and restrict law-abiding citizens, we can see how the system has lost touch with its purpose. The individual who wishes to pray at a public school event is now public enemy no. 1. The soldier who risked his or her life by taking up arms in defense of our Constitution is denied a firearm upon their return home. Instead of upholding the rule of law, there are those in the government who would rather undermine it at every opportunity to further a left-wing agenda. This two-tier justice system works perfectly well as long as one is on the correct tier.

Our framers built a Constitution with Jehovah at the center and the laws He provided as our foundation. The Code of Hammurabi may have made for a great historical discovery for the French archaeologist who discovered it in 1901, but its relevance to our laws compared to the Ten Commandments is nonexistent. So, with the base of our laws set, these learned men began the arduous task of putting together a document to represent the newly formed republic. Looking back to the royal charter of rights agreed to by King John of England, better known as the Magna Carta (1215), they saw equality for all under the law, fair trials for the accused, church free from governmental interference, and the right for free citizens to own property. The 1689 English Bill of Rights outlined fundamental liberties and concepts that may sound familiar as well:

- Freedom of speech in parliament
- Freedom to bear arms for self-defense
- Freedom from cruel and unusual punishment and excessive bail
- Freedom of fines and forfeitures without a trial

Our framers formed our judicial system by emphasizing the law's equal application and not whether one can swim like Michael Phelps.

When done, our framers had created a constitutional republic. Article 4, Section 4 of the US Constitution, makes clear that each state maintains a republican form of government. When we recite the Pledge of Allegiance, we do so to honor our flag (nation), which is a constitutional republic, not a democracy. Our Founders were careful to exclude such a word knowing that it could easily lead to a tyrannical majority.

The glaring difference between a republic and democracy is the source of its authority. In a democracy, whichever way the prevailing winds are blowing will determine its moral path at any given time.

Let's see what some of our Founding Fathers had to say about democracy and republicanism:

- John Adams: "Remember, democracy never lasts long. It soon wastes, exhausts, and murders itself."
- Benjamin Rush: "A simple democracy is the devil's own government."
- Noah Webster: "Citizens should early understand that the genuine source of correct republican principles is the Bible, particularly the New Testament, or the Christian religion."
- James Madison: "Had every Athenian citizen been a Socrates, every Athenian assembly would still have been a mob."

Before Madison traveled to Philadelphia in 1787 for the Constitutional Convention, Virginia's young assembly member buried himself in books on failed democracies throughout history. He concluded the demise of all these previous democracies was the rule of demagogues and mobs.

In "Federalist No. 10," Madison warned of impetuous gangs as factions and defined them as *"united and actuated by some common impulse of passion, or of interest, adversed to the rights of other citizens, or to the permanent and aggregate interests of the community"*—what we today recognize as Antifa.

To prevent mob rule and give our republic a divided government, Madison proposed his Virginia Plan, a government made up of three branches (legislative, executive, and judicial).

Side note: During the Peloponnesian War, the Athenians abided by the "might makes right" philosophy when it came to imposing their will. Tragically, for the peaceful people on the island of Melos, this meant accept Athens as their new sovereignty or be destroyed. After the Melians refused to submit, the Athenians laid siege to the island, killing all the men and enslaving the women and children. In Thucydides's *History of the Peloponnesian War*, the Athenian general gives account to the lack of morality by stating, *"The strong do what they can, and the weak suffer what they must."*

Therein lies the dangers of mob rule as we march toward single-party dominance.

No One Is above the Law

With the rule of law and our Constitution under constant attack by the liberal elite, a two-tier justice system has emerged. For anyone skeptical or who thinks this author's assessment isn't warranted, I would ask to observe some of the blatant double standards that exist.

Classified Information:

- When Machinist Mate First Class Kristian Saucier took six pictures of his work area in a restricted area of the nuclear-powered attack submarine USS *Alexandria*, the Navy sailor was tried, convicted, and served a year in prison.

• When secretary of state Hillary Clinton kept top-secret classified material on a private server, and then acid washed said server after it was subpoenaed by the FBI, destroying 33,000 emails in the process, she was told that she'd been a bad little girl by FBI Director Comey and never to do it again.

WTF no. 1: How was it that a naïve decorated sailor with no harmful intent or malice toward his country served one year in the brig, and Hillary commits about a half a dozen felonies and goes scot-free? Fortunately, in this particular case, justice was finally served when Saucier was pardoned by President Trump in 2018 while Hillary was sentenced to remain married to a pedophile with an obsession for blue dresses.

Perjury:

• What do Bill Clinton, John Brennan, and James Clapper all have in common? All three lied under oath; however, not one of them had the pleasurable experience of having twenty-nine FBI agents raid their home in the early morning hours with a FROG team of specially trained agents hovering in the nearby Fort Lauderdale waters.

• As for Roger Stone, he lied under oath and was given the full Gestapo treatment—FROG team and all. Stone was so dangerous that before lunch on the very same day the KGB carted him away—my bad, I mean FBI. The judge allowed him to post bond and return to the comfort of his hideout.

WTF no. 2: How Brennan and Clapper can show their faces on news programs as though they speak with moral superiority is absolutely laughable. But the chutzpah has to go to Bubba. President Clinton was caught lying five times to Independent Counsel Kenneth Starr during his deposition. When Bubba was asked, "Did you have an extramarital affair with Monica Lewinsky?" He answered under oath,

"No." However, after the stained blue dress *burst* onto the scene, the Rhodes Scholarship recipient used the excuse that he thought having "oral sex" performed on him was different than "sexual relations." Once again, in the Clinton fantasy island world of delusional thinking, the forty-second president truly believed he was forthcoming in his answer.

But this next one has to be my favorite. When William Jefferson Clinton was asked if he had touched Monica Lewinsky's breast while he was in the Oval Office, Slick Willy replied, *"That is not my recollection."*

All right, people. Let's get real. First, for the record, I'm happily married and would never stray from my beautiful wife for three simple reasons: she's my best friend, I love her and respect her with all my heart, and her hot Colombian blood would do a Lorena Bobbitt on my private parts faster than a hot knife through melted butter. That said, before taking my vows, I can remember each and every time I rounded first base and slid safely into second. So I'm pretty sure if I was the president of the United States hanging out (no pun intended) in the Oval Office, I'd remember touching a twenty-two-year-old White House intern's breast. So, Bubba, I'm sorry, but *"That's not my recollection"* has to be the lamest bullshit excuse of an excuse in the history of sorry-ass excuses. But from one guy to another, I give you props for trying. Now hurry up, it's your turn to relieve Stephanopoulos and rub Hillary's bunions!

Taxes:

- Since Trump took office in 2016, the media had been obsessed with obtaining 45's tax returns—and apparently, so was the attorney general of New York State Letitia James and Manhattan's district attorney Cyrus Vance, both Democrats. Together, the two had been on a KGB fishing expedition. Instead of investigating crimes, the two went with the "show me the man, and I'll show you the crime" methodology of doling out their form of justice. As for Trump's taxes and the bias Empire State politicians, I guess we'll just have to wait to see if they can reel in the orange-hair whale.

- Does anyone know how much Joe Biden is worth? Does anyone know how a guy who's been in public service his entire life owns numerous multimillion-dollar properties? Does anyone know who the mysterious "Big Guy" is in Hunter's infamous emails referring to that person's 10 percent finder's fee cut? Does anyone know why Hunter has been giving his father 50 percent of everything he makes? Does anyone know why the IRS hasn't opened up an investigation on Biden Inc.? *These questions—and many others—will be answered in the next episode of... Soap.*

WTF no. 3: This is a perfect example of the hypocrisy and dangers we find in today's powerful elite. Those in power do whatever the hell they please and then use their positions to seek vengeance against their adversaries.

Impeachment No. 1:

- Congress impeached President Trump for threatening to withhold aid from a country that nine and a half people out of ten couldn't find on a map. The Democrats insisted that Trump's actions showed he intended to influence the presidential election.
- Pelosi withheld hundreds of billions of already appropriated money for small businesses struggling during the pandemic crisis for political purposes. So as businesses closed their doors at an alarming rate, Crazy Nancy was doing the same thing she was accusing Trump of doing. The only difference was Trump was being accused of screwing Ukrainians (which he never did) while Pelosi openly stuck it to the American working-class people with the sole purpose of influencing an election.

WTF no. 4: The despicable part of the 2020 impeachment charade against Trump was the fact that it was nothing more than a fulfillment of a campaign promise made by bloodthirsty Dems.

Sadly, with the new precedent set so law, impeachment proceedings will no longer be used on the rarest of occasions. Instead, it will be a weapon to be implemented when opposing political parties control the House and the executive branch.

I want to make a *prediction*. As I write this book, the Hunter Biden scandal is just getting started. As the dominos begin to fall, you will hear Democrat leaders in an attempt to distract from seeking the truth cry, *"This is nothing but a political hitjob."* Funny, because when the left was trying to get Trump via a political hit job, they preached, "No one is above the law." Hypocrisy; double standards; and their motto, "Do as thee, not as me," are some of the fine qualities representing the heart of today's political leaders.

Note: The rights given to us by our Creator and recognized by our Founders are under attack from this very same party that has lost its way. Tragically, the document that acknowledges these rights is the same one that those on the left are now doing their best to destroy in the attempt to separate us from God. This separation and the rewriting of our United States Constitution is the endgame. Once God is dismissed from society, the secular government will remove all references to His existence and then replace any individual's rights with the community, otherwise known as *communism*.

Faith

> *Without faith no one can please God. Whoever comes to God must believe that he is real and that he rewards those who sincerely try to find him.* (Heb. 11:6 ERV)

I'm going to take a shot in the dark and say not too many atheists lined up to buy a book titled *Godless v. Liberty*, but if someone had by mistake, I'm guessing somewhere between the introduction and chapter 1, my book would've found its way onto the kindling pile. As for the agnostic who is committed to *nothing* or for people like my good Canadian buddy Jeff, who subscribes to the "Chinese buffet" philosophy when describing his views of picking and choosing what he likes regarding his Jewish faith, this section of the book is for them.

The Bible

So how can God's existence and all his beautiful gifts be obscured to some but not to others? The answer lies in one's perspective. Most of us, as individuals, believe that we are at the center of the universe. Wherever that person is at any particular moment becomes "here" and everyone else who is not there is elsewhere. The thought that maybe the person doing the observing is the one who is elsewhere never seems to cross that person's mind. Why? It's because of perspective. So if I read a book that has never been proved wrong and has had prophecy after prophecy come to fruition, of course, I'm going to believe. Conversely, if someone never read the book or barely skimmed through some pages because they found it uninteresting, then that person's perspective would be completely different.

Hopefully, when I'm done making a case for the power of faith, it will help bring those willing to open up their hearts and minds closer to our Creator, along with a newfound appreciation for the greatest book ever written, the Bible. There is another reason for me to take the time to explain the authenticity of the Bible. Although hundreds of prophecies listed in the Bible have already come to fruition, there are still many more waiting to be fulfilled. To comprehend what is coming, I believe it's imperative to appreciate what has already occurred. Or another way of saying it would be to borrow George Santayana's words: *"To know your future, you must know your past."*

In a span of over 1,600 years, the Bible was written in Greek, Hebrew, and to a lesser extent, Aramaic. Forty authors across three continents wrote the sixty-six books comprising of the Bible. Yet, somehow, the entire Bible is harmonious, truthful, and honest. Impressive, yes, but I know this still isn't enough to convince my buddy Jeff, who, by the way, is the slowest golfer on the planet. So here we go! Please try and keep up, Mr. Gossack.

No Strings Attached

In ancient times, many believed that the planet was flat and maybe even sat on a giant beast. It wasn't like they had the luxury of Doppler radar to see that we were just one big unattached rock flying through the universe. However, in Job (26:7), considered to be the oldest book in the Bible, it stated 3,500 years ago:

"He spreads out the northern skies over empty spaces; he suspends the earth over nothing."

In Isaiah 40:22 ERV, the scriptures reveal to us that the earth is round:

"It is the Lord who sits above the circle of the earth."

Deep-Sea Fishing

I'm going to go out on a limb and say that in Job's time, there weren't any deep-sea diving cameras or high-tech submarines roaming around the ocean floor. If my assumption is correct, how can one explain the following verse's origin from anywhere else but God?

"Hast thou entered into the springs of the sea? Or hast thou walked in the search of the depth? (Job 38:16)

At the time, no one knew the sea had springs on the bottom of the ocean floor.

Where's Dino?

In the book of Job, God speaks of a great "behemoth." When the verse was written, the Museum of Natural History's dinosaur exhibition was still a few millennials away from opening. So there was no way of knowing that the creature described in the text could've existed. The scripture recounts an animal as having a *"tail the size of a tree"* and *"bones like bars of iron"* (Job 40:15–24).

Cleanliness Is Next to Godliness

Long before humankind could see deadly microscopic organisms, God instructed us to wash our hands and feet. Dozens of verses address the issue in the Bible and the importance of hygiene.

In James 4:8, we're told to *"cleanse your hands, you sinners, purify your hearts…"*

Isaiah 1:16 tells us, *"Make yourselves clean; remove the evil of your deeds from before my eyes…"*

For those that were ill, Leviticus 14:8–9 gives us the first instructions on quarantining: *"And he who is to be cleansed shall wash his clothes and shave off all his hair and bathe himself in water, and shall be clean. And after that he may come into the camp, but live outside his tent for seven days…"*

If this one scripture had been heeded during the Black Death, millions of lives would've been saved.

In Vienna during the mid-nineteenth century, a young doctor named Ignaz Semmelweis was alarmed by the death rate of mothers giving birth. Dr. Semmelweis connected the lack of hygiene, specifically, doctors failing to wash their hands in between deliveries, contributing to the high death rate. He wasn't able to see the culprit but still had the solution. He ordered every doctor to wash their hands before seeing their next patient. The death rate plummeted immediately from 30 percent to less than 2 percent.

In Genesis 17:12, it states, *"And he that is eight days old shall be circumcised among you, every man child in your generations, he that is born in the house…"*

The scripture gives a specific number of days (eight) when the circumcision is to take place. Maybe to some skeptics, this is just a random number. However, in recent years medical science has shown that it's at this exact moment when the baby's immune system is at its healthiest and the coagulating factor in the blood is at its peak before reversing. In my view, this is anything but a coincidence. Come to think of it, maybe that's why there's no such word in the Hebrew language for *coincidence*.

Blood

It was only a little over a century ago that the practice of blood-letting to prevent or cure ailments was still in use. Just in the twentieth century alone, we went from learning the different blood types to discovering DNA. Today we can reveal more about our health from a simple blood test than at any time in our existence. However, the Bible told us the answers to our health were in the blood thousands of years ago:

> *For the life of the flesh is in the blood...* (Lev. 17:11)

> *Only be sure that thou eat not the blood: for the blood is the life; and thou mayest not eat the life with flesh.* (Deut. 12:23)

God Must be a Sailor

Navy Commander Matthew Fontaine Maury (1806–1873) was home one day listening to his wife read the Bible. When she came to the verse Psalms 8:8 that described *"paths in the sea,"* he asked for her to read it to him again. After listening carefully, Maury realized that God put *paths in the sea* and now needed to find them. The Navy Commander readied himself to set sail but not before observing another verse he thought could prove helpful:

> *Goeth toward the south, and turneth about unto the north; it whirleth about continually, and the wind returneth again according to his circuits.* (Eccles. 1:6)

So, along with discovering the ocean paths that Jehovah spoke of, Maury, known as the father of oceanography, tracked the Northern and Southern Hemispheres' winds, something previously written in the Bible two thousand years earlier. Maury's discovery of the warm and cold continental currents of the ocean and wind patterns significantly reduced the length of future voyages. To this day, the commander's book *Sailing Directions and Physical Geography of the Sea, and Its Meteorology* is still in use.

Going, Going, Gone!

Long before scientist discovered the Second Law of Thermodynamics (the degeneration of all things physical), the Bible let us know that the earth is dying:

> *O Lord, in the beginning you made the earth, and your hands made the sky. These things will disappear, but you will stay. They will all wear out like old clothes.* (Heb. 1:10–11 ERV)

> *Lift up your eyes to the heavens, and look upon the earth beneath: for the heavens shall vanish away like smoke, and the earth shall wax old like a garment, and they that dwell therein shall die in like manner: but my salvation shall be for ever, and my righteousness shall not be abolished.* (Isa. 51:6)

> *Long ago, you made the world. You made the sky with your own hands! The earth and sky will end, but you will live forever! They will wear out like clothes, you will change them. But you never change. You will live forever!* (Ps. 102:25–27 ERV)

Can You Hear Me Now?

As a child, I used to play the telephone game with my little sister, Gwen. We'd take two paper cups, some of my mother's yarn, and pretend we were switchboard operators. Truth be told, I could never understand what the hell she was saying, so I'd have to pull the cup away from my ear and yell to her, "What," but we enjoyed it just the same. Well, that is until Mom noticed all her yarn missing. Fast-forward several decades, and somehow I'm able to talk to my little sis 1,300 miles away in real-time and can hear her as if she were standing right next to me. How is this possible?

The answer lies in Einstein's theory of special relativity, which calculates the speed of light at traveling at a dizzying 186,000 miles per second. Since I'm not a scientist, I'm unable to explain how this is done, but somehow our speech can be sent using light waves traveling at that same speed as light.

In Job 38:35 (NASB), God asks:

"Can you send forth lightnings that they may go And say to you, 'Here we are'?"

It wasn't until more than three millennials later when British scientist James Clerk Maxwell (1831–1879) hypothesized that light waves and electricity were from the same origin. Samuel Morse (1791–1872) used electrical signals to revolutionize long-distance communications via the telegraph. And, in 1988, long after God was using electricity at the speed of light to communicate with Job, AT&T laid the first fiber optic cable across the Atlantic.

"If You Build It, He Will Come"

Jehovah gave Noah some very specific instructions when it came time to build his ark. He told him where he wanted the window and door to be placed, how many levels, the type of wood (gopher), and who was to be on the exclusive passenger list. In the instruction manual, God gave Noah the exact measurements:

"And this is the fashion which thou shall make it of: The length of the ark shall be three hundred cubits, the breadth of it fifty cubits, and the height of it thirty cubits" (Gen. 6:15).

Now, I'm guessing Noah might've been a lot like Kevin Costner's character Ray Kinsella in the movie *Field of Dreams*. Ray heard a voice tell him to construct a baseball field in the middle of his farm. And like Noah, both men had to ignore the naysayers who thought they were crazy. However, instead of Shoeless Joe Jackson showing up upon completion, Noah had *"every living thing of all flesh, two of every sort shalt thou bring into the ark, to keep them alive with thee; they shall be male and female"* (Gen. 6:19).

Some may believe the ark Noah built was nothing more than a myth, a legendary story passed down through generations. But if this was just merely a good bedtime story, how can one explain the phenomenon that took place in Holland in the seventeenth century?

In 1609, a ship was built to the same dimensions Jehovah provided Noah with (30:5:3). What took place next gave birth to a maritime empire in the Netherlands, along with the beginning of a new era in shipbuilding. By 1900, the shipbuilding ratio of 30:5:3 could be found on every large vessel that sailed the seas ("Lloyd's Register of Shipping," *World Almanac*).

Note: Some may doubt there was an ark, but there's scientific proof a global flood occurred. I want to point to two facts. One, all major religions write of an epic flood at some time in their recordings. Two, 85 percent of all rocks found on the earth's surface are composed of sedimentary rock, indicating at some point they were submerged in water.

Let It Rain!

When I was a young student at Saint Patrick's parochial school in Bay Ridge, Brooklyn, I did an oral presentation titled "God's Fountain." I went in front of my classmates and explained the cycle by which water circulated around the planet through a process involving the evaporation of H_2O from the earth's oceans and returning in the form of precipitation. All these years later, I can still recall two remarkable facts. First is the constant recirculation of water that we experience today is the same rain that had fallen on the pharaohs in Egypt thousands of years ago. Second, those in the science field didn't understand the complete water cycle until the 1600s.

So thousands of years prior to my school project, and long before scientist understood the whole "rain sequence thingy," the Bible was already explaining the cycle to us:

> *If the clouds be full of rain, they empty themselves upon the earth...* (Eccles. 11:3)

It is he that buildeth his upper chambers in the heavens, and hath founded his vault upon the earth; he that calleth for the waters of the sea, and poureth them out upon the face of the earth; Jehovah is his name. (Amos 9:6)

All the rivers run into the sea, Yet the sea is not full; unto the place from which the rivers come, There they return again. (Eccles. 1:7)

Note to my buddy Jeff: Let me know when all these little *facts* start to paint the bigger picture that the Bible is the most incredible book ever written! But just in case my frozen friend north of the border is still doubting, here are some prophecies mentioned in the Bible that have come to fruition to the letter:

Daniel

Maybe I'm not supposed to choose a favorite, but if there's one story in the Bible that I love to read over and over again, it's the Book of Daniel. It's the one book Jesus urged more than any other to study to reveal God's plans for the end times and those of His enemies. Here was a nobleman forced into slavery, and through Daniel's faithfulness to God, rose in rank and stature among his captives, including their king, Nebuchadnezzar.

When the king struggled to interpret a dream that was haunting him, he summoned his astrologers and ordered these wise men to explain the vision's meaning to him. One slight problem, the king would not describe the dream to them. The astrologers argued without knowing the details of the king's dream that their task was impossible. As if these men weren't under enough pressure, the king told them if they failed that he'd kill them. When Daniel heard of the pending execution and the reason behind it, he asked to see the king.

The king asked Daniel, "Are you able to tell me what I saw in my dream and interpret it?" Daniel replied, "No wise man, enchanter, magician or diviner can explain to the king the mystery he has asked about, but there is a God in heaven who reveals mysteries. He has shown King Nebuchadnezzar what will happen in days to come. Your dream and the visions that passed through your mind as you were lying in bed are these… Your Majesty looked, and there before you stood a large statue—an enormous, dazzling statue, awesome in appearance. The head of the statue was made of pure gold, its chest and arms of silver, its belly and thighs of bronze, its legs of iron, its feet partly of iron and partly of baked clay. While you were watching, a rock was cut out, but not by human hands. It struck the statue on its feet of iron and clay and smashed them. Then the iron, the clay, the bronze, the silver and the gold were all broken to pieces and became like chaff on a threshing floor in the summer. The wind swept them away without leaving a trace. But the rock that struck the statue became a huge mountain and filled the whole earth. This was the dream, and now we will interpret it to the king. Your Majesty, you are the king of kings. The God of heaven has given you dominion and power and might and glory; in your hands he has placed all mankind and the beasts of the field and the birds in the sky. Wherever they live, he has made you ruler over them all. You are that head of gold. After you, another kingdom will arise, inferior to yours. Next, a third kingdom, one of bronze, will rule over the whole earth. Finally, there will be a fourth kingdom, strong as iron— for iron breaks and smashes everything—and as iron breaks things to pieces, so it will crush and break all others. Just as you saw the feet and toes were partly baked clay and partly of iron, so this will be a divided kingdom; yet it will have some of the strength of iron in it, even as you saw mixed with clay. As the toes were partly iron and partly clay, so this kingdom will be partly strong and partly brittle. And just as you saw the iron mixed with baked clay, so the people will be a mixture and will not remain united, any more than iron mixes with clay. In the time of those kings, the God of heaven will set up a kingdom that will never be destroyed, nor will it be left to another people. It will crush all those kingdoms and bring them to an end, but it will itself endure forever. This is the meaning of the vision of the rock cut out of a mountain, but not by human hands—a rock that broke the iron, the bronze, the clay, the silver and the gold to pieces. The great God has shown the king what will take place in the future. The dream is true and its interpretation trustworthy. (Dan. 2:26–45 ERV)

Daniel's interpretation of King Nebuchadnezzar's dream shows that the statue's gold head represents Babylon as the first empire. When the Persian king Cyrus the Great conquered Babylon in 539 BC, the event gave way to the Persian Empire's rise (chest and arms of silver). When the Greeks defeated the Persian Empire, they became the next great world power (belly and thighs of bronze). As prophesized, each empire rose and fell. Daniel 7:23–24 describes ten horns representing ten kings, along with the "little horn" that appears and uproots three more. If the "little horn" is understood to be Greece, then the three empires that follow are Rome, the United Kingdom, and the United States of America. Each one of these three realms can find its roots stemming back to the previous empire. If all this is true, then the earth's last empire is upon us and God's Kingdom is near.

Thanks to the Dead Sea Scrolls discovered in 1947, we know that Daniel wrote his prophecies well before any of the nations listed rose to power. That means there can be only one of two possibilities. Either Daniel was a heck of a good guesser, or he was a prophet from God? Since I'm looking forward to the rest of Daniel's prophecy coming to fruition and God's Kingdom coming to earth, I'm prayerful it's the latter.

King of Kings

In Matthew 4:4, when Jesus tells Satan: *"Man shall not live by bread alone, but by every word that comes from the mouth of God,"* he is letting us know that the scriptures are the Word of Divine authority. Later in Matthew, Jesus explains to us that *"until heaven and earth pass away, not an iota, not a dot, will pass from the Law until all is accomplished,"* meaning every prophecy written in the Bible will come to pass.

The prophecy written in Zechariah 9:9 speaks of the day when the Son of God will ride *"into Jerusalem on a donkey."* When Jesus did just that, he fulfilled a centuries-old prophetic scripture of the coming of the Messiah, "the anointed one" or, as translated from Hebrew to Greek, "Christ." However, since many people rode into Jerusalem on a donkey, it's fair to seek more definitive evidence that Jesus was indeed the Messiah. After all, if it's proven that Jesus is not, then all the Scriptures that follow cannot be trusted. Conversely, if we can prove that Jesus is the Messiah, then we know the *"scriptures cannot be broken" (John 10:35)*, and God's Word *"is the truth" (John 17:17)*. This is truly an all-or-nothing proposition.

So what scriptures prove to us that Jesus is indeed the Son of God?

Jesus's Birth (Micah 5:2 ERV)

> But you, Bethlehem Ephrathah, are the smallest town in Judah.
> Your family is almost too small to count, but the "Ruler of Israel" will come from you to rule for

Me. His beginnings are from ancient times, from
long, long ago.

Jesus was born in Bethlehem from the bloodline of King David.

Born of a Virgin Mother (Isa. 7:14)

> *Therefore the Lord himself shall give you a*
> *sign; Behold, a virgin shall conceive, and bear a son,*
> *and shall call his name Immanuel.*

Jesus was conceived and born by Mary the Blessed Virgin through the Holy Spirit. By nature, Mary's son was Immanuel (God is with us), but by name, He was Jesus.

Rejected (Isa. 53:3 ERV)

> *He is despised and rejected of men; a man of*
> *sorrows, and acquainted with grief: and we hid as*
> *it were our faces from him; he was despised, and we*
> *esteemed him not.*

Jesus was the Lamb God sacrificed to pay the ransom for the sins of the world. God's only begotten Son was despised and rejected by his own as well as His enemies. Jesus was crucified with criminals (Isa. 53:12) and hated without cause (Ps. 35:19). His detractors mocked him (Ps. 22:7–8) while they spat upon the Son of God (Isa. 50:6). And, as it was foretold over a thousand years before it occurred, Jesus's garments were cast for lots after His crucifixion (Ps. 22:18).

The Messiah Will be a Prophet (Deut. 18:15)

> *The Lord your God will send to you a prophet.*
> *This prophet will come from among your own peo-*
> *ple. And he will be like me. You must listen to him.*

In Luke 21, Jesus prophesized the destruction of the Temple and how *"not one stone will be left upon another."* Less than a generation later, in AD 70, the Temple was torn down by Titus's Roman soldiers.

In Matthew 24, the disciples ask Jesus, *"When shall these things be and what shall be the sign of the end of the world?"* Jesus's answer shines light on what is to come:

> *Be careful! Don't let anyone fool you. Many people will come and use my name. They will say, "I am the Messiah." And they will fool many people. You will hear about wars that are being fought. And you will hear stories about other wars beginning. But don't be afraid. These things must happen before the end comes. Nations will fight against other nations. Kingdoms will fight against other kingdoms. There will be times when there is no food for people to eat. And there will be earthquakes in different places. These things are only the beginning of troubles, like the first pains of a woman giving birth. Then you will be arrested and handed over to be punished and killed. People all over the world will hate you because you believe in me. During that time many believers will lose their faith. They will turn against each other and hate each other. Many false prophets will come and cause many people to believe things that are wrong. There will be so much more evil in the world that the love of most believers will grow cold. But the one who remains faithful to the end will be saved. And the Good News I have shared about God's kingdom will be told throughout the world. It will be spread to every nation. Then the end will come. Daniel the prophet spoke about the terrible thing that causes destruction. You will see this terrible thing standing in the holy place... because it will be a time of great trouble. There will*

be more trouble than has ever happened since the beginning of the world. And nothing as bad as that will ever happen again. False messiahs and false prophets will come and do great miracles and wonders, trying to fool the people God has chosen, if that is possible. Now I have warned you about this before it happens. Right after the trouble of those days, this will happen:

> *"The sun will become dark,*
> *and the moon will not give light.*
> *The stars will fall from the sky,*
> *and everything in the sky will be changed."*

Then there will be something in the sky that shows the Son of Man is coming. All the people of the world will cry. Everyone will see the Son of Man coming on the clouds in the sky. He will come with power and great glory. He will use a loud trumpet to send his angels all around the earth. They will gather his chosen people from every part of the earth. The fig tree teaches us a lesson: When its branches become green and soft, and new leaves begin to grow, then you know that summer is very near. In the same way, when you see all these things happening, you will know that the time is very near, already present. I assure you that all these things will happen while some of the people of this time are still living. The whole world, earth and sky, will be destroyed, but my words will last forever.

In the scripture, Jesus is telling us what will transpire before the end of the world as we know it. In 2 Timothy, Paul the Apostle echoes these words when he speaks of the *"perilous times that shall come."* In those days, we shall see an increase in floods, droughts, famines, pestilence, blasphemers, masses void of natural affection, lovers of pleasures more than God, unholy, and children no longer honoring their parents. All one has to do is turn on the six o'clock news or read the newspaper to see with clarity that this prophecy is coming to fruition right before our eyes. However, knowing the exact time when *"heaven and earth shall pass away,"* Jesus is clear that only the Father knows. So for all those false prophets out there predicting exactly when the world will end, the Bible tells us differently.

A Message of Freedom (Isa. 61:1–2)

> *The Spirit of the Lord God is on me. The Lord has chosen me to tell good news to the poor and to comfort those who are sad. He sent me to tell the captives and prisoners that they have been set free, He sent me to announce that the time has come for the Lord to show his kindness, when our God will also punish evil people. He has sent me to comfort those who are sad.*

These words were written over seven centuries before Jesus was born. Throughout Jesus's ministry, He spread the good news to the poor and comforted the sad with the promise of God's Kingdom.

Betrayal (Ps. 41:9 ERV)

> *My best friend, the one I trusted, the one who ate with me—even he has turned against me.*

The prophecy came to fruition when the betrayer, Judas Iscariot, gave up the Son of God for thirty pieces of silver to the Sanhedrin in the Garden of Gethsemane by kissing Jesus and calling him "Rabbi." In John 17:11–12 (ERV), Jesus prays to His Father:

> *Now I am coming to You. I will not stay in the world, but these followers of mine are still in the world Holy Father, keep them safe by the power*

of your name—the name you gave me. Then they will be one, just as you and I are one. While I was with them, I kept them safe by the power of your name—the name you gave me. I protected them. And only one of them was lost—the one who was sure to be lost. This was to show the truth of what the Scriptures said would happen.

These are just a few of the many prophecies that assure us that Jesus is indeed the Messiah.

More Prophecies Fulfilled

The Balfour *Declaration* of 1917, named after Lord Balfour, committed the United Kingdom to establish in Palestine a national home for the Jewish people. Lord Balfour believed the Almighty chose him to be the one to carry out the task of restoring the Jewish people to their homeland, and in doing so, fulfilling a significant ancient prophecy. On May 14, 1948, the State of Israel was established and immediately recognized by President Truman. Over sixty years later, this "rebirth of Israel" was acknowledged by Israel's Prime Minister Benjamin Netanyahu during an address he gave to his cabinet:

> The Balfour Declaration recognized the land of Israel as the national home for the Jewish people and started the international movement that led to Israel's establishment.

So what is the significance of Israel gaining statehood in 1948? To answer this question and understand the prophecy that is coming to fruition in our lifetime, let's take a look at an overview of Israel and what the Bible has to say:

In 586 BC, the First Temple built by Solomon was destroyed by the Neo-Babylonian Empire. A portion of the population, including Daniel, was taken into exile and brought to Babylon. The

Second Temple building commenced upon the return of the Jews to Jerusalem in 538 BC and was completed twenty-three years later. This Temple stood for several centuries until it too was laid to rubble by Titus's army in 70 AD. During the siege, over a million Jews were killed, while many thousands were forced into slavery.

For nearly two-thousand years, the Jewish people spread throughout the globe without a state of their own. Under the Alhambra Decree in 1492, about 200,000 Jews were expelled from Spain. They fled into many neighboring countries, with most immigrating to Poland. A year later, 137,000 Jews were expelled from Sicily, and a few years after that, Portugal and several German cities dismissed their Jewish population. Throughout the following centuries, antisemitism grew. In the mid-eighteenth century, many Jews immigrated back to Palestine under the influence of Messianic predictions. Following America's Revolutionary War, George Washington wrote to the Jewish community in Rhode Island to promise them their right to exercise their religion freely. In his letter, Washington assures their safety, stating, *"Which gives bigotry no sanction...persecution no assistance."* At the time, America and its leaders were predominately Protestant, proving the young nations' commitment toward the First Amendment's religious liberties. By 1930 there were fifteen million Jews scattered throughout the globe. The United States was home to four million while Poland, the Soviet Union, Romania, and Palestine made up a significant portion of the Jewish population. From 1938 to 1945, the Holocaust was responsible for the death of nearly six million Jewish people.

After reading the previous paragraph, one may still find it astounding, and against all odds, that on November 29, 1947, the United Nations approved the creation of a Jewish State, something the prophecies accurately predicted thousands of years ago. The timing of such a remarkable occurrence should not go unnoticed. At the start of the 1940s, there was a serious threat to the Jewish people's existence. Before the decade was over, they would go from their darkest moments to having several prophecies come to fruition, including their return to Palestine.

In the Book of Ezekiel, the priest was given God's task to explain to his people why Jerusalem was destroyed and the preceding banishment from the promised land. In Jehovah's judgment for their breaking of the covenant, He removed the gifts bestowed upon the Jewish people. All of their land, including Jerusalem, the Temple, and the monarchy, were no more. However, all was not lost. In Ezekiel 11:17 and 34:13, the prophet offers hope:

> *Therefore say, Thus saith the Lord God; I will even gather you from the people, and assemble you out of the countries where ye have been scattered, and I will give you the land of Israel.*

> *And I will bring them out from the people, and gather them from the countries, and will bring them to their own land, and feed them upon the mountains of Israel by the rivers, and in all the inhabited places of the country.*

In Deuteronomy 4:27 (ERV) and 30:3–5 (ERV), Moses tells his people:

> *And the Lord shall scatter you among the nations. And only a few of you will be left alive to go to the countries where the Lord will send you.*

> *Then the Lord your God will be kind to you. The Lord your God will make you free again! He will bring you back from the nations where he sent you. Even if you were sent to the farthest parts of the earth, the Lord your God will gather you from there and bring you back. The Lord your God will bring you into the land your ancestors had, and the land will become yours. He will do good to you, and you will have more people in your nation than they ever had.*

In 2 Kings 19:30, Jeremiah writes: *"And the remnant that is escaped of the house of Judah shall yet again take root downward, and bear fruit upward."*

Believe

Here is how some have expressed their reverence for the most remarkable book ever written:

George Washington: "It is impossible to rightly govern the world without God or the Bible."

Ronald Reagan: "Within the covers of the Bible are all the answers for all the problems men face."

Ulysses S. Grant: "The Bible is the sheet-anchor of our liberties."

Charles Dickens: "The New Testament is the very best book that ever was or ever will be known in the world."

Andrew Jackson: "That book…is the rock upon which our republic rests."

Robert E. Lee: "In all my perplexities and distresses, the Bible has never failed to give me light and strength."

Sir Isaac Newton: "I have a fundamental belief in the Bible as the Word of God, written by men who were inspired. I study the Bible daily… I find more sure marks of authenticity in the Bible than in any profane history whatsoever."

Theodore Roosevelt: "No educated man can afford to be ignorant of the Bible."

Mark Twain: "Most people are bothered by those passages of Scriptures they do not understand, but the passages that trouble me are those I do understand."

Dwight Eisenhower: "Our civilization is built upon its [the Bible's] words. In no other book is there such a collection of inspired wisdom, reality, and hope."

Abraham Lincoln: "I believe the Bible is the best gift God has given to man."

John Adams: "It contains more philosophy than all the libraries I have seen."

Our sixth president, John Quincy Adams, frequently wrote to his son George Washington Adams on the Bible and its teachings. Here's an excerpt from one of those letters:

> *The first and almost the only book deserving of universal attention is the Bible. I have myself for many years made it a practice to read the Bible once every year. I have always endeavored to read it with the same spirit and with the same temper of mind which I now recommend to you; that is, with the intention and desire that it may contribute to my advance in wisdom and virtue.*

Our framers recognized the Words of wisdom found in the Bible and the God-given rights bestowed to the individual. When Jefferson writes in the Declaration of Independence, *"We hold these truths to be self-evident, that all men are created equal, that they are endowed by their Creator with certain unalienable rights, that among these are Life, Liberty, and the pursuit of Happiness,"* he is documenting for the first time in human history, a republic that acknowledges the rights bestowed upon by God.

Note: It needs to be recognized that only white men were afforded these rights at the time of Jefferson's writings. Women still weren't permitted to vote, and the evil institution of slavery was allowed to continue. So, although the words in the United States Constitution read *"to form a more perfect Union,"* the reality was the young Judeo-Christian republic still had a ways to go to right many wrongs.

So strong did Alexander Hamilton believe in these God-given rights that he wrote, *"The sacred rights of mankind are not to be rummaged for among old parchments or musty records. They are written, as with a sunbeam in the whole volume of human nature, by the hand of Divinity itself, and can never be erased or obscured by mortal power."*

When Benjamin Franklin addressed the delegates at the Constitutional Convention in 1787, he first reminded each and every one of them that they needed God to be their friend and ally.

He said, *"If a sparrow cannot fall to the ground without His notice, is it probable that an empire can rise without His aid?"* From that day forward, Franklin led a prayer at the Convention at the start of each day.

The Critics

There will always be the skeptics when it comes to God and the Bible. To this day, there are those who say Jesus never existed and that the Bible is nothing more than a great work of fiction written by "creatively smart men of their time." If that's true, why then hasn't anyone come forward to disprove the Bible is the Word of God? Think about it. The New Testament has been around for thousands of years, and the Old Testament longer than that, but no one has been able to disprove their contents. On the contrary. The Bible is proven more authentic with every archaeological find. The discovery of the Dead Sea Scrolls in 1947 corroborated many of the Old Testament Scriptures, especially the books of Daniel and Isaiah.

In 1906, German archaeologist Hugo Winckler discovered the great lost empire of the Hittites. Since the Scriptures make dozens of references to the Hittite Empire and there hadn't been any proof it ever existed, critics were quick to point to the lack of evidence as proof that the Bible was flawed. Winckler unearthed thousands of clay tablets proving that not only did the Hittites exist, but they thrived.

Evangelist Josh McDowell has authored or coauthored over 150 books in his career. In his book, *The Beauty of Intolerance,* McDowell explains how our "Founding Fathers established a new democracy in America…on the premise that humanity was fallen and thus there was a need for a rule of law to curb natural tendencies to follow our own wants and lusts." Is it any wonder as our society grows further away from Jehovah, Jesus, and the Bible that people gain in lust and selfishness? The naysayers will do everything to detract from a book offering a relationship with Jehovah through Jesus Christ while eagerly defending governments under Satan's control.

Here's a final thought on the Bible provided by Josh McDowell:

> *Now here's the picture: 1,600 years, 60 genera-*
> *tions, 40-plus authors, different walks of life, differ-*
> *ent places, different times, different moods, different*
> *continents, three languages, writing on hundreds of*
> *controversial subjects and yet when they are brought*
> *together, there is absolute harmony from beginning*
> *to end.*

Now that I've made the case as to why I believe the Bible is the Word of God, hopefully, we may better understand our responsibilities toward Him, along with the love He has for us. In doing so, we may now attempt to understand what is to come.

Chapter 9

Only the Father Knows

*But that day and hour knoweth no man, no, not
the angels of heaven, but my Father only.*

—Matthew 24:36

I n AD 95, a man by the name of John was exiled to the island of Patmos. Whether this was the same beloved disciple who wrote the Gospel and Letters of John or a different person by the same name, in my view, makes little difference. What's important are the words provided to him by Jehovah describing the Revelation of Jesus Christ. Trying to decipher the symbolic meaning, however, may not be so easy at times. The Irish playwright George Bernard Shaw described it as "A curious record of the visions of a drug addict." Between a beastly seven-headed sea monster, dragons, 144,000 high priests called to duty as missionaries, the sea and moon turning to blood, the unleashing of four apocalyptic horses, and the sounds of trumpets could be a bit intimidating trying to wrap one's mind around. Then there's Revelation 6:12–14 (ERV) that needs no decoding:

> *Then I watched while the Lamb opened the
> sixth seal. There was a great earthquake, and the
> sun became as black as a sackcloth. The full moon
> became like red blood. The stars in the sky fell to
> the earth like a fig tree dropping its figs when the*

wind blows. The sky was split in the middle and both sides rolled up like a scroll. And every mountain and island was moved from its place.

As one can see, there's a lot going on in the only apocalyptic book included in the Bible. To simplify things, I've taken the liberty of breaking Revelation down into three sections: the good, the bad, and the ugly. Understand, the purpose will be to offer a brief overview of the book as it relates to what is going on in the world today and how it shows that we are living in the last days. Yes, the end is near, but what many fail to realize is that Armageddon will usher in a new kingdom, God's Kingdom. That's the good news, but first...

The Bad and The Ugly

The Book of Revelation describes the prophecy of what is to happen before, during, and after Jesus's second return. Some theologians believe that the predictions chronicled have already occurred—this Christian eschatological view is known as *preterism*. It's this author's view that John wrote about events that are still yet to come in the last days—otherwise known as the *futurist approach*. Having listed in the previous chapter all the prophecies that have come to fruition word for word the first time Jesus came, there's no reason, for me anyway, not to believe the warnings listed in Revelation won't come to pass as precisely written. However, the symbolism used in John's writings leaves room for interpretation.

Note: The symbols John describes in Revelation enabled him to express the spiritual experiences he was envisioning. Although the symbolism used may seem foreign today, it would've been consistent with his day's Jewish apocalyptic literature.

In the first verse of chapter 13, John describes a gruesome beast rising from the sea with seven heads and ten horns, and upon his horns ten crowns, and marked with the name of blasphemy. Then John saw another beast come out of the earth. This beast is the false prophet who will force everyone to display the beast's mark of 666.

Without it, no one will be allowed to trade. But how will this come about? Well, we know the devil is the great deceiver who's resourceful and cunning. So the Antichrist won't be brash and dividing, nor will this person be unintelligent or look hideous as Hollywood portrays. On the contrary, this individual will be charismatic and articulate. There will be those who will quickly fall under the spell of this individual's false promises of peace and security when, in fact, his or her goal is just the opposite. This should come as no surprise to anyone, but Satan isn't looking forward to Jesus's return. The prince of darkness has enjoyed ruling over the Earth and will do whatever it takes to retain such power. Who do you think is responsible for all the distractions that are in our lives today? Here's a hint, it's not God. We have 24/7 entertainment at the tip of our fingertips. Violence, pornography, and drugs are so much a part of our society that many have become desensitized to its destructive ways. The Bible foretold of this occurring in Matthew 24:12 (ERV):

"There will be so much more evil in the world that the love of most believers will grow cold."

Satan does not want us to be focused, so he puts roadblocks between Jehovah and us. Through his political minions, he has made God an unwelcomed guest in our schools, made killing babies legal, and changed the definition of marriage. But because my beliefs do not coincide with the secular left, I'm considered the crackpot. Think about the spiritual deterioration that has transpired in our nation in just one generation. What we are witnessing is the devil's last-ditch effort to remain in power. I know many will read these words and ridicule me the same way they did with Noah. But make no mistake, there's another flood coming that will wash away the sins of the earth, starting with Satan. My goal is not to be sucked further into Satan's world but to prepare myself for the second coming of Jesus. Instead of building an ark, I'm building up my spiritual strength because I know things are going to get a whole lot worse before they get better.

In Revelation, Jesus wastes little time telling us just that. The book opens with Jesus's seven letters to the seven churches. He warns them there will be more suffering to come to those loyal to Him. The churches will be forced to choose between compromise and faithfulness. And the devil will cast God's followers into prisons while imposters infiltrate the synagogues.

In chapter 6, John of Patmos describes the worthy Lamb opening the first four seals. With each opening, the Lamb reveals the Four Horsemen of the Apocalypse. The riders unleashed represent God's intervention to bring about a social upheaval for those persecuting Jehovah's people. The first horseman wears a golden crown and rides a white horse. He sets forth to conquer. Upon opening the second seal, God sends forth a red horse whose rider carries a sword that will take peace from the earth. After the third seal is peeled back, a black horse appears whose rider holds a scale for weighing. In these last days of war and upheaval, inflation will make money worthless, and food will be in short supply. Finally, with the fourth seal opening, God sends a horse whose rider is pale and goes by Death's name. Following him is Hades.

> *And power was given unto them over the fourth part of the earth, to kill with sword, and with hunger, and with death, and with the beasts of the earth.* (Rev. 6:8)

More than any other book, it was Daniel's recorded prophecies that Jesus urged His followers to study to reveal God's plans for the end times. In these prophecies, Daniel interprets King Nebuchadnezzar's dream of an enormous statue made of four metal types, each symbolizing a sequence of kingdoms. These kingdoms represented nations that were to follow Babylon and bring much violence upon the earth. That is, until one day when God will send His Kingdom to replace all the nations. It's not until Daniel has a dream of his own that he discovers how this will take place.

At first, Daniel has difficulty understanding his vision until an angelic messenger helps him with its revealing. In the dream, Daniel sees a series of four beasts representing man's prideful nations. There's a lion, a bear, a leopard with four wings on its back, and, finally, a super beast. The last animal displays an array of horns, a common symbol for kings in the Old Testament, with one prominent horn in the image of an arrogant king. The ruler of this ultimate evil empire puts himself above God and goes on to persecute his people. The Ancient of Days, as Daniel refers to God, comes and sets up His throne. He defeats the super beast and exalts the Son of Man on the clouds beside Him.

Side note: In ancient times, similar to now, animals were used to symbolize kingdoms. Today, China is the dragon; the United Kingdom a roaring lion; the old Soviet Union a bear; and the United States of America a bald eagle, a meat-eating carnivore that feeds on flesh. Once these nations put themselves above the Almighty, they turn into wild beasts. Like all governments under Satan's control, they make false promises in order to lure as many as they can away from Jehovah and closer to the devil. The resourceful prince of darkness has an ingenious way of executing his plan. Satan has redefined right and wrong by masking the feeling of guilt and lowering public morals to below the level of depravity. Please don't take my word for it. Simply look at our country and ask the obvious question: Today, right now as a nation, are we honoring Jehovah? Or are we part of the pattern of the violent beasts that have come before us?

However, not all is doom and gloom. Daniel tells us that God will destroy the beast and, in doing so, will rescue His people and the world.

The Good

In northern Israel, there's a city that goes by the name Mount Megiddo. Napolean Bonaparte described the twenty-mile-long, fourteen-mile-wide valley as the world's most perfect battlefield. *Megiddo* is the Hebrew word for "Armageddon." It will be here, at Mount Megiddo, that all the earth's armies will gather for one final glorious battle. In the prophecy, Jesus returns from heaven on a white horse carrying with Him the Word of God. At this Second Coming of Jesus, He halts the conflict and kills Satan *"with the breath that comes from His mouth. The Lord will come in a way that everyone will see, and that will be the end of the Man of Evil"* (2 Thess. 2:8 ERV). Revelation concludes with a marriage between heaven and earth. God comes to live forever with His people and will make all things new, including the heavens and earth.

Note: *Armageddon* appears only once in the Bible (Rev. 16:16). But the weight of this one word has encapsulated the end of times more than any other. With all the wars that have taken place in this area over the millenniums and the region's current history of volatility, can there be any doubt that Mount Megiddo will be where the *final battle* takes place?

After the battle, John sees a vision of Jesus's followers raised from the dead in the first resurrection. They share in the Kingdom for one thousand years before Satan rallies for one last futile effort to regain its power on earth. Finally, the devil is destroyed for good, and the rest of the dead are brought back to life.

After God's final judgment, John sees a new heaven and a new earth. There will be a union between the two, with Jehovah coming to dwell among His people. In this new creation, *"God shall wipe away all tears from their eyes; and there shall be no more death, neither sorrow, nor crying, neither shall there be any more pain: for the former things are passed away"* (Rev. 21:4)

Many believe the book of Revelation tells the story of the end of times. As we have read, it's not the end but a new beginning. It's not a book of despair but one of hope and everlasting life. History will come to an end, and a new world with Jehovah and Jesus sitting to His right will forever reign...or not.

In my view, this is a simple choice between option *A* or *B*. Either one believes or doesn't. Either there is a God, or there isn't. The Bible is the Word of God, or it's not. The prophecies will continue to be 100 percent accurate, or they won't. The world will end as we know it; or all the evil, corruption, abominations, and evildoers will continue forever.

If one believes as I do, the answer to each of the above choices is simple. Of course, there is a God and vengeance will be His. The day is coming when He will destroy evil, and a New Jerusalem will be upon us. So for those of us who believe, what should we be doing, if anything? When Jesus was asked this very question, He said to rely on the wisdom given by the Holy Scriptures:

> *All Scripture is given by God. And all Scripture is useful for teaching and for showing people what is wrong in their lives. It is useful for correcting faults and teaching the right way to live. Using the Scriptures, those who serve God will be prepared and will have everything they need to do every good work.* (2 Tim. 3:16–17 ERV)

It will be this wisdom that leads to salvation through faith in Jesus Christ.

Jesus tells us to stand strong in our faith and to be watchful. As for when this will all come to pass, no one knows the day or time, not the Son nor the angels in heaven, only the Father knows. So we are to *"be sober-minded; be watchful. Your adversary the devil prowls around like a roaring lion, seeking someone to devour"* (1 Pet. 5:8).

As I've previously explained, I'm not trying to sway atheists into believing in God or what is written in the Bible. For whatever their rationale, they've made a decision and are sticking to their convictions. I disagree with their position but show no ill will to them for their beliefs. It's the *casual* believer that I have difficulty understanding. Assuming we're not some scientific, cosmic accident as the atheists would have us believe, why then would anyone bury their head in the sand and choose to stay in the darkness when Jesus has given us the gift of light? Through His Words, He has given us the gift of wisdom, but still, people would instead choose ignorance over enlightenment. All we have to do is accept God's love:

> *And I say unto you, Ask, and it shall be given you; seek, and ye shall find; knock, and it shall be opened unto you.* (Luke 11:9)

I have a theory I'd like to share with you that I've coined the Nobel Effect.

Alfred Bernhard Nobel was born in Stockholm, Sweden, in 1833. The gifted chemist invented an explosive that changed the world's industrial future and made the young inventor one of his era's wealthiest men. Unfortunately, Noble's success wasn't without scars.

His youngest sibling, Emil's death in 1864, had an enormous impact on Noble's life and the direction that followed. While experimenting with the volatile nitroglycerine in the family lab, Emil and four other employees were killed. The accidental explosion made Nobel determined to find a way to make nitroglycerine safer to use. Following his brother's death, Noble isolated himself until he came up with a solution: an absorbent mineral called diatomaceous earth, also known as kieselguhr. The mixture of nitroglycerin and the porous siliceous kieselguhr created a hugely impactful but stable explosive. Noble named his invention after the Greek word for power, *dunamis*, or better known to us as dynamite.

Then in 1888, the passing of another brother occurred that proved to be even more life-altering than Emil's had been to Noble.

Ludvig Immanuel Noble was the older brother of Alfred. He was enormously successful and, like his younger brother, one of the wealthiest men in the world. Ludwig owned an oil company in Russia that produced half of the world's petroleum at the time. He invented the first oil tankers and redesigned refineries and pipelines to be more efficient. The first tank steamer built in the United States was from plans designed by Ludvig. The visionary businessman introduced banking and profit sharing to his employees. Ludwig improved working conditions in his factories, something unheard of in those days, by building recreational areas for his workers to enjoy. I think it's fair to say this guy was no *Fredo Corleone*—sorry, Chris.

Side note: Following the Bolshevik Revolution (1917–1923), the Nobel brothers, who had one of the largest oil companies in the world located in Russia, were *kindly* relieved of their fortune, in the spirit of *fairness*, by comrades working for the communist regime. I'll assume people like Bernie and AOC would agree with such an equitable arrangement as long as it wasn't their money or business being confiscated.

When Ludwig died from a heart attack, many media outlets incorrectly announced that it was Alfred who'd passed. One French newspaper's headline wrote:

THE MERCHANT OF DEATH IS DEAD
Dr. Alfred Noble, who became rich by finding ways to kill more people faster than ever before, died yesterday.

Having been visited by Charles Dickens's Ghost of Christmas Yet to Come in the form of a brutal premature obituary, Noble decided he wanted to alter how his story was to be told. Desperate to change his image, Noble revised his will to award monetary prizes to those who confer the *"greatest benefit on mankind."* The five areas were physics, chemistry, medicine, literature, and peace. Economics would be added later by the foundation in 1969. Noble died one year after updating his last will and testament. He bequeathed 94 percent of his wealth (nearly two hundred million dollars) to the foundation that bears his name.

As is the case in all of our lives, Noble adjusted his life's direction as his surroundings changed. I have little doubt that he would've liked to have made nitroglycerin safer to use prior to Emil's tragic accident. However, as we saw, it wasn't until the impact of losing his younger brother that made him focus his efforts entirely on finding a solution. After the death of his older brother, Ludwig, Noble displayed a similar intensity to change the perception of his life. By seeing his obituary while still alive, Alfred Noble realized he was given a gift. The great inventor was shown before departing the Earth how he'd be remembered and decided to change the outcome. If Noble were a man filled with pride or in denial, he would've never seen the offering God bestowed upon him. Instead, the premature obituary motivated Noble not only to change himself but the world.

Is there still time for humanity to change our obituary, or has our race already crossed the Rubicon? As we approach the cliff of self-destruction, what will our obituary read?

"Man destroys man"

"Smartest to dumbest"
"What could've been"

I don't know precisely how all this will unfold or when Jesus will return. However, I don't need an explosion or a preemptive obituary for me to awaken to the fact that life is a gift from God and should be cherished by honoring Him. So even if the atheists are right and the Bible is nothing more than some interesting stories, can anyone think that the world we're living in is sustainable or that man himself can fix what is so obviously broken? I believe there's only one answer to both questions: no!

To this author's bewilderment, some choose to ignore what's coming. Governments think they're above God and can rule without His presence. People would rather live a life of debauchery in darkness than live with the illumination of knowledge. Remember, only the Father alone knows the day and time this will all end. He's watching as two trains are heading toward each other on a collision course at full speed. On one train is an out-of-control Satan doing everything in its powers to blind us to God's truth, while the other train is us, a mix of believers and nonbelievers who can't seem to exist without war and bloodshed. Whether one wishes to heed the warnings offered by Jesus is entirely up to each person's free will. Just like it's a choice to listen to the weather forecast before leaving the house. However, whether we choose to prepare for the storm or not, it's still coming. For me, I choose to be watchful and ready because the Second Coming will occur like a thief in the night, at which point *the day of the Lord* will have arrived. A day, in my view, that cannot come soon enough, Amen!

Chapter 10

Author's Summation

*Make three correct guesses consecutively, and you
will establish a reputation as an expert.*

—Canadian Educator Laurence J. Peter

As I write this final chapter, our country is in the midst of change. The seventy-eight-year-old Joseph Robinette Biden Jr. has taken over as the forty-sixth president of the United States. The fact that the politician committed plagiarism, regularly shows signs of senility, chose the most liberal senator in Congress as his running mate, and has suspiciously profited nicely from our adversaries during five decades in public service didn't seem to deter voters. I'll go out on a limb by stating Biden's victory had more to do with the hatred for the fat orange-hair guy than it was about his own qualifications. And, of course, those mass mail-in ballots sure came in handy.

Now that the Democrats control both chambers of Congress and the executive branch, it will be interesting to see how this one-party rule will shape America going forward. If liberal-leaning states like Califonia and New York are the prelude, let the "tax and spend" commence, along with roaming blackouts, lawlessness, and job-killing Green New Deal initiatives that will do next to nothing to help the environment. But who knows? Maybe by 2024, we'll be thankful Joe Biden was our president or, and I'm just shooting in the dark here, asking ourselves, "How the hell did this idiot get elected?"

As we move forward as a country, something to keep in mind is that Trump—love him or hate him—was elected because of a broken political system. The American people are tired of elected officials going to Washington to represent their own best interests and not those of their constituents. The poster child for that corrupt, dysfunctional government has been Uncle Touchy-Feely Joe Biden. I'm no Nostradamus, but if anyone thinks America will be better off in 2024 than it was in the disaster known as 2020, you're in for one hell of a surprise.

As for Trump and the infamous January 6 *rally*, he simply couldn't help himself. For you millennials, you'll have no idea what I'm talking about, but it was reminiscent of a Ralph Kramden self-implosion. Every time the hard-luck Brooklyn bus driver's mother-in-law would come to visit, he'd be so close to getting through her stay without an incident, but at the last moment, he couldn't control himself any longer. *Ralphie boy* would have one of his classic meltdowns by blowing his top and calling her "a blabbermouth."

Well, for the Donald, he'd gone 206 weeks without a major gaffe, but with two weeks left to go in his term, he gave his enemies a belated Christmas present. Regardless if one thinks Trump incited a riot or not, the fact is when our Capitol was under attack, the once-reality TV star who never passed a camera without stopping somehow couldn't find his way down to the 24/7 press room to condemn the violence immediately. Instead, he acted like a petulant child. As far as he was concerned, it was time to show Congress he wasn't happy and neither were his far-right knuckleheads, like Viking-wearing helmet man QAnon Shaman. The self-inflicted wound by 45 was born out of hate and anger and, in my opinion, all but ended the Trump political dynasty.

There is no other emotion that will produce worse results than the toxic combination of hate and anger. Take a moment and think of some of the most regrettable things you've ever done in your life, and I'll bet you that these were significant contributors. Trump did a tremendous job as president while under incessant attacks from idiots on both sides of the aisle. Sadly, he let his pride get in the way, and because of it, his legacy will be remembered more for one day than the other 1,460 other days in office.

Pride goes before destruction, a haughty spirit before a fall. (Prov. 16–18 NIV)

Does It Matter?

Until Jesus's return, we must make the best of an imperfect government run by imperfect beings. While writing this book, my goal was to illustrate where we've been as a na tion and where I believe we're sadly heading. I combined a historical, political, and apocalyptic account of what is to come. So the question for many is if this corruptible world is in Satan's hands and the world as we know it will someday end, why should we bother? For starters, through our free will, we can tell Satan to go to hell. Maybe we can't destroy the devil, but we can certainly choose not to be its accomplice. Imagine if every person in the world opened their eyes the way Alfred Nobel had. And therein lies the dichotomy of the human race. We created fire to survive and use it to kill, the wheel to further our civilization and tanks to destroy it, the nail to build shelter and to crucify the innocent, man conquered flight only to see it used to deliver two atomic bombs, discovered life-saving medicines while drug addiction destroys lives, brought the world closer together via the Internet as the addiction to pornography grows faster than any epidemic the world has ever known.

So as we await the New Jerusalem, the human race will flourish and flounder simultaneously. Fascism will return under the guise of protecting us from, you guessed it, fascism. After tickling our ears, socialism will sound so good that the masses will welcome it the same way the Russian people had after the Bolshevik Revolution over a century ago. In case not everyone is convinced, our leaders will use *experts* to assure us this time will work.

The Experts

I'm thinking about becoming an *expert*. I've noticed most experts make good money, live in nice houses, and people seem to respect them an awful lot. The best part is they don't ever seem to have to account for when they're wrong. Good money, a sweet crib, respectability, and zero accountability, hell, I really want to be an *expert*. One problem. Where exactly does one go to acquire such a title?

At the outset of the pandemic, we were advised by *experts* not to wear a mask. The surgeon general of the United States, Jerome Adams (not the sharpest tool in the shed), said it could actually spread the virus if we did. Here's a tweet the "Nation's Doctor" sent in the early days of the pandemic: *"Seriously people—STOP BUYING MASKS! They are NOT effective in preventing general public from catching #Coronavirus…"* After that, any credibility this *expert* might've had was gone. New York City's former health commissioner, Dr. Oxiris Barbot, told us early on that the Wuhan virus was nothing to fear and gave her *expert* stamp of approval to go about business as usual. Now she was a doctor and a commissioner and sounded really smart. The only problem was she was dead wrong too. Nancy Pelosi was hugging her constituents in San Francisco's Chinatown at the beginning of the outbreak. I'm not sure if she's an *expert* on anything, but at the time, she was third in line to the presidency, so I'm thinking she must've been at least advised by *experts* there was nothing to fear. Sadly, Crazy Nancy and her *experts* were wrong as well.

As I write this passage, the United States has just passed five hundred thousand deaths attributed to the virus from hell. As for all you *experts* out there, here's a piece of advice. If you don't know what the hell you're talking about, keep your mouth shut. As for those *experts* who knowingly spread misinformation, you have blood on your hands. But, of course, that's only my non*expert* opinion!

Side note: I was playing the standard six-hour round of golf with my good buddy Jeff and his neighbor, who I hadn't met before. For convenience, and maybe lacking a bit of creativity on my part, let's nickname him Mr. Personality. I noticed he hadn't much to say on the course and was even less chatty over lunch. However, once the conversation turned to the pandemic, the individual who rationed his words more than a mime was all of a sudden a conversationalist. For the next several minutes, I sat back and listened to Mr. Personality describe Trump's handling of the COVID-19 as a "complete fiasco." According to the self-proclaimed *expertise* of Mr. Personality, "If Trump had implemented a national mask mandate, lives would've been saved." Instead of educating Mr. Personality on the Tenth Amendment and state's rights, I continued to remain quiet until Jeff's neighbor echoed a Biden talking point by saying, "We need to listen to the *'experts.'"*

There's a reason why people shouldn't discuss politics or religion at social gatherings, and today's unsolicited monologue by Mr. Personality was no exception. I restrained myself for as long as I could, but once the magic word of *expert* came into the conversation, I could no longer hold back. So I asked Jeff's neighbor what exactly makes someone an *expert*. The apparent Ivy League grad with the pink Polo shirt provided me with a textbook meaning, saying, "It's someone who has extensive knowledge in a particular field." Keeping Mr. Personality's definition in mind, I asked him a follow-up question of what he felt was an acceptable percentage of being wrong before one should be stripped of the title of *expert*. Visibly uncomfortable with my push back, and probably sensing I was one of the few people on the planet not impressed with his self-inflated intellect, he returned the question to me without attempting to answer. Not missing a beat, I replied, "Zero." Both Jeff and his neighbor laughed and then ridiculed me for my answer. They thought it was ridiculous to think anyone can be right 100 percent of the time. I agreed and then explained:

"If someone's an expert, then the only options they have when asked a question in their field of expertise is the correct one or what they believe to be the correct one. Using the mask mandate as an example, when Dr. Fauci was asked if the public should wear masks, he gave a definitive answer of 'no.' He never said under certain circumstances or that he wasn't sure. Both of which would've been acceptable answers. However, within a few months, the expert doctor did a complete reversal. For the record, that's not the sign of an expert but rather a dishonest idiot. But, in fairness to Dr. Faucci, this is only my nonexpert opinion. And just in

case Dr. Fauci hadn't lost all credibility, nearly a year into the pandemic, the expert told us we should start wearing two masks. So let me see if I have this right. The expert has gone from no masks to wearing 'a' mask to now wearing two masks. At this rate, we'll all be in bubbles, thanks to the rock-solid expert advice of Dr. Fauci."

To no surprise, Mr. Personality went back to his mime impersonation as he sipped on his Blush Zinfandel Spritzer through a paper straw.

Note: To all our public officials out there. You should have more faith in the American spirit. If you advised us to wear a face covering but not to buy masks because of the fear of a shortage of PPEs for our first responders, the vast majority of us would've complied. Instead, once again, those we've entrusted to advise us honestly, aka *experts*, have insulted the American citizens' intelligence, and in doing so, have lost our trust—or at least mine.

To be fair to Dr. Fauci, he's not the first *expert* to offer advice that turned out to be 100 percent wrong. Let's take a look at some other geniuses who cost lives thanks to their *expert* advice:

- Robert McNamara was the secretary of defense during the 1960s under both the Kennedy and Johnson administrations. Perhaps no individual had more influence in escalating the United States involvement in the Southeast Asia conflict than the Harvard Business School graduate.

  In his 1995 book *Retrospect*, McNamara made a desperate attempt to offer his mindset for why he felt at the time the Vietnam War was necessary but, in *retrospect*, a mistake. As early as 1965, Defense Secretary McNamara is on record claiming he advised President Johnson, nearly ten full years before the war ended, that at best, the United States had only a one in three chance of winning the war militarily.

  If anyone out there can follow this logic, you're a wiser person than me. According to the *expert* MacNamara, he knew we couldn't win the war militarily but was still in favor of an escalation in troops. This sounds like one of those John Kerry's "I was in favor of the war before I was against it" nonsensical idioms. As a veteran myself who loves his country and for the 58,479 souls that perished in Vietnam, damned be you, Mr. MacNamara.

• Does anyone ever wonder why we never hear the phrase "slam dunk" outside the basketball arena anymore? Remember the days when prosecutors would get up to a podium and declare their case was a slam dunk or some late-night oil snake salesperson claiming their product was a slam dunk to cure boldness, ugliness, stupidity, pimples, or whatever miracle someone was seeking at three in the morning? Well, we can thank the former director of intelligence at the CIA, George Tenet, for removing the sales slogan from our vernacular. Tenet stood in front of the international community, declaring a "slam dunk" that Saddam Hussein had weapons of mass destruction (WMDs). There was one slight problem with the intel officer's *expert* assessment: he was wrong. The news should come as no surprise since Tenet made a bad habit of such blunders while heading the CIA.

In 2005 the inspector general's report found that Tenent failed miserably in identifying al Qaeda as a significant threat leading up to the attacks that took place on 9/11. And, in case anyone had forgotten about the torture detention center in Abu Ghraib that broke countless international laws, not to mention the scarring of America's reputation, that too was authorized by none other than the *expert* himself, CIA director George Tenet.

So let me see if I have the whole picture here. In Tenet's *expert analysis*, the director had Sadaam as an imminent threat with WMDs who immediately needed to be removed. But when it came to al Qaeda and the numerous attacks leading up to 9/11, Inspector Clouseau sees nothing to sound the alarm bells.

Below is a list of some of the terror attacks carried out by al Qaeda leading up to the September 11, 2001, attack.

Since we're not all qualified to be labeled an *expert* in the intelligence field the way Tenet was, it's understandable if the rest of us idiots miss the glaring pattern of escalating terrorist activity by al Qaeda:

- 1992: The Yemen Hotel bombing objective was to kill US Marines. But for the grace of God, no soldiers were hurt.
- 1993: The first World Trade Center bombing killed six and injured over a thousand.
- 1995: A car bomb targeting Americans was detonated in Riyadh, Saudi Arabia, killing five US citizens and wounding an additional thirty.
- 1998: The simultaneous bombing of two American embassies in Kenya and Tanzania combined for 224 killed (12 Americans) and 4,500 wounded.
- 2000: The bombing of the USS *Cole* killed 17 sailors and injured 39 others.

So how does Washington, D. C., deal with such incompetence? They have a ceremony in the East Room of the White House and wrap a medal around this idiot's neck. Not just any medal, but the Presidential Medal of Freedom, the highest honor a civilian can receive. You just can't make this stuff up!

Thanks to Tenet's *expert intelligence* leading up to the Second Gulf War, nearly ten thousand American soldiers have been killed and another forty thousand seriously wounded. Who knows, maybe it's time to wrap another medal around this *expert's* neck.

- *"If you already have health insurance, the only thing that will change for you under this plan is the amount of money you will spend on premiums. That will be less."*

That wasn't just President Obama preaching those words, but all the pundits who championed the cause via their *expert analysis* of the Affordable Care Act. Premiums would go down, those who were uninsured would now be covered, and, best of all, if we liked our plan, we could keep it. One question: How'd that work out?

There's no way of knowing the exact number of people who lost their health insurance because of the skyrocketing jump in premiums. Nor is there any way of knowing how many of those people missed their annual checkups, screenings, and tests because they no longer could afford the (Un) Affordable Care Act. However, thanks to the government under-delivering and over-promising, people died.

I do have one question regarding the ACA. If it was so good for the American people, how come Congress didn't switch their health insurance onto the exchange? I'll take a shot in the dark and say the *experts* advised them not to.

Yippie! The idiots finally got one right!

My Expert Summation on Experts

If anyone is ever fortunate enough to talk with incredibly successful people, please ask them what they think of experts. I can promise you they may respect and even admire such people but fall way short of blind acceptance. In fact, when given a choice between trusting an expert's opinion or their own instincts, people like Gates, Bezos, Jobs, and Zuckerberg will put money on their intuition over pencil pushers any day of the week. After all, if any of these men listened to the *experts* when starting their businesses, I doubt we'd know their names today.

Do you ever wonder what the *experts* were thinking right before the stock market crash of 1929 or the housing bubble of 2008? My guess is they were telling their clients, *"Mortimore, it's a slam dunk. Buy, Mortimor, buy!"* And like sheep to the slaughterhouse, they did. But now we're supposed to listen to a new administration when they tell us to "trust the experts" when it comes to making decisions on how we should live our lives during the pandemic. Call me a bit of a cynic, but I'm not all in on this idea. To me, it sounds a lot like the left's socialism mantra of "this time will be different" nonsense. The left is banking on the masses will do as told because, after all, they promise peace and security in return for our compliance. In case anyone has forgotten, that would be the same "peace and security" Chamberlain waved in the air upon his return from Munich. Once again, how'd that work out?

While the *experts* tell us to lockdown or the sky will fall, people are losing their jobs, businesses, and self-worth. All because the *experts* "think" what they're proposing will work. We don't need *experts* to tell us wearing masks and social distancing are good ideas. However, telling people to stay locked inside their homes while life passes is asinine and statistically unwarranted. For our children, it's nothing less than abuse.

I have two *predictions* when it comes to the *experts* and current events. My first is research will show that continuous lockdowns were a mistake. Of course, since I'm not an expert, I'm relying on the lost wisdom known as common sense. Second, the *experts* will make it official that Joe Biden won the election legitimately and that there wasn't enough widespread fraud that could've overturned the results. The *experts* will go as far as to say that mail-in ballots, not absentee ballots, showed "no significant cases of fraud." So here's my question for all you *experts* that have taken the painstaking time to look into the 2020 election: *how much fraud was there?*

I don't think it's too much to ask to have accountability when it comes to our elections. Since every vote should count, and fraudulent votes disenfranchise the entire process, I think it's only fair to know the exact number of fraudulent votes that were cast. Of course, we'll never get a precise number, but that won't stop the *experts* from emphatically declaring Biden the legitimate winner and that there was no widespread fraud. Making me ask, how does anyone know for sure when no one can offer an accurate accounting of the election? Try that game with the IRS. *"I know my taxes are a bit off, but I'm confident it's not enough to warrant a full-scale audit."* I'm sure right after your fifth cavity search from some bureaucratic pencil pusher with fat fingers, you'll catch on that in the real world, close enough doesn't work.

But don't worry, I'm sure the *experts* will have everything fixed in time for the 2024 election. After all, we're the idiots, and they're the *experts*!

Side note: When my father passed many years ago, I was given the unenviable task of settling his estate. One issue that needed to be resolved was his car. Two days after his death, I called the auto insurance company to cancel his policy and let them know that my dad was deceased. The agent on the other end of the phone offered their condolences and then said something that nearly knocked me off my seat: "Yes, we know. We've already canceled the policy." Now tell me, how is it my father's name was removed from the account within forty-eight hours, but dead people are still on voter rolls? Here's a thought, maybe we should hire Geico to secure our elections.

Hope

What is hope? For Red in *Shawshank Redemption*, hope could be a dangerous thing. For his friend Andy Dufresne, "hope is a good thing, maybe the best of things, and no good thing ever dies." For the record, I like Andy's definition over Red's.

After Pandora foolishly released all the wickedness from her box into the world, there was one thing left remaining inside to offset it all, hope!

The Bible is filled with scriptures offering the gift of hope. From the hope of eternal life (Titus 3:7) to a future free from evil (Jer. 29:11). When Jesus speaks of all things being possible for those who believe (Mark 9:23), He is referring to hope. In Romans (8:24–25 ERV), Jesus says of hope:

> *We were saved to have this hope. If we can see what we are waiting for, that hope is not really hope. People don't hope for something they already have. But we are hoping for something we don't have yet, and we are waiting for it patiently.*

I sometimes wonder if America's success is not also our curse. Never has a country experienced so much wealth, prosperity, and technological advancements as these United States have. In many ways, we are the envy of the world and the reason so many risk their lives trying to make the journey here. Our poor are overweight, and our wealthy travel the globe in flying machines. Scientific know-how has made life easier in nearly every aspect of our lives. Water runs freely from a faucet while appliances do everything from clean our clothes to preserving our food. Thanks to Thomas Edison, we've bottled the energy from a star and are no longer restricted to daylight. Since the start of the twenty-first century, Apple, Amazon, Facebook, and Google have provided more content than all the previous years known to man combined.

So one would think that we'd be happy living during a time of such prosperity, but as a whole, we're not.

According to the American Foundation for Suicide Prevention, in 2018, suicide was the tenth leading cause of death in this country. There were 1.4 million attempts and 48,344 suicide deaths. The highest group at risk were middle-aged White men (BowFOGs) while men, in general, were 3.5 times more likely to kill themselves than women. But why?

I have a theory that dates back to Greek mythology.

King Tantalus had it all, but like a petulant child, he tempted fate by pushing his cruelty and arrogance to the limit. Thinking he was wiser than the gods, Tantalus invited them to dinner, hoping to trick them into eating the forbidden flesh of a human. Tantalus's idea behind killing his son and making him into a stew was to prove that he could outwit even the all-knowing gods. However, when Zeus learned of the diabolical plot, he brought Tantalus's son back to life and then banished the evil king to Hades for an eternity of thirst and hunger. Although Tantalus stood in a pool of water with a tree filled with fruit dangling over his head, the branches were just out of reach while the water would agonizingly drain lower whenever he attempted to bend down to drink from it. Today we know this torment by the king's name, tantalize.

Similar to Tantalus, we've become like restless children tempting our fate to see how far we can go before we end up destroying ourselves. We have so much to be thankful for, but somehow, we find new ways to be miserable. The only winner in this stew of discontent is Satan. After stirring the pot with hate to feed a society hungry for anger, the prince of darkness sits back to watch its handiwork play out, knowing his goal of keeping a wedge between God and us is working.

Speaking from personal experience, the times in my life when I was furthest away from God was when I found myself most in despair and without hope. I certainly wasn't looking at the glass half full but rather irritatingly empty. Once I stopped thinking about myself and started thinking of others, I took my first step toward recovery. My second step proved to be the scariest. I knew if I kept God away, it was a matter of time before I'd eventually end my life, so I asked for His forgiveness. Not long after, Jehovah blessed me by bringing my wife, Diana, into my life.

The Colombian-born immigrant came to the States, as many do, seeking a new life filled with hope. When she decided to go to America, she was a twenty-eight-year-old single mother who couldn't speak a word of English and had what little money she'd saved stolen from her at gunpoint. I write about Diana's perseverance in *Gardenia's Garden: Trusting in God's Path.* I love telling my wife's story to illustrate how we can all accomplish great things when we keep God in our lives.

One other point I'd like to make regarding my wife. Before I met Diana, I may have known people who migrated to America, but I never took the time to understand their stories. There's something to be said about those who choose to be an American compared to those of us who are fortunate enough to be born here. For those of you out there who think this country is awful, may I recommend going to an American swearing-in ceremony? My wife was sworn-in with over one hundred other people, and another two hundred or so of us present as guests. After the group took their pledge, there wasn't a dry eye in the room, including yours truly. The joyous tears I experienced in the room that day are the proudest I've ever been as an American.

In Nascar, for safety purposes, they install what's called restrictor plates to limit the airflow, which in turn curtails the car's power. It seems like in today's society that we have a metaphorical restrictor plate put on us at a young age for no good reason. Today's watered-down curriculum would be unrecognizable to those who lived during the early days of our republic. Back then, a student needed to be proficient in three languages (English, Greek, and Latin) before acceptance into a university. Today we have a multiple-choice test (SAT/ACT) to help in determining college admittance. Soon these tests will be replaced with an even lower standard. Don't be surprised if an applicant is given higher marks based on their zip code, skin color, and socioeconomic ranking one day. All in the name of fairness, diversity, equality, and unquestioned conformity. I have to believe somewhere Socrates is shaking his head and asking himself, *"So they put me to death for corrupting the minds of the youth, but this system of education is perfectly acceptable? More hemlock, please."*

Unfortunately, as a society, not only have our expectations been lowered over the years, but our standards as well. Our dumbed-down curriculum was supposed to leave no child behind when, in fact, it's left the US nearly dead last in math and science.

*In 2018, the Organization for Economic Co-operation and Development (OECD) report showed Singapore in first place while the US finished in twenty-eighth.

* In the same year, according to CNBC, 24 percent of American students had not acquired "basic skills," ranking it the second-worst high-income country in the world.

Here are my two cents for parents:

Fight! Be your child's advocate. Fight like hell for the competitive school choice option. Our eyes have shown us the utter failure of public schools in the inner cities. But still, the bureaucrats want us to believe what they tell us and not what we see. They tell us that our children are behind because of the new boogie man known as systemic racism. Of course, the left conveniently leaves out that these schools, school boards, city councils, and mayors are predominately run by Democrat African Americans. If there is any discrimination to be found, it's from corrupt Black officials cheating minority students out of a proper education. So my advice to all parents is the following:

- Fight for the best possible education because our children deserve nothing less.
- Hold our elected leaders accountable.

- Don't lower your child's expectations the way the government does.
- The public library should be your child's home away from home.
- Regardless of one's religious beliefs, all children should read the Bible. It's the greatest history book ever written. Most of our Founding Fathers read the Bible cover to cover before their sixth birthday. Six! It's amazing what the mind can accomplish when there aren't so many distractions around (TV, computers, phones, video games, etc.).
- Finally, buy them George Washington's *Rules of Civility and Decent Behavior* and read it together.

Your children have the power to shape their lives. The only question is, will it be a life lived in fear and dependence or hope and prosperity?

A Few of My Heroes

I want to thank all the libs who pushed through to read up to this point in the book. I'm sure it hasn't been easy to absorb some, if not all, of this Bowfog's material. As a token of my appreciation, I'd like to tell you about my favorite Democrat president, Harry S. Truman, along with some of my other heroes.

Give Em' Hell

It was January 12, 1969, when two amazing things occurred in history. I successfully completed my potty training course that I'd been failing miserably for the previous two and a half years, and Broadway Joe Namath delivered the biggest upset in professional football history. Ever since watching that game with my dad, I've been a romantic when it comes to rooting for the underdog. Maybe that's why Harry S. Truman, outside of Washington and Lincoln, is my favorite president.

The five-foot-nine-inch Midwestern senator from Missouri with poor eyesight and a hair-trigger temper was so unlikely to be chosen as FDR's running mate that when his name came up for consideration, Roosevelt's chief of staff quipped, "Who the hell is Truman?" After being tapped by Roosevelt to be his VP, *Time* magazine gave a less than glowing endorsement by describing Truman as "the mousy little man from Missouri."

In three months, Harry S. Truman went from being the Democrat senator of Missouri to vice president to the presidency of the United States. Truman may have inherited the title of his predecessor, but not the respect. Considered a country bumpkin out of his league, the uncomplimentary slogan "To err is Truman" was slung from both sides of the aisle.

Truman overcame the personal attacks and proved to be the right leader at the right time. As a reminder that the ultimate decision-making and consequences laid with him, the commander in chief kept a sign on his desk that read, The *buck stops* here! In what had to be his most difficult decision while in office, Truman chose to use the atom bomb on Hiroshima and Nagasaki. Although controversial, it undoubtedly saved hundreds of thousands of American lives.

During Truman's administration, the thirty-third president implemented a new policy to deal with the growing global threat of communism. The Truman Doctrine, as it was known, was created when the British government decided they would no longer supply military and economic assistance to the Greek government to help fight against the insurrection of communism. The United States' new foreign policy strategy was designed to help nations like Greece preserve international peace and, in the long run, the United States' security. The idea, according to Truman, was to "support free people who are resisting attempted subjugation by armed minorities or by outside pressure."

Under Truman's leadership, America stood up to communism, rebuilt Europe under the Marshall Plan, and was the first to recognize Israel as a state. Known as the American Airlift, Truman took decisive action against the Soviets blockade in West Berlin by providing life-saving supplies to over two million people for nearly a year. Winston Churchill said of Truman that he "more than any other man…saved civilization."

Even after all his significant accomplishments, Truman left office with the lowest approval rating of any president before him and a minuscule Army pension of $112.56 a month. It wasn't like the World War I veteran didn't have ample opportunities after leaving the White House to cash in on endorsement fees offered by several corporations. As Truman wrote in his memoir as to why he declined such overtures, he said, *"I could never lend myself to any transaction that would commercialize on the prestige and dignity of the office of the presidency."*

As that sinks in, think about how much money some presidents have made in just the past half a century?

- Gerald Ford went the Hunter Biden route after leaving office by accepting high-paying positions on prominent corporate boards.
- If one wishes to book Jimmy Carter for a webinar, just go to bigspeak.com and have your credit card ready.
- Ronald Reagan received millions shortly after leaving the White House for a couple of speeches in Japan.
- Bush 41 and 43 have done nicely over the years on the speaking circuit, commanding $80,000 to $100,000 a gig.
- But the real lottery winners in this presidential sweepstakes has to go to Clinton and Obama. Their commitment to "public service" has made them so wealthy that they can afford multiple luxurious homes in some of the most expensive zip codes in America. Combined, the two prostitutes, I mean presidents, are worth over a zillion dollars. Okay, maybe my numbers are a little off, but I'm just following the same accounting procedures that calculated Biden receiving eighty million votes from his basement in the 2020 election. For the record, that would be the accounting firm of *I'll Just Make This Shit Up As I Go Along, LLP.*

So while modern presidents stuff their pockets with cash like game show contestants in money-blowing booths, thanks to President

Truman's integrity of practicing what he preached, Missouri's little mouse showed that the buck truly did stop with him.

John Locke (1632–1704)

Known as the Father of Liberalism, John Locke was a theologian, physician, and philosopher. The seventeenth century Englishman lived during a time known as the Enlightenment, also referred to as the Age of Reason 1685–1815. This new way of thinking was ushered in by visionaries like Galileo, Kepler, Hobbes, Bacon, Newton, and Locke. These men were changing Europe with their minds, not their swords. Indeed a revolutionary idea for a continent that was finally emerging out of the Middle Ages' darkness.

For Locke, it was his political philosophies in which he wrote in the *Two Treatises of Government* that would have the most influence for that "City upon a Hill" known as America. Our framers, and more specifically, Thomas Jefferson, used his 1689 book as a blueprint for what would later be known as the Declaration of Independence. Former president of the Continental Congress, Richard Henry Lee, known for his defiant motion at the Convention to separate from Great Britain, was quoted as saying that Locke's book was so influential it was as if they copied the Constitution directly from his masterpiece.

Many historians consider Locke to be one of the most influential people when it came to establishing our nation, and without question, one of the least credited.

Note: In Locke's Two Treatises of Government, *the theologian cites the Bible over 1,500 times to illustrate the proper way to operate a civic government.*

Locke's revolutionary idea that God created men to be by nature free was an affront to the monarchy, who held a different opinion regarding their subjects (did I hear someone yell, "*Pull!*"). In part, his revolutionary philosophy was to govern from the bottom up, once again leaving the royalty throughout Europe scratching their crowns.

In Locke's writing, he stated: "The reason why men enter into society, is the preservation of their property. Men would not quit the freedom of the state of nature…were it not to preserve their Lives, Liberties, and Fortunes."

I'll assume those last few words by Locke were the inspiration behind Jefferson's "Life, Liberty, *and the* Pursuit of happiness" found in the Declaration of Independence. It would be these natural rights of the people that Locke, and later Jefferson, deemed the government's duty to protect.

Locke's political philosophy and influence on our framers can be seen with another one of his radical ideas: the separation of powers we find in our Constitution.

Benjamin Rush (1746–1813)

A signer of the Declaration of Independence and revered as the Father of American Medicine, his contemporaries considered Rush to be one of the most influential framers. The Evangelical Christian man deeply believed in the importance of a personal relationship with God through Jesus Christ. By having this spiritual connection and an understanding of the Bible, all social issues would diminish. These Christian principles inspired Rush in starting our nation's first Sunday schools, Bible Society, and Abolitionist Society. Dr. Rush explained, in living by the Bible, man becomes both "humanized and civilized."

On July 4, 2014, in honor of the United States' 238th birthday, *Borgen Magazine* compiled a list of who they believed to be the ten most important founding fathers. In order they were the following:

1. George Washington
2. John Adams
3. Thomas Jefferson
4. James Madison
5. Benjamin Franklin
6. Samuel Adams
7. Patrick Henry
8. Thomas Paine
9. Alexander Hamilton
10. Gouverneur Morris

Below is a letter I submitted to the Borgen publication dated July 6, 2014, regarding their omission of Dr. Benjamin Rush's name from their list.

Dear Editor,

> *Who am I to question your publication's decision regarding choosing our most significant founding fathers. It would be as if you compiled a list of your favorite top ten desserts, and because my liking for strawberry shortcake was omitted, I took offense.*
>
> *No, my issue isn't with who's on your list, but who's not.*
>
> *His name is Doctor Benjamin Rush. One of fifty-six signers of The Declaration of Independence, his contributions to our country is too numerous to list in this brief correspondence. However, I took the liberty of noting a few regarding the framer known as both the Father of American Medicine & the Father of Public Schools:*
>
> - *Rush served as the Surgeon General during the Revolutionary War*
> - *Founded the Sunday School movement*
> - *Created the nation's first Bible Society*
> - *Started the nation's first Abolitionist Society*
> - *Established the first institution for women's higher education*
> - *Published the first psychiatric textbook in the US (1812)*
>
> *In closing, I would like to leave you with this thought. Upon the doctor's death in 1813, publications across America wrote that Benjamin Rush was one of the three most influential founders behind George Washington and Benjamin Franklin.*

If your publication should compile a similar list in the future, I hope you'll consider making it a Top 11.

Respectfully,

Rush, whose forward-thinking proclaimed that the two most important people in America were schoolmasters and mothers, promised that the Bible would always be in the curriculum of public schools. *He forewarned that any future generation that removed the Bible from the classroom would spend most of their days fighting crime.* I ask, do not these prophetic words ring true?

Gouverneur Morris (1752–1816)

No other framer spoke more during the Constitutional Convention of 1787 than Gouverneur Morris. Known as the Penman of the Constitution, Morris was not only behind the words found in the document but also in the actual writing. We've all seen his famous cursive penmanship flowing through the Constitution that starts with the words: "*We the People.*"

When France embarked on its constitution, Morris extended his assistance along with some advice. Serving as the Minister Plenipotentiary to France, Morris began the proceedings by stressing the importance of teaching religion and man's duties towards God. Only then could a constitution have any hope of survival.

At the Constitutional Convention, Morris addressed the delegates regarding his opposition to slavery. He pleaded with his fellow representatives that it was incongruous to say that a slave was both a man and property. Denouncing slavery as an evil institution, Morris went on to warn of the hell that was to come if the nation continued down such an abhorrent path. To my knowledge, Gouverneur Morris never claimed to be clairvoyant, but it's this author's opinion, at a minimum, he possessed uncanny foresight.

At the time of the Constitutional Convention, there were nearly seven hundred thousand slaves in the United States. By 1860, that number had swelled to almost four million. The hefty price forewarned by Morris and many of the other delegates during the Convention came two generations later during the Civil War. The North would lose 360,222 men and the South 258,000.

Here's another vision Morris had prior to his death in 1816:

> *The proudest empire in Europe is but a bubble*
> *compared to what America will be, must be, in the*
> *course of two centuries, perhaps of one.*

Alexis de Tocqueville (1805–1859)

On May 11, 1831, a ship arrived in New York harbor carrying France's version of Lewis and Clark. Who were these two young pioneers, and what was the adventurous journey they were about to embark on?

They were the aristocrat Alexis de Tocqueville and his fellow magistrate Gustave de Beaumont. The two men crossed the Atlantic not to seek out and explore new lands but something much more elusive. Their quest was in search of an idea that took root in the summer of 1776.

After the French Revolution in 1789, France's people modeled their republican government after America's. What followed was a breakdown of civil order that led directly to the emergence of the tyrannic dictator Napoleon Bonaparte. So why did one country flourish under republicanism and another collapse? The question itself perplexed Tocqueville and made him want to see for himself what a functional, prosperous republic resembled. So when the minister of the interior commissioned Tocqueville and his long-time friend Beaumont to visit the States to conduct a study on our prison system, the young Frenchmen pounced on the opportunity.

Tocqueville and his companion dutifully carried out their mission for the Interior. However, at every opportunity, Alexis, using his status as an emissary, would add cities and set up meetings with men of importance to learn more about how America was able to thrive under republicanism.

In the nine months that the two men were in North America, they traveled as far north as Quebec and as deep into the south as New Orleans. They visited major cities like New York; Albany; Niagara Falls; Philadelphia; Baltimore; Detroit; Cincinnati; Nashville; Memphis; and, finally, Washington, D. C. They met with political leaders from every branch of government, including sitting President Andrew Jackson; former president John Quincy Adams; Supreme Court Chief Justice John Marshall; Senator Henry Clay; and the last surviving signer of the Declaration of Independence and its sole Catholic signatory, ninety-four-year-old Charles Carroll. The entire time, Tocqueville asked questions and feverishly took notes.

He soon realized that unlike Europe's pursuit for virtue in their citizens, America's quest, as Alexander Hamilton had anticipated, was self-interest.

Tocqueville noted, "The doctrine of self-interest well understood...has been universally accepted; one finds it at the foundation of all actions; it pierces into all discussions."

It was this pursuit of "self-interest" via profit-seeking individuals that Tocqueville observed as the driving force behind the American spirit and not constitutions, communities, or righteousness. However, Tocqueville conceded that the men in America obtained traits emblematic of those with virtue despite this pursuit of wealth, which was in contrast to how European gentlemen sought righteousness. What materialized from this self-made success was the unlikely organizing of charitable support within the community via the church, free from government interference.

Side note: Some years later, when Federick Douglass was asked what slaves wanted from freedom, he echoed the sentiments observed by Tocqueville by stating:

"What the slave wants most in freedom is the free pursuit of self-interest. The undisturbed possession of the natural fruits of his own exertions. After that, there's really little left for society and government to do."

In Tocqueville's attentiveness to find the answer as to why America succeeded where other nations failed, he concluded it laid in two unique institutions:

The first was America's freedom of the press (newspapers). Unlike in Europe, this open practice shed light where none previously existed. In doing so, according to Alexis, the influence of public opinion creates a natural balance of power. Tocqueville said, "Newspapers make political life circulate in all sections of this vast territory and open public affairs to the inspection of every reader." The openness Tocqueville witnessed in America would force public men to be held accountable, and in doing so, expose potential Caesers.

The other institution Tocqueville credits with the success of America's republic were the churches (volunteer organizations).

Whereas in Europe, the governments were more responsible for social programs, Tocqueville observed that people in the States looked toward their church. Each congregation would watch over their members, which in turn created security, morality, and less dependence on the government. Tocqueville concluded since there was a limited role by the government, then political overreach would be less inclined.

In 1835 and 1840, Tocqueville published his observations in two volumes titled *Democracy in America*. His work possessed a unique perspective in the sense that as an outsider whose family was severely impacted by the French Revolution, he could see the possible pitfalls in our newfound liberty. Tocqueville had concerns regarding the American Republic's longevity and warned of the downfall that awaited if and when the press and church no longer functioned as intended. His other worry was the downfall of liberty by the righteous seeking *fairness* in all aspects of life. Tocqueville witnessed firsthand in France the dangers of a public's demand for such equality.

News flash: We are not created equal. I can't dunk a basketball like Michael Jordan, paint like Picasso, or sing like Andrea Bocelli. The mere thought of nuclear physics hurts my brain cells. No, we are not meant to be equals, but rather individuals protected equally under the law. As we strive toward a more perfect union, we must be careful not to conflate equality with conformity. Suppose we allow the government to implement a utopian playing field and regulate equality. The result will not lift us as a society but limit everyone to the lowest common denominator. No longer will the bar be set high for those to achieve their full potential, but so low that it will stunt growth. And all this will be done by bleeding heart liberals who hide their snobbery in the form of misguided benevolence for all the little idiots of the world who they think couldn't survive without their big brother and big sister's help. The result is a society completely dependent on the state and a government growing exponentially more intrusive.

Once the government believes they are granting our liberty instead of defending it, these rights we hold so dear will be no more. So here's an idea. How about we stick to the actual meaning of the word *equality* as it pertains to the American people:

> We hold these truths to be self-evident, that all men are created equal, that they are endowed by their Creator with certain unalienable Rights, that among these are Life, Liberty, and the pursuit of Happiness.

John Quincy Adams (1767–1848)

Over the years, there have been numerous congressional members who've taken the leap from the Capitol Building to the White House, but there's only been one president in history to reverse course. John Quincy Adams's post-presidential service as a United States congressman began in 1831 and ended in 1848 upon his sudden death while working at his desk surrounded by his fellow legislators. Adams, an archenemy of slavery, lobbied his fellow members of Congress to abolish the immoral practice. Known in the chambers as the Hell Hound of Abolition, his fellow members grew tired of his relentless crusade against slavery. When asked by one of his colleagues why he kept fighting a losing proposition, he replied, *"I do this because the duty is ours—results are God's."* After years of determination, the man who dedicated his entire life to public service was finally able to persuade enough of his fellow congressman to go along with his three-part plan to end slavery. Tragically for the Union, his

1843 petition was dead on arrival upon reaching the upper chamber of the Senate.

A year before his death, Adams befriended a freshman congressman from Hodgenville, Kentucky. The senior statesman took it upon himself to mentor his junior legislator, detailing his plans on how to end slavery. The two became so close in such a short period that the lanky six-foot-four youngster was bestowed the honor as a pallbearer at the former president's funeral. The humble representative from Kentucky lost his seat in the next election, but thirteen years later, in 1860, he'd win the most important election in US history. Shortly after being sworn in, Abraham Lincoln started acting on a plan that was first introduced to him by his mentor, John Quincy Adams.

In 1820, Adams made an observation regarding immigration that would be wise for today's Congress to heed:

> Children will cling to the prejudices of this country, and partake of that proud spirit... [referring to the importance of immigrants assimilating to the US]. This is a land, not of privileges, but of equal rights. Privileges are granted by European sovereigns to particular classes of individuals. The governments are the servants of the people, and are so considered by the people, who place and displace them at their pleasures.

Martin Luther

In 1521, Martin Luther was summoned to appear before the Holy Roman Emperor Charles V to recant his writings of the "Disputation on the Power and Efficiency of Indulges." More commonly known as the "Ninety-Five Theses," Luther proposed a list of questions and propositions for debate regarding what he believed were several corruptible acts by the church. At the top was the papal practice of selling "indulgences," a sweet moneymaker for the Roman Catholic Church that promised forgiveness of sins via a "*donation*." In his defiant refusal to recant, Martin Luther proclaimed, *"Unless I am convicted by scripture and plain reason, my conscience is captive to the Word of God. Here I stand, I can do no other, so help me God. Amen."*

When Luther nailed his "Ninety-Five Theses" to the Wittenberg Castle church's door on October 31, 1517, his intent was never to start a separate church. He would've considered the mere thought sacrilegious. Instead, Luther's goal was to reform the only church he ever knew and root out its corruption.

Thanks to Johannes Gutenberg's half-century-old printing press, Luther's "Ninety-Five Theses" spread to the people of Europe faster than any other publication up until that time. Pope Leo X reacted by excommunicating Luther from the church while the Holy Roman Emperor Charles V issued a death warrant known as the Edict of Worms. However, Charles's order to kill Luther *"without consequence"* was opposed by many who supported the Augustinian monk. These protestors, *protestari* in Latin, would become known as the Protestants. As for Luther and his attempt to reform the church, at the core of the issue was his belief that *"neither the Church nor the pope can establish articles of faith. These must come from Scriptures."*

In his writings, Luther broached the subject of the construction cost of Saint Peter's Basilica:

"Why does not the pope, whose wealth today is greater than the wealth of the richest Crassus, build the basilica of St. Peter with his own money rather than with the money of poor believers?"

How do you think that went over in the Vatican? Here's a quick visual. Picture Nancy Pelosi dressed in that all-white pantsuit of hers she wore at the 2020 State of the Union Address. Replace Trump's torn-up speech with Luther's "Ninety-Five Theses," add a three-tiered papal tiara and some red shoes to her ensemble, and I think we're pretty close to what Pope Leo X looked like after reading Luther's "Disputation on the Power and Efficacy of Indulgences."

In the end, it was God-fearing men like Martin Luther, John Calvin, and numerous lesser-known individuals who risked life and limb to reform the medieval Christian Church in the hope of restoring Christianity to its scriptural foundation.

Clarence Thomas

Of all the Supreme Court justices who have ever donned the black robe, without question, Clarence Thomas's path was the least likely. Raised in the poverty-stricken Deep South without a father in the home, Thomas tells his story in his 2007 memoir *My Grandfather's Son*. In the book, the descendent of West African slaves described what life was like early on in his childhood:

"Never before had I known the nagging, chronic hunger that plagued me in Savannah. Hunger without the prospect of eating and cold without the prospect of warmth—that's how I remember the winter of 1955."

For reasons never fully explained, at the age of seven, Thomas and his younger brother were sent to live with his maternal grandparents. The balance of a warm, doting grandmother and a strict hardworking grandfather provided the structure the young boy had been missing. Upon their arrival, Daddy, as Thomas would respectfully address his grandfather, laid down the law to the two boys by announcing, "The damn vacation is over."

On the day the Bull Street Library in Savannah was desegregated, Daddy brought Clarence there and told him that it was his responsibility to honor those who fought for such equality by taking full advantage of the knowledge that awaited him. As far as Clarence's grandfather was concerned, children were expected to "rise early, work hard, and keep their opinion to themselves." Traits that Daddy, a man of modest means, hoped would further be reinforced by sending Thomas to a Catholic school.

In Thomas's brutally honest memoir, he recounts telling his demanding grandfather that slavery was over. To which Daddy quickly retort, "Not in my house."

If not for Clarence's grandparents, there's little doubt I'd be writing about a Justice Thomas. However, I can't help but wonder how many other budding Justice Thomas's are out there but because of a fatherless home, poverty, and no guidance, they never reach their full potential.

To my bewilderment, the government believes it can do a better job in the home than parents. They can't. All the liberal policies meant to help are no substitute for God, love, and a foundation based on Judeo-Christian values.

In 1980 while delivering a speech to fellow Black conservatives, Thomas recalled his sister's dependence on welfare: "She gets mad when the mailman is late with her welfare check." For Thomas, the quote illustrated the toxic combination of dependency and entitlement. Worse, he could see the vicious cycle taking root with the next generation of welfare recipients by his sister's children having "no motivation for doing better or getting out of that situation."

Sadly, in 1999, Thomas's words came to fruition when Mark Thomas, his sister's son, was sentenced to thirty years in prison. Justice Thomas took custody of his nephew's six-year-old son, and as Daddy did for him, Thomas enrolled the boy in a Catholic school.

Thomas viewed the court-ordered school busing of Black children to White schools and affirmative-action policies amounted to racial discrimination. In his own experience in finding work after law school, the Justice explained how he was at a disadvantage due to affirmative action. It was difficult for those interviewing him to believe he was as bright as his grades indicated. Thomas writes more on his experience as a Black man in a big city:

> *At least southerners were upfront about their bigotry: You knew exactly where they were coming from. Not so the paternalistic big-city whites who offered you a helping hand so long as you were careful to agree with them, but slapped you down if you started acting as if you didn't know your place.*

Mother Teresa

On May 24, 1931, a young twenty-year-old girl named Agnes Gonxha Bojaxhiu took her vows as a Sister of Loreto. On that day, the Albanian-born missionary chose the name Teresa after St. Theresa of Lisieux, known as the Little Flower of Jesus. The planet had not yet heard of the "Little Flower," but before the century was over, her impact on humanity would be felt worldwide.

The year was 1946 when the fragile health Mother Teresa received "the call within a call," as she put it. She was on a train when Jesus came calling for her:

"And when that happens, the only thing to do is to say 'Yes.' The message was quite clear, I was to give up all and follow Jesus into the slums—to serve Him in the poorest of the poor."

For the second time in her young life, she gave up the luxuries of comfort to fulfill her extraordinary vision with only her faith to guide her.

In 1964 when Pope Paul VI gifted his ceremonial limousine to her, she immediately had it sold to raise money for the leper colony. When Beirut was under siege in 1982, Mother Teresa brokered a brief ceasefire between the Palestinians and Israelis, no small feat, so she could rescue thirty-seven children trapped in a hospital. Mother Teresa led the Red Cross workers across the war zone to the hospital, where she successfully evacuated the children.

Of all the anecdotes told of Mother Teresa's selfless acts, it's the "baker story" that perhaps best illustrates her commitment to her work and God. Mother Teresa went to a local bakery to beg for food for the children who had nothing to eat. Fed up with the unwelcomed solicitation, the baker spat on her extended hand. Mother Teresa responded by way of the Scripture: "Do not resist an evil person. If anyone slaps you on the right cheek, turn to them the other cheek also" (Matt. 5:39 NIV). So, while holding out her other hand, she humbly let the baker know that she would keep his saliva for herself but to please give bread to her hungry children. Realizing the error of his ways, the baker was no longer angry but ashamed of his actions. From that day forward, the baker generously donated bread to help feed the children at the orphanage.

Side note: In the category of *"It Never Ceases to Amaze Me,"* hate was somehow able to find its way to even someone like Mother Tereasa. In Christopher Hitchens' book, a title not worthy of repeating, the idiot accuses the "saint of the slums" of glorifying poverty to suit her cause. Other detractors had criticized the Nobel Peace Prize recipient for her "controversial" stance on abortion and birth control. The only thing that would've been controversial is if the Catholic nun had "pro views" on either of the aforementioned issues. But leave it to the holier than thou left to impose their moral superiority on even a saint. You just can't make this stuff up!

Harry "Black Harry" Hosier (1750–1806)

Black Harry, as he was known by to his fellow Christians, was one of the most influential preaching voices in early America. Founding Father Benjamin Rush praised the ex-slave as the greatest orator of his time. Fellow Methodist minister Henry Boehm said of Harry, "His voice was musical, and his tongue as the pen of a ready writer. He was unboundedly popular, and many would rather hear him than the bishops."

Harry Hosier often quoted Bible verses with great accuracy, which in itself is an impressive accomplishment. However, the fact that he was illiterate and couldn't read a word of scripture made his retention of the Bible all the more astounding. Using his blessed oratory skills, Hosier transcended race and became the first African American to preach to an all-White congregation.

Sadly, the academic world controlled by the left has silenced Harry Hosier's Christian voice by keeping him out of today's secular school books. Maybe that can explain why nearly no one, including in the African American community, has heard of the Methodist preacher who brought biblical truths to life to anyone within earshot.

John Adams

It can't be easy following greatness, but for the final person on my list, that's precisely what happened.

When John Adams succeeded George Washington as commander in chief, the contrast in leaders could not have been further apart. The stoic Washington was a Southerner who owned slaves, while the Massachusettes-born Adams strongly opposed the institution. The learned Adams was Harvard educated and wasn't shy in sharing his political philosophies, whereas the self-taught Washington was more at home on a farm or a battlefield than a classroom. Washington stood nearly a foot taller than the portly five-foot-six Adams, and unlike his predecessor, could easily be lost in a crowded room. Washington had both sexes' admiration: women were attracted to him while men wanted to be like him. As for Adams, he had no such burden.

However, what Adams did possess more than any of his contemporaries was unwavering principles. When nearly all of the other Founding Fathers owned slaves, Adams disavowed slavery completely and famously remarked that the American Revolution would not be complete until all slaves were freed. Although several of his peers publicly denounced its existence, sadly, it did not deter them from owning slaves privately. For example:

James Madison described slavery as "the most oppressive dominion ever exercised by man over man." George Washington said of slavery that it was his "only unavoidable subject of regret." Thomas Jefferson used terms like "moral depravity" and "hideous blot" in describing the bondage. He even believed slavery to be the single greatest threat to America's survival. Yet still, each of these men was a slave owner.

Many years before John Adams became America's second president, he had a law practice in Boston. In an environment growing less tolerant of British occupation, and on the eve of the thirteen colonies declaring their independence, Adams took the unenviable task of representing the British soldiers involved in killing five colonists during a confrontation with a mob. The tragic incident became known as the Boston Massacre. Although a patriot at heart, Adams, a man who respected the rule of law above all else, advocated vigorously on behalf of the accused. As would be the case throughout his life, the future second president did what he thought was right, not what was popular. In what would be the two "firsts" in America's judicial system (although technically still under British law), the jury was sequestered and the standard of reasonable doubt was applied.

Capt. Thomas Preston, along with six other British soldiers, were acquitted. The two Redcoats found guilty of manslaughter were sentenced to having their hand branded. Some may think the mixed verdict would've spurred violence, but the colony accepted the outcome in large part due to the respect and professionalism displayed by Adams throughout the trial.

John Adams was a God-fearing man who treated his wife as an equal partner, not a subordinate. The family man instilled Christian values in his children and raised a future president. That president, John Quincy Adams, was advised by his father never to be without a book and never stop searching for knowledge.

A Final Thought

America is still the greatest nation on earth. However, with the passing of each national emergency, we find our liberties peeled away one by one. During the Second World War, the excuse was the possible threat of Japanese Americans, so they were rounded up and sent to internment camps. After 9/11, the Patriot Act did less to prevent terrorism and more for the American government to spy on ordinary law-abiding citizens. The pandemic that started in 2020 turned democratically elected governors into tyrannical dictators. Not even churches were safe from their draconian policies.

So where is this leading us as a nation?

I want to share an excerpt from "The Federalist Papers No. 8" that I believe shows the uncanny foresight of Alexander Hamilton when it comes to this very issue. Please keep the following in mind the next time a politician promises peace and security at the expense of our God-given rights.

> Safety from external danger is the most powerful director of national conduct. Even the ardent love of liberty will, after a time, give way to its dictates. The violent destruction of life and property incident to war, the continual effort and alarm attendant on a state of continual danger, will compel nations the most attached to liberty to resort for repose and security to institutions which have a tendency to destroy their civil and

political rights. To be more safe, they at length
become willing to run the risk of being less free.

For the left to achieve their goal of complete dominance, they
will use every crisis as an opportunity to extend their socialist ideology. Along the way, they will do all they can to eradicate any opposing
views. Instead of debating important issues of the day, the radical left
would rather silence the opposition while shredding the Constitution
in the process.

In GODLESS V. LIBERTY, godless is winning. There's another
kingdom on the horizon that will be free of death, pain, and evil. But
until that day comes, we must fight to preserve the liberties bestowed
upon us by God and protected under the Constitution of the United
States of America.

Amen!

Epilogue

On September 10, 2001, I stopped by a Home Depot in Northern New Jersey to pick up supplies for a project I'd started earlier that summer. Attempting to stay within my budget, I sold an old toy to pay for a new one. My sacrifice, if I dare call it that, was a pristine classic 1984 Crossfire Corvette. The finishing touch on the home renovation was a Master Spa hot tub. The fully loaded "Master Blaster Edition" was to be delivered later that week. Wanting to stay on schedule, I planned on finishing some prep work and then head to Brooklyn later that evening to meet up with my drinking buddies. I had an apartment in the city, so my routine on Monday nights was to drink throughout the evening and then sleep throughout the following day. If you haven't figured it out yet, I was single at the time, living a life of decadence and debauchery. I had my self-pity excuses to justify such a lifestyle. They all started with "me" and "I," and needless to say was absent from spiritual guidance. To help understand it better, one cannot be immersed in the lifestyle I was living and still have room for empathy, compassion, and God. The two worlds simply cannot coexist. The worst part was that I knew I was making a foolish decision at the time but didn't care. After all, my mindset was, the world sucked and there was nothing I could do about it. The truth was, all the hot tubs and Corvettes in the world couldn't change the fact that my life was empty because I was missing the most important thing of all—a relationship with Jehovah through our Lord Jesus Christ.

The next day, Tuesday, September 11, 2001, I had nothing scheduled except to call to confirm my jacuzzi's Friday delivery. What should've been another uneventful, mundane day in my life turned out to be anything of the sort.

I write about the horrific events of that day, and the days that followed, in *The Blue Pawn: A Memoir of an NYPD Foot Soldier*. I compare the sadness that fell upon the city to a black cloak engulfing all that was in its path. It took weeks for the dust to settle, but when it did, I witnessed firsthand the power of the human spirit. Every day I went to "the pile," civilian volunteers lined the Westside Highway to offer us first responders bottles of water, gloves, or to share a kind word of gratitude. The surreal experience exposed to me the crazy dichotomy of good and evil within the same human race.

The world is a violent place, and if the book of Revelation is correct, which I believe it is, I *predict* more 9/11s are still to come. So how should we live? Well, for me, it's three steps: stay spiritually healthy, live by the truth, and never forget evil exists.

In my view, I would think the easier of the three would be to stay conscious of the existence of evil. However, for bleeding-heart liberals who wish to social engineer our way out of everything, it seems to be the most difficult. For some reason, they believe everyone is good, or if they're not, easily redeemable (except, of course, for half of all Trump supporters who Hillary has declared irredeemable). Even if a thug is caught on video doing something heinous, the endless defense attorney excuses commence: it had to be because he was molested; ate too much sugar; was a victim of White privilege; suffered from White privilege; corrupt cops; systemic racism; or the catchall, the system failed 'em.

On an individual basis, maybe these legal tricks don't seem so destructive. But as the secular left gains power in crucial government positions, they transfer these pacifist beliefs into their policy; failing to remember two essential points:

1. The government's top priority is to protect its citizens.
2. Evil's priority is to destroy them.

The result of ignoring these two critical points led to millions of deaths in World War II. The appeaser, Neville Chamberlain of Great Britain, a scared, weak bureaucrat, signed a deal with the devil, Adolf Hitler. Upon Chamberlain's return from Munich, he waved a white sheet of paper into the air and naively proclaimed, *"Peace for our time."* But that turned out not to be the case. I don't understand? Hitler and Chamberlain both signed that white piece of paper that the prime minister was so proudly waving in the air agreeing to peace between the Anglo-German people but somehow war broke out anyway.

So what went wrong?

A victim to a con can only work if there's one of three things present; greed, stupidity, or despair. Sadly, for Chamberlain, he possessed two out of the three. It was his lack of wits, along with a sense of desperation for wanting to believe, that blinded the prime minister from seeing the evil that stood before him. Hitler, just like his mentor Satan, was a master of disguises. There's no doubt the German chancellor used his charm and gifted orator skills to lure his prey into a false sense of security. Hitler may have even come across as magnanimous toward his British counterpart. All the while knowing he had zero intentions of honoring the agreement.

So why sign it?

For Hitler, it was a no-brainer. He obtained Czechoslovakia without a shot being fired, all for *promising* there'd be no more aggression on his part. After all, the Fuhrer signed that promissory note giving his word to be a good little Nazi. So Chamberlain and the French prime minister Edouard Daladier, who also took part in the agreement, went back to their respective countries with swollen egos over their great accomplishment.

And what was that accomplishment exactly?

The short answer is, they obtained Herr Hitler's autograph on a lovely white birch sheet of paper—and that's it!

It was so typical of the elitist left to think their intellect could save the day—no doubt, playing right into Hitler's hands. So while the French and British prime ministers toasted to their gifted displays of diplomacy, Hitler went back to working on the blueprints for his Third Reich's thousand-year reign.

"Peace for our time" lasted exactly eleven months, when on September 1, 1939, Germany's Panzer IV tanks roared into Poland. It took two full days for Britain and France to declare war on Germany.

Rumor has it Chamberlain and Daladier were busy on the phone with each other the entire time repeating:

"But we have his signature," while the other protested, "This isn't fair."

Fair? I'll tell you what's not fair—having one's country (Czechoslovakia) carved up like some Ron Popeil chopper dicer isn't fair. That gives me an idea. Let's cast Hitler as the pitch guy in this late-night infomercial production known as the "Munich Agreement." Since Mussolini was there, let's put him as the Fuhrer's little sidekick. Every time Hitler says something, we'll have Mussolini standing next to him, nodding his head in agreement with that twenty-pound chin going up and down like a bobblehead doll.

Munich Agreement Scene 1 Take 1…and action:

> HITLER: But wait, if you act right now, I'll throw in this once-in-a-lifetime limited edition autograph.

> *Audience (Chamberlain and Daladier) politely applaud.*

> *Mussolini, on cue, does that annoying up and down bobblehead thing to show his approval.*

> HITLER: But I'm not done. If you agree in the next five minutes to my terms, you'll not only get the mark of the beast, which, let's face it, is worth much more than the price of that minuscule Czech country, but I'll throw in—I can't believe I'm doing this—my signature on none other than genuine 100 percent white birch paper extracted from trees grown deep in the Bavarian forest.

> *Cue the audience. Mad applause!*

Cue *the annoying Italian guy to do his bobblehead thing again.*

HITLER: I'll give you all this for a one-time pay-
     ment of only two signatures. And because
     I'm feeling extra giddy today, I'm going to
     throw in a one-time worthless promise that
     I won't come to either of your countries
     (Britain and France) and kick your asses.

Audience goes wild with joy over the prospects of peace and security while the two appeasers stumble to retrieve their pens.

Mussolini takes a break from doing his bobble thing so he can lean over to kiss the Fuhrer's ass.

Go to black...

In case you're wondering, it wasn't an oversight by my info-mercial casting director regarding the Czech emissary at the Munich meeting because there wasn't any. That's right. As four men filled with hubris discussed the Czechoslovakian people's fate, no one thought it necessary for one of their representatives to be present. Once again, the elitists decided what would be best for those less fortunate.

I believe the Munich Agreement best illustrates precisely how not to deal with evil. But here we are at the start of the twenty-first century talking of socialism, fascism, and appeasement all over again.

As I think back upon Ronald Reagan's line, *"We can have peace this second, if we surrender,"* gives me pause when it comes to today's leaders.

This leads to my final *prediction.*

The stronger the secular left grows in America, the more likely it will be to produce the next Chamberlain, and with it, the next Hitler. I don't say this to be hyperbolic. I say it, so maybe a young child reading this will be inspired to be the next great conservative leader of the free world. Maybe there's the next Ronald Reagan or Margaret Thatcher out there who will stand up to evil and have peace through strength. Instead, we have leaders like Obama and Biden sending our modern-day version of Chamberlain in the likes of John Kerry over to Vienna (2015), promising pallets of cash to Iranian leaders in return for a piece of paper with Satan's signature attached. Sound familiar?

Winston Churchill once said that "It's human nature to forget, but the left seems to make a habit out of it."

To which I say, "Ain't that the bloody truth!"

Articles

Real Men Read
Sun Sentinel
March 12, 2020

On Thursday, March 5th, I, along with over thirty adult male volunteers from Broward, were cordially invited to Thurgood Elementary school in Fort Lauderdale to participate in a celebration of reading. The event, Real Men Read, was an opportunity for male role models in the community to connect with young students via the gift of a children's book. This investment in our children's future was made possible by the mobilizing community group HandsOn Broward, along with a collection of several other county organizations, including the one I volunteer for: Reading Pals.

The book I chose to read to Ms. Mejia's third-grade class was House Mouse Senate Mouse by Peter and Cheryl Barnes. The poetic rhyme children's book explains how a bill becomes a law. Using Miss Tufmouse's second-grade class as the catalyst behind the movement to declare a National Cheese for the United Mouses of America, the students request the help of the Squeaker of the House and the Senate Mousejority Leader. After many debates, compromises, and skillful navigation of the party leaders, a bill was finally ready for the president to sign into law. Our new National Cheese would be…

"We are city mice, country mice, large mice and small—We like many cheeses—in fact, like them all! But we're Americans first! So now, if you please, let's agree that American is our National Cheese!"

I finished my visit by declaring American Cheese the law of the land and then readied myself to go. However, not before Ms. Mejia's third-grade class presented me with an oversized thank you card with the students' names and hand outlines.

There's something special going on in Broward County. All one has to do is visit a school like Thurgood Marshall or Margate Elementary (my assigned Reading Pals school) to see firsthand how today's educators are shaping the hearts and minds of our most precious resource, our children. Due to the leadership of Principals Michael Billins and Thomas Schroeder, along with over fifteen-thousand other professional educators in the county, I feel confident in saying our future is in excellent hands.

Through the United Way, Reading Pals is a one-on-one statewide volunteer-based literacy program that puts mentors with students from Pre-K through third grade.

I Knew I Had to get Myself to Ground Zero
Michael d'Oliveira
editor@newpelican.com

Deerfield Beach—On the eve of the September 11th attacks in 2001, Dean Simpson's life was in shambles.

Simpson, 53, a former New York City police officer was struggling to find purpose five years after a disability forced his early retirement from "the job I once said I'd work for free."

Add to that, his father, Jim Simpson, also a former police officer and "my mentor, my rock, and my best friend" had died of Non-Hodgkin's Lymphoma in June of 2001.

"Without a healthy routine or something in my life to care about, I began to drink heavily during the night and sleep throughout the day. I'd reached a point that I either wanted to be intoxicated or unconscious—anything else has become pure hell."

In his 2018 book, "The Blue Pawn: A Memoir of an NYPD Foot Soldier," Simpson, a Gulf War veteran and Deerfield Beach resident, details his experience on September 11th as well as his past struggles with alcoholism, depression and contemplating suicide.

After his father died, Simpson got a part-time gig as a bouncer at The Wicked Monk, a bar near his Brooklyn apartment. It's where he was until 5 a.m. on the morning of the attacks.

By the time Simpson woke up, the world had already changed. He just didn't know it yet.

When he entered a store to get coffee, the news was on the TV.

"I took off my ultra-dark glasses to see what was being broadcasted: The World Trade Center buildings were no longer," he wrote.

After the initial shock, Simpson's feelings of depression and worthlessness resumed. He found himself in a pew at church, asking Jesus to take him instead of the people he knew were dying.

"While I sat there trying to explain to God that my life had less meaning than those he was taking from their families, I already knew my offering was in vain."

He went home and put on his old uniform.

But the uniform made him realize how much weight and muscle mass he had lost since leaving the force. A feeling of inadequacy, of being less than what his uniform was supposed to represent, washed over him.

He was shaken into action after a television reporter compared the attacks to Pearl Harbor 60 years earlier, "I knew I had to get myself to Ground Zero."

What he found there reminded him of Dante's Inferno.

Gone were the towers and with them the typical hustle, bustle and noise of lower Manhattan. "A gray, thick dust clung to everything in sight."

Few survivors were found during the 20 days and nights Simpson spent at the site helping to remove debris. But it was far more than the number he expected would be found—zero.

"Each day as I entered the pile, there were ordinary citizens lined along the barricade thanking me, a stranger, for my service," he wrote. "Hundreds of ordinary men and women giving their support in the rescue by handing out bottles of water, gloves, masks and anything else they thought could help in our efforts." He witnessed "grown men cry like babies, while their brethren comforted them with a hug."

His decision to leave the site for good came when he and the other rescue workers recognized that there were no more survivors.

It was time to recover those who perished. As he left for the last time, he spotted a blue dress shoe.

It had some dried blood on it and Simpson prayed the shoe was the only thing its owner lost that day. But there was no way to know.

"One thing I did know was life as we knew it, for everyone in NYC and throughout the country, was never going to be the same."

Simpson's life later changed for the better in December of 2001 when he took a pledge to no longer let alcohol control him. Today, he lives with his wife, Diana, and stepdaughter, Nathaly, and occupies much of his time with writing and volunteering to help children and his fellow veterans.

Coming Christmas of 2022, the Godless Series continues with *Godless v. Trust*

CPSIA information can be obtained
at www.ICGtesting.com
Printed in the USA
LVHW011022050122
707889LV00003B/36